Kissinger & Detente

Kissinger
&
Detente

Edited by Lester A. Sobel

Contributing editors: Hal Kosut, Joseph Fickes and
Stephen Orlofsky

FACTS ON FILE, INC.   NEW YORK, N.Y.

Kissinger & Detente

© Copyright, 1975, by Facts on File, Inc.

Library of Congress Catalog Card No. 75-20839
ISBN 0-87196-243-8

9 8 7 6 5 4 3 2 1
PRINTED IN
THE UNITED STATES OF AMERICA

Contents

Introduction

THE MOST WIDELY APPROVED ACCOMPLISHMENT of the late Nixon Administration is the reduction of overt antagonism between the United States and its two major Communist adversaries—the Soviet Union and the People's Republic of China. Despite some criticism of this policy, there seems to be general agreement that, at the least, the fruit of detente will be a lessening of the danger of war.

The man usually acclaimed as the "architect" of the U.S. policy of detente is the former Harvard professor Henry Alfred Kissinger, who took over as Assistant to the President for National Security Affairs when the Nixon Administration assumed office in 1969 and who in 1973 added the role of Secretary of State to his growing list of duties.

While Dr. Kissinger unquestionably was a (if not the) central figure in formulating and carrying out the detente policy, many observers and Kissinger himself point out that actions to promote detente had been proposed and in some instances started at least as far back as the Eisenhower Administration. It is also noted that Nixon,

1

well-known as a bitter enemy of communism both at home and abroad, had been suggesting detente long before Kissinger, who had been a political foe of Nixon's, agreed to join the Nixon team. In any case, as Kissinger and others observe, Nixon was in charge of U.S. international relations at the time the detente policy was inaugurated and when the critical negotiations were started. It was Nixon who decided to adopt the policy, who chose Kissinger to play his key role in detente, who made the vital decisions, whether based on Kissinger's recommendations or not, and who bore the fundamental responsibility for the policy's ultimate success or failure.

It has been suggested, by Kissinger among others, that Nixon became President just when the time was ripe for the diplomatic change of course that detente represented. The nuclear weapons race was making the threat of mutual annihilation too pressing to permit the continuation of older policies of confrontation and of going to the brink of war. The economic cost of developing and building up ever more sophisticated and expensive arsenals was becoming more than the antagonists could bear. Worldwide economic problems ranging from food and energy shortages to balance-of-payments woes prompted the potential belligerents to seek new sources of supply, of trade or of technology by rapprochment with ideological foes. Even the Vietnam War played a part. In the case of the U.S. and China, as Dr. Kwan Ha Yim pointed out (in *China & the U.S. 1964-72,* FACTS ON FILE, 1975), "it was in the intractability of the war [so expensive in human and economic currency] that the adversaries came to terms with the need for embarking on a new course away from their antagonistic relationship."

In the U.S., it was said, detente was made more feasible by the changover from a Democratic administration to a Republican one. This assertion was based on the 1949 "loss of China," the overthrow of the Chinese Nationalists by the Communists, a defeat that some Republicans blamed on "soft-on-communism" Democrats. Democratic Administrations since 1949 have sometimes been accused of being excessively afraid to attempt anything that could lead to similar charges, especially in the Far East. Republicans, considering themselves to be untainted by history on the communism issue, felt free to negotiate with Communist nations without too much worry about criticism. Dwight D. Eisenhower, thus, had been uninhibited in ending the Korean War, and Richard M. Nixon had been considered similarly free to bargain for the departure of American fighting men from Vietnam.

Detente was said to have been sought by the Russians and Chinese also for political reasons of a quasi-parochial nature. The long-standing Sino-Soviet rift, which involved matters ranging from border disputes to disagreement over Communist ideology and rivalry for leadership of international communism, had erupted in several brief and inconclusive military clashes. There seemed to be little doubt that the two Communist adversaries truly feared and distrusted each other. The Chinese charged that the Soviet Union was in league with the U.S. in a revisionist plot against the Chinese ideal of pure communism. Such accusations may seem ludicrous in the West but apparently were taken with some seriousness in Communist circles, as were Soviet charges linking the U.S. with the Chinese Communists. According to some observers, at least one reason the Communist rivals sought to improve relations with the U.S. was the hope that they could thereby break up an alliance that endangered them.

Such considerations as those outlined above provide perspective for Kissinger's role in the policy of detente, but they probably detract little if at all from the portrayal of Kissinger as the key man in the achievement of detente. Kissinger headed the studies on the basis of which the Nixon Administration charted its course towards detente, and he was the principal American representative in some of the most important negotiations through which detente progressed. Both critics and admirers of Kissinger agree that he deserves a major share of credit or blame for the policy's successes or failures.

The official described as the Nixon Administration's "essential" man was born in Fürth, Germany May 27, 1923. His Orthodox Jewish parents named him Alfred Heinz Kissinger, and he spent his early years in a country where Nazi anti-Semitism was becoming increasingly venomous. Kissinger's father was dismissed as a teacher because he was a Jew. Young Kissinger was denied admission to a Gymnasium, for the same reason, and he was a victim of beatings by anti-Semitic youths. To escape persecution, the family moved in 1938 to New York, where young Kissinger's names were Americanized to Henry Alfred. A good student, Kissinger received straight-A marks in high school and then studied in evening courses in City College while he worked during the day in a shaving-brush factory.

Kissinger was drafted in 1943 and became a naturalized U.S. citizen in the Army. He served in Europe during the Battle of the Bulge, later became a German interpreter, then a Counter-Intelligence Corps interrogator and, although an enlisted man, was appointed military government administrator in the town of Krefeld.

Returning to the U.S., Kissinger studied at Harvard, was graduated summa cum laude and was elected to Phi Beta Kappa. He remained at Harvard for graduate study, headed the Harvard International Seminar, undertook various studies for the government, for the Council on Foreign Relations and for other organizations and became a full professor at Harvard. Kissinger served as director of the Rockefeller Brothers Fund special studies project and was active in Nelson A. Rockefeller's unsuccessful campaign for the Republican Presidential nomination in 1968.

Kissinger was furious when Nixon won the nomination, and Nixon presumably knew that Kissinger was said to have denounced him bitterly as "unfit to be President." Yet shortly after Nixon actually was elected President in November 1968, he offered Kissinger the post of Assistant to the President for National Security Affairs—and Kissinger accepted.

As the President's chief adviser on international affairs and defense, Kissinger quickly became one of the nation's most controversial people. Sen. Stuart Symington (D, Mo.), commenting on Kissinger's "unique and unprecedentedly authoritative role," as revealed in a series of *New York Times* articles, told the Senate March 2, 1971 that Kissinger "emerges as clearly the most powerful man in the Nixon Administration next to the President himself." Discussing Kissinger's power, Symington said:

Dr. Kissinger is Assistant to the President for National Security Affairs. In that position he heads the staff of the National Security Council. That staff consists of some 110 people. The fiscal year 1972 budget request for the National Security Council staff is $2.3 million, almost four times the amount expended in 1968—the amount requested for outside consultants alone is nearly $500,000.

. . . The function of the National Security Council is "to advise the President with respect to the integration of domestic, foreign, and military policies relating to national security." The staff of the Council was intended to advise the members of the Council. Instead, however, said staff operates as an in-house policy shop for the President himself.

With this broad mandate, Dr. Kissinger has established under the National Security Council a complex structure of six committees which formulate and review policy options on a wide range of subjects before they are forwarded to the President. Dr. Kissinger himself is chairman of all six committees. . . . Perhaps the most powerful of the six committees is the Senior Review Group which, unlike the other more specialized committees, deals across the board with those most critical policy issues which are of special interest to Congress and the people as well as to the administration. . . .

Some say it is the advisory voice of Dr. Kissinger that has been heard the loudest with respect to all major decisions that involve the United States in Indochina—more so than that of either the Secretary of State or the Secretary of Defense; in fact reports have been circulated that one major military decision in this area was made within the White House, without prior consultation with the Joint Chiefs of Staff. . . .

Another committee chaired by Dr. Kissinger, the so-called 40 Committee—named for the Presidential directive which set it up—is described as one which supervises covert intelligence operations. . . .

Underlying all these six committees as well as the National Security Council staff, Dr. Kissinger has set up six interdepartmental groups according to specific regions of the world—Europe, the Middle East, Africa, and so forth. Each group is headed by an Assistant Secretary of State.

. . . Do these Assistant Secretaries of State, as heads of interdepartmental groups under the National Security Council, report directly to Dr. Kissinger, or do they report to the Secretary of State? If the former, anyone experienced in the actual operation of the executive branch knows that Dr. Kissinger is Secretary of State in everything but title, with this organizational arrangement a vital key to the formulation of foreign policy.

One result of the function of these interdepartmental groups has been to place certain broad categories of executive branch communicators beyond the reach of legitimately interested members of Congress. As example, on more than one occasion within the past year, members of the Foreign Relations Committee who sought to discuss pending policy matters with executive branch officials have been told by those officials that their ability to discuss the subject in meaningful terms was limited because it was a matter pending within the National Security Council process. . . .

Dr. Kissinger has other official powers. As example, he is a member of the new Council on International Economic Policy. This Presidential council . . . is designed to "pull together military and economic aid, international trade and monetary, financial, investment and commodities matters into a cohesive body of policy, taking into account the requirements of foreign policy." . . .

Sitting as he does in such a broad seat of authority, Henry Kissinger is clearly the best-informed administration official on White House policy; and he is permitted to lobby the decisions of the executive branch to the news media, to representatives of foreign countries, to the Cabinet, to the military, to government boards and commissions, and also to various private groups and individuals, without any accountability of any kind whatever to the Congress. . . .

Symington, however, joined the majority Sept. 21, 1973 in the 78-7 Senate vote to confirm Kissinger on his nomination by Nixon to be Secretary of State. The debate that preceded the nomination reviewed much of the controversy over Kissinger. Sen. Alan M. Cranston (D, Calif.) was one of the many Senators who voted to confirm Kissinger despite his "very mixed feelings" about the nominee. Cranston's remarks appear to summarize many of the views expressed during the debate:

. . . There is no doubt in my mind that some of the results of Dr. Kissinger's policies have been creative steps toward peace. In fact, he had a major hand in ending the Cold War. . . .

Most outstanding is the breakthrough with China and the Soviet Union. Dr. Kissinger's outstanding contributions have been to realize that these two countries are no longer behaving like revolutionary powers but integral members of the international system—and to act on that realization. He knows that, at least for the time being, these countries are willing to play by the rules, and he gets along well with their leaders partly because they share a concern with maintaining the status quo.

In some ways the breakthrough with China was just lying there, waiting to be harvested by anyone fortunate enough to be President at the right time. A foolish policy had already withered and fallen. Meanwhile, the Chinese were worried about the sharp deterioration in their relations with the Russians and did not want a hostile confrontation with both superpowers at the same time.

But Dr. Kissinger did more than just pick up the pieces. He negotiated a major breakthrough on the emotionally charged issue of Taiwan—long a stumbling block to better relations with Peking. He arranged for President Nixon to visit China with Chinese leaders. And he did all this without unduly alarming the Russians.

Similarly, his politics of détente with the Soviet Union were carried out without damaging relations with China. The high degree of Sino-Soviet tension and mutual resentment makes this feat particularly supreme. . . .

It is this style which is most frequently admired. But, I suggested a moment ago, even more impressive is Dr. Kissinger's ability to act on a fresh perception of the international system, namely, the perception that two powers formerly hostile to us and presently hostile to each other could simultaneously become—within limits—partners of American diplomacy.

His triumph in the field of arms limitation was a natural fruit of this perception. The SALT [Strategic Arms Limitation Talks] agreements—and the sophistication they reflect—are already important steps. If the momentum behind them continues, they can become major accomplishments of our time. . . .

Another byproduct of détente may have been the absence of a major war in the Middle East. I believe that Soviet restraint in this area is partly due to the overall improvement in relations with the United States. Dr. Kissinger deserves some credit for the fact that there has been no major outbreak of violence since 1967.

Unfortunately, the record of Henry Kissinger's diplomacy also shows some minuses.

Many, many lives were lost while Dr. Kissinger was adviser to the President because of the bloody and needless prolongation of the Vietnam war and the bombing of Cambodia and Laos. . . .

Bangladesh has dropped out of the headlines. But only two years ago an entire people became the target of massacre, pillage, and rape, and the United States lined up with the oppressors. There were so-called balance-of-power reasons for supporting Pakistan, notably our delicate but steadily ripening friendship with Pakistan's ally, China, combined with the need to offset what appeared to be a growing Soviet-Indian alliance. But these ''reasons'' produced a policy that effectively condoned slaughter on an appalling scale.

On a less violent level, the United States has mishandled our relations with Tokyo. Unfortunately, the time and effort that went into nurturing better relations with the Russians and the Chinese was not devoted as well to our important and loyal friends in Japan. . . .

Preoccupation with the Soviet Union and China also entailed the neglect of most of the countries of the developing world, particularly Africa and Latin America. They do not fit into Dr. Kissinger's world of major powers and legitimacy and balances. . . .

Another casualty suffering from U.S. neglect is the United Nations. . . . The American contribution to the international debate over the oceans and the seabed has been highly constructive. But this is an exception. I would like to see similar initiatives in other U.N. activities. . . .

In 1973, the year in which Kissinger became Secretary of State, he and Le Duc Tho of North Vietnam were awarded the Nobel Peace Prize for negotiating for the end to U.S. participation in the fighting in Vietnam. This award was the most controversial in the prize's history, and Tho announced that he would not accept the prize because "peace has not really been established in South Vietnam. . . ."

Later in 1973—and again in 1974—the Gallup Poll announced that Kissinger headed the list of men whom Americans admired most. He had been fourth on the list in 1972.

THIS BOOK IS AN ACCOUNT OF THE EFFORT to reduce overt antagonism between the U.S. and its two major Communist adversaries during the Nixon Administration and the early days of the Ford Administration. This record is preceded by a presentation of Henry Kissinger's views on the U.S.' policy of detente. The narrative of events consists largely of the record compiled by FACTS ON FILE in its weekly coverage of world events. As in all FACTS ON FILE works, a conscientious effort was made to keep this volume free of bias and to make it a balanced and accurate reference tool.

LESTER A. SOBEL

New York, N.Y.
October, 1975

Kissinger on Detente

A summary of official U.S. policy on detente was presented by Secretary of State Kissinger to the Senate Committee on Foreign Relations Sept. 19, 1974 in a statement entitled "Detente With the Soviet Union: The Reality of Competition and the Imperative of Cooperation." With minor deletions this statement follows.

SINCE THE DAWN OF THE NUCLEAR age the world's fears of holocaust and its hopes for peace have turned on the relationship between the United States and the Soviet Union.

. . . Tragic as the consequences of violence may have been in the past, the issue of peace and war takes on unprecedented urgency when, for the first time in history, two nations have the capacity to destroy mankind. . . .

The destructiveness of modern weapons defines the necessity of the task; deep differences in philosophy and interests between the United States and the Soviet Union point up its difficulty. These differences do not spring from misunderstanding or personalities or

9

transitory factors: They are rooted in history and in the way the two countries have developed. They are nourished by conflicting values and opposing ideologies. They are expressed in diverging national interests that produce political and military competition. They are influenced by allies and friends whose association we value and whose interests we will not sacrifice.

Paradox confuses our perception of the problem of peaceful coexistence: if peace is pursued to the exclusion of any other goal, other values will be compromised and perhaps lost; but if unconstrained rivalry leads to nuclear conflict, these values, along with everything else, will be destroyed in the resulting holocaust. However competitive they may be at some levels of their relationship, both major nuclear powers must base their policies on the premise that neither can expect to impose its will on the other without running an intolerable risk. The challenge of our time is to reconcile the reality of competition with the imperative of coexistence.

There can be no peaceful international order without a constructive relationship between the United States and the Soviet Union. There will be no international stability unless both the Soviet Union and the United States conduct themselves with restraint and unless they use their enormous power for the benefit of mankind.

Thus we must be clear at the outset on what the term "détente" entails. It is the search for a more constructive relationship with the Soviet Union reflecting the realities I have outlined. It is a continuing process, not a final condition that has been or can be realized at any one specific point in time. And it has been pursued by successive American leaders, though the means have varied as have world conditions.

Some fundamental principles guide this policy:

The United States cannot base its policy solely on Moscow's good intentions. But neither can we insist that all forward movement must await a convergence of American and Soviet purposes. We seek, regardless of Soviet intentions, to serve peace through a systematic resistance to pressure and conciliatory responses to moderate behavior.

We must oppose aggressive actions and irresponsible behavior. But we must not seek confrontations lightly.

We must maintain a strong national defense while recognizing that in the nuclear age the relationship between military strength and politically usable power is the most complex in all history.

Where the age-old antagonism between freedom and tyranny is concerned, we are not neutral. But other imperatives impose limits on our ability to produce internal changes in foreign countries. Consciousness of our limits is recognition of the necessity of peace—not moral callousness. The preservation of human life and human society are moral values, too.

We must be mature enough to recognize that to be stable a relationship must provide advantages to both sides and that the most constructive international relationships are those in which both parties perceive an element of gain. Moscow will benefit from certain measures, just as we will from others. The balance cannot be struck on each issue every day, but only over the whole range of relations and over a period of time.

The Course of Soviet-American Relations

In the first two decades of the postwar period, U.S-Soviet relations were characterized by many fits and starts. Some encouraging developments followed the Cuban missile crisis of 1962, for example. But at the end of the decade the invasion of Czechoslovakia brought progress to a halt and threw a deepening shadow over East-West relations.

During those difficult days some were tempted to conclude that antagonism was the central feature of the relationship and that U.S. policy. . .had to be geared to this grim reality. Others recommended a basic change of policy; there was a barrage of demands to hold an immediate summit to establish a better atmosphere, to launch the SALT talks [Strategic Arms Limitation Talks], and to end the decades-old trade discrimination against the Soviet Union. . . .

These two approaches reflected the extremes of the debate that had dominated most of the postwar period. . . .

For many Americans, tensions and enmity in international relations are anomalies, the cause of which is attributed either to deliberate malice or misunderstanding. Malice is to be combated by force, or at least isolation; misunderstanding is to be removed by the strenuous exercise of good will. Communist states, on the other hand, regard tensions as inevitable byproducts of a struggle between opposing social systems.

Most Americans perceive relations between states as either friendly or hostile, both defined in nearly absolute terms. Soviet foreign policy, by comparison, is conducted in a gray area heavily influenced by the Soviet conception of the balance of forces. Thus Soviet diplomacy is never free of tactical pressures or adjustments, and it is never determined in isolation from the prevailing military balance. For Moscow, East-West contacts and negotiations are in part designed to promote Soviet influence abroad, especially in Western Europe—and to gain formal acceptance of those elements of the status quo most agreeable to Moscow.

The issue, however, is not whether peace and stability serve Soviet purposes, but whether they serve our own. Indeed, to the extent that our attention focuses largely on Soviet intentions we create a latent vulnerability. If détente can be justified only by a basic change in Soviet motivation, the temptation becomes overwhelming to base U.S.-Soviet relations not on realistic appraisal but on tenuous hopes: a change in Soviet tone is taken as a sign of a basic change of philosophy. Atmosphere is confused with substance. Policy oscillates between poles of suspicion and euphoria.

Neither extreme is realistic, and both are dangerous. The hopeful view ignores that we and the Soviets are bound to compete for the foreseeable future. The pessimistic view ignores that we have some parallel interests and that we are compelled to coexist. Détente encourages an environment in which competitors can regulate and restrain their differences and ultimately move from competition to cooperation.

American Goals. America's aspiration for the kind of political environment we now call détente is not new.

The effort to achieve a more constructive relationship with the Soviet Union is not made in the name of any one administration or one party or for any one period of time. It expresses the continuing desire of the vast majority of the American people for an easing of international tensions and their expectation that any responsible government will strive for peace. No aspect of our policies, domestic or foreign, enjoys more consistent bipartisan support. . . .

In the postwar period repeated efforts were made to improve our relationship with Moscow. The spirits of Geneva, Camp David, and Glassboro were evanescent moments in a quarter century otherwise marked by tensions and by sporadic confrontation. What is new in the current period of relaxation of tensions is its duration, the scope of the relationship which has evolved, and the continuity and intensity of consultation which it has produced.

A number of factors have produced this change in the international environment. By the end of the '60s and the beginning of the '70s the time was propitious—no matter what administration was in office in the United States—for a major attempt to improve U.S.-Soviet relations. Contradictory tendencies contested for preeminence in Soviet policy; events could have tipped the scales toward either increased aggressiveness or toward conciliation.

● The fragmentation in the Communist world in the 1960s challenged the leading position of the U.S.S.R. and its claim to be the arbiter of orthodoxy. The U.S.S.R. could have reacted by adopting a more aggressive attitude toward the capitalist world in order to assert its militant vigilance; instead, the changing situation and U.S. policy seem to have encouraged Soviet leaders to cooperate in at least a temporary lessening of tension with the West.

● The prospect of achieving a military position of near parity with the United States in strategic forces could have tempted Moscow to use its expanding military capability to strive more determinedly for expansion; in fact, it tempered the militancy of some of its actions and sought to stabilize at least some aspects of the military competition through negotiations.

● The very real economic problems of the U.S.S.R. and Eastern Europe could have reinforced autarkic policies and the tendency to create a closed system; in actuality, the Soviet Union and its allies have come closer to acknowledging the reality of an interdependent world economy.

● Finally, when faced with the hopes of its own people for greater well-being, the Soviet government could have continued to stimulate the suspicions of the Cold War to further isolate Soviet society; in fact, it chose—however inadequately and slowly—to seek to calm its public opinion by joining in a relaxation of tensions.

For the United States the choice was clear: To provide as many incentives as possible for those actions by the Soviet Union most conducive to peace and individual well-being and to overcome the swings between illusionary optimism and harsh antagonism that had characterized most of the postwar period. . . .

We sought to explore every avenue toward an honorable and just accommodation while remaining determined not to settle for mere atmospherics. We relied on a balance of mutual interests rather than

Soviet intentions. When challenged—such as in the Middle East, the Caribbean, or Berlin—we always responded firmly. And when Soviet policy moved toward conciliation, we sought to turn what may have started as a tactical maneuver into a durable pattern of conduct.

Our approach proceeds from the conviction that, in moving forward across a wide spectrum of negotiations, progress in one area adds momentum to progress in other areas. If we succeed, then no agreement stands alone as an isolated accomplishment vulnerable to the next crisis. We did not invent the interrelationship between issues expressed in the so-called linkage concept; it was a reality because of the range of problems and areas in which the interests of the United States and the Soviet Union impinge on each other. We have looked for progress in a series of agreements settling specific political issues, and we have sought to relate these to a new standard of international conduct appropriate to the dangers of the nuclear age. By acquiring a stake in this network of relationships with the West, the Soviet Union may become more conscious of what it would lose by a return to confrontation. Indeed, it is our hope that it will develop a self-interest in fostering the entire process of relaxation of tensions.

The Global Necessities. In the late 1940s this nation engaged in a great debate about the role it would play in the postwar world. We forged a bipartisan consensus on which our policies were built for more than two decades. By the end of the 1960s the international environment which molded that consensus had been transformed. What in the '50s had seemed a solid bloc of adversaries had fragmented into competing centers of power and doctrine; old allies had gained new strength and self-assurance; scores of new nations had emerged and formed blocs of their own; and all nations were being swept up in a technology that was compressing the planet and deepening our mutual dependence.

Then as now, it was clear that the international structure formed in the immediate postwar period was in fundamental flux and that a new international system was emerging. America's historic opportunity was to help shape a new set of international relationships— more pluralistic, less dominated by military power, less susceptible to confrontation, more open to genuine cooperation among the free and diverse elements of the globe. This new, more positive international environment is possible only if all the major powers—and especially the world's strongest nuclear powers—anchor their policies in the principles of moderation and restraint. They no longer have the power to dominate; they do have the capacity to thwart. They cannot build the new international structure alone; they can make its realization impossible by their rivalry.

Détente is all the more important because of what the creation of a new set of international relations demands of us with respect to other countries and areas. President Ford has assigned the highest priority to maintaining the vitality of our partnerships in Europe, Asia, and Latin America. Our security ties with our allies are essential, but we also believe that recognition of the interdependence of the contemporary world requires cooperation in many other fields. Cooperation becomes more difficult if the United States is perceived by allied public opinion as an obstacle to peace and if public debate is polarized on the issue of whether friendship with the United States is inconsistent with East-West reconciliation.

One important area for invigorated cooperative action is economic policy. . . . Clearly, whatever the state of our relations with the U.S.S.R., the international economic agenda must be addressed. But the task would be infinitely more complex if we proceeded in a Cold War environment.

International economic problems cut across political dividing lines. All nations, regardless of ideology, face the problems of energy and economic growth, feeding burgeoning populations, regulating the use of the oceans, and preserving the environment.

At a minimum, easing international tensions allows the West to devote more intellectual and material resources to these problems. As security concerns recede, humane concerns come again to the fore. . . . The climate of lessened tensions even opens prospects for broader collaboration between East and West. . . .

In the present period mankind may be menaced as much by international economic and political chaos as by the danger of war. Avoiding either hazard demands a cooperative world structure for which improved East-West relations are essential.

The Evolution of Detente—The Balance of Risks & Incentives

The course of détente has not been smooth or even. As late as 1969, Soviet-American relations were ambiguous and uncertain. To be sure, negotiations on Berlin and SALT had begun. But the tendency toward confrontation appeared dominant.

We were challenged by Soviet conduct in the Middle East ceasefire of August 1970, during the Syrian invasion of Jordan in September 1970, on the question of a possible Soviet submarine base in Cuba, in actions around Berlin, and during the Indo-Pakistani war. Soviet policy seemed directed toward fashioning a détente in bilateral relations with our Western European allies, while challenging the United States.

We demonstrated then, and stand ready to do so again, that America will not yield to pressure or the threat of force. We made clear then, as we do today, that détente cannot be pursued selectively in one area or toward one group of countries only. For us détente is indivisible.

Finally, a breakthrough was made in 1971 on several fronts—in the Berlin settlement, in the SALT talks, in other arms control negotiations—that generated the process of détente. It consists of these elements: An elaboration of principles; political discussions to solve outstanding issues and to reach cooperative agreements; economic relations; and arms control negotiations, particularly those concerning strategic arms.

The Elaboration of Principles. Cooperative relations, in our view, must be more than a series of isolated agreements. They must reflect an acceptance of mutual obligations and of the need for accommodation and restraint.

To set forth principles of behavior in formal documents is hardly to guarantee their observance. But they are reference points against which to judge actions and set goals.

The first of the series of documents is the statement of principles signed in Moscow in 1972. It affirms: (1) the necessity of avoiding confrontation; (2) the imperative of mutual restraint; (3) the rejection of attempts to exploit tensions to gain unilateral advantages; (4) the renunciation of claims of special influence in the world; and (5) the willingness, on this new basis, to coexist peacefully and build a firm long-term relationship.

An Agreement on the Prevention of Nuclear War based on these principles was signed in 1973. It affirms that the objective of the policies of the United States and the U.S.S.R. is to remove the danger of nuclear conflict and the use of nuclear weapons. But it emphasizes that this objective presupposes the renunciation of *any* war or threat of war not only by the two nuclear superpowers against each other but also against allies or third countries. In other words, the principle of restraint is not confined to relations between the United States and the U.S.S.R.; it is explicitly extended to include *all* countries.

These statements of principles are not an American concession; indeed, we have been affirming them unilaterally for two decades. Nor are they a legal contract; rather, they are an aspiration and a yardstick by which we assess Soviet behavior. We have never intended to "rely" on Soviet compliance with every principle; we do seek to elaborate standards of conduct which the Soviet Union would violate only to its cost. And if over the long term the more durable relationship takes hold, the basic principles will give it definition, structure, and hope.

Political Dialogue & Cooperative Agreements. One of the features of the current phase of U.S.-Soviet relations is the unprecedented consultation between leaders. . . . [Consultation provides] a mechanism for the resolution of differences before they escalate to the point of public confrontation and commit the prestige of both sides.

The channel between the leaders of the two nations has proved its worth in many crises; it reduces the risk that either side might feel driven to act or to react on the basis of incomplete or confusing information. . . .

But crisis management is not an end in itself. The more fundamental goal is the elaboration of a political relationship which in time will make crises less likely to arise.

It was difficult in the past to speak of a U.S.-Soviet bilateral relationship in any normal sense of the phrase. Trade was negligible. Contacts between various institutions and between the peoples of the two countries were at best sporadic. There were no cooperative efforts in science and technology. Cultural exchange was modest. As a result, there was no tangible inducement toward cooperation and no penalty for aggressive behavior. Today, by joining our efforts even in such seemingly apolitical fields as medical research or environmental protection, we and the Soviets can benefit not only our two peoples but all mankind; in addition, we generate incentives for restraint. . . .

Each project must be judged by the concrete benefits it brings. But in their sum—in their exchange of information and people as well as in their establishment of joint mechanisms—they also constitute a commitment in both countries to work together across a broad spectrum.

The Economic Component. During the period of the Cold War, economic contact between ourselves and the U.S.S.R. was virtually nonexistent. Even then, many argued that improved economic relations might mitigate international tensions; in fact, there were several congressional resolutions to that effect. But recurrent crises prevented any sustained progress.

The period of confrontation should have left little doubt, however, that economic boycott would not transform the Soviet system or impose upon it a conciliatory foreign policy. The U.S.S.R. was quite prepared to maintain heavy military outlays and to concentrate on capital growth by using the resources of the Communist world alone. Moreover, it proved impossible to mount an airtight boycott in practice since, over time, most if not all the other major industrial countries became involved in trade with the East.

The question, then, became how trade and economic contact—in which the Soviet Union is obviously interested—could serve the purposes of peace. On the one hand, economic relations cannot be separated from the political context. Clearly, we cannot be asked to reward hostile conduct with economic benefits, even if in the process we deny ourselves some commercially profitable opportunities. On the other hand, when political relations begin to normalize, it is difficult to explain why economic relations should not be normalized as well.

We have approached the question of economic relations with deliberation and circumspection and as an act of policy, not primarily of commercial opportunity. As political relations have improved on a broad basis, economic issues have been dealt with on a comparably broad front. A series of interlocking economic agreements with the U.S.S.R. has been negotiated side by side with the political progress already noted. The 25-year-old Lend-Lease debt was settled; the reciprocal extension of most-favored-nation (MFN) treatment was negotiated, together with safeguards against the possible disruption of our markets and a series of practical arrangements to facilitate the conduct of business in the U.S.S.R. by American firms; our government credit facilities were made available for trade with the U.S.S.R.; and a maritime agreement regulating the carriage of goods has been signed.

These were all primarily regulatory agreements conferring no immediate benefits on the Soviet Union but serving as blueprints for an expanded economic relationship if the political improvement continued.

This approach commanded widespread domestic approval. It was considered a natural outgrowth of political progress. At no time were issues regarding Soviet domestic political practices raised. Indeed, not until *after* the 1972 agreements was the Soviet domestic order [specifically, Soviet restrictions on the emigration of Jews— and other Soviet citizens] invoked as a reason for arresting or reversing the progress so painstakingly achieved. This sudden ex post facto form of linkage raises serious questions:

● For the Soviet Union, it casts doubt on our reliability as a negotiating partner.

● The significance of trade, originally envisaged as only one ingredient of a complex and evolving relationship, is inflated out of all proportion.

● The hoped-for results of policy become transformed into preconditions for any policy at all.

We recognize the depth and validity of the moral concerns expressed by those who oppose, or put conditions on, expanded trade with the U.S.S.R. But a sense of proportion must be maintained about the leverage our economic relations give us with the U.S.S.R.:

● Denial of economic relations cannot by itself achieve what it failed to do when it was part of a determined policy of political and military confrontation.

● The economic bargaining ability of most-favored-nation status is marginal. MFN grants no special privilege to the U.S.S.R.; in fact it is a misnomer, since we have such agreements with over 100 countries. To enact it would be to remove a discriminatory holdover of the days of the Cold War. . . .

● Trade benefits are not a one-way street; the laws of mutual advantage operate, or there will be no trade.

● The technology that flows to the U.S.S.R. as a result of expanded U.S.-Soviet trade may have a few indirect uses for military production. But with our continuing restrictions on strategic exports, we can maintain adequate controls—and we intend to do so. Moreover, the same technology has been available to the U.S.S.R. and will be increasingly so from other non-Communist sources. Boycott denies us a means of influence and possible commercial gain; it does not deprive the U.S.S.R. of technology.

● The actual and potential flow of credits from the United States represents a tiny fraction of the capital available to the U.S.S.R. domestically and elsewhere, including Western Europe and Japan. But it does allow us to exercise some influence through our ability to control the scope of trade relationships.

● Over time, trade and investment may leaven the autarkic tendencies of the Soviet system, invite gradual association of the Soviet economy with the world economy, and foster a degree of interdependence that adds an element of stability to the political equation.

The Strategic Relationship. We cannot expect to relax international tensions or achieve a more stable international system should the two strongest nuclear powers conduct an unrestrained strategic arms race. Thus, perhaps the single most important component of our policy toward the Soviet Union is the effort to limit strategic weapons competition.

The competition in which we now find ourselves is historically unique:

● Each side has the capacity to destroy civilization as we know it.

● Failure to maintain equivalence could jeopardize not only our freedom but our very survival.

● The lead time for technological innovation is so long, yet the pace of change so relentless, that the arms race and strategic policy itself are in danger of being driven by technological necessity.

● When nuclear arsenals reach levels involving thousands of launchers and over 10,000 warheads, and when the characteristics of the weapons of the two sides are so incommensurable, it becomes difficult to determine what combination of numbers of strategic weapons and performance capabilities would give one side a militarily and politically useful superiority. At a minimum, clear changes in the strategic balance can be achieved only by efforts so enormous and by increments so large that the very attempt would be highly destabilizing.

● The prospect of a decisive military advantage, even if theoretically possible, is politically intolerable; neither side will passively permit a massive shift in the nuclear balance. Therefore the probable outcome of each succeeding round of competition is the restoration of a strategic equilibrium, but at increasingly higher levels of forces.
● The arms race is driven by political as well as military factors. While a decisive advantage is hard to calculate, the *appearance* of inferiority—whatever its actual significance—can have serious political consequences. With weapons that are unlikely to be used and for which there is no operational experience, the psychological impact can be crucial. Thus each side has a high incentive to achieve not only the reality but the appearance of equality. In a very real sense each side shapes the military establishment of the other.

If we are driven to it, the United States will sustain an arms race. Indeed, it is likely that the United States would emerge from such a competition with an edge over the Soviet Union in most significant categories of strategic arms. But the political or military benefit which would flow from such a situation would remain elusive. Indeed, after such an evolution it might well be that *both* sides would be worse off than before the race began. . . .

The Soviet Union must realize that the overall relationship with the United States will be less stable if strategic balance is sought through unrestrained competitive programs. Sustaining the buildup requires exhortations by both sides that in time may prove incompatible with restrained international conduct. The very fact of a strategic arms race has a high potential for feeding attitudes of hostility and suspicion on both sides, transforming the fears of those who demand more weapons into self-fulfilling prophecies.

The American people can be asked to bear the cost and political instability of a race which is doomed to stalemate only if it is clear that every effort has been made to prevent it. That is why every President since Eisenhower has pursued negotiations for the limitation of strategic arms while maintaining the military programs essential to strategic balance.

There are more subtle strategic reasons for our interest in SALT. Our supreme strategic purpose is the prevention of nuclear conflict through the maintenance of sufficient political and strategic power. Estimates of what constitutes "sufficiency" have been contentious. Our judgments have changed with our experience in deploying these weapons and as the Soviets expanded their own nuclear forces. When in the late 1960s it became apparent that the Soviet Union, for practical purposes, had achieved a kind of rough parity with the United States, we adopted the current strategic doctrine.

We determined that stability required strategic forces invulnerable to attack, thus removing the incentive on either side to strike first. Reality reinforced doctrine. As technology advanced, it became apparent that neither side *could* realistically expect to develop a credible disarming capability against the other except through efforts so gigantic as to represent a major threat to political stability.

One result of our doctrine was basing our strategic planning on the assumption that in the unlikely event of nuclear attack, the President should have a wide range of options available in deciding at what level and against what targets to respond. We designed our strategic forces with a substantial measure of flexibility, so that the U.S. response need not include an attack on the aggressor's cities— thus inviting the destruction of our own—but could instead hit other targets. . . . In our view such flexibility enhances the certainty of retaliation and thereby makes an attack less likely. Above all, it preserves the capability for human decision even in the ultimate crisis.

Another, at first seemingly paradoxical, result was a growing commitment to negotiated agreements on strategic arms. SALT became one means by which we and the Soviet Union could enhance stability by setting mutual constraints on our respective forces and by gradually reaching an understanding of the doctrinal considerations that underlie the deployment of nuclear weapons. Through SALT the two sides can reduce the suspicions and fears which fuel strategic competition. SALT, in the American conception, is a means to achieve strategic stability by methods other than the arms race.

Our specific objectives have been:

1. To break the momentum of ever-increasing levels of armaments;
2. To control certain qualitative aspects—particularly MIRVs [multiple independently targeted reentry vehicles];
3. To moderate the pace of new deployments; and
4. Ultimately, to achieve reductions in force levels.

The SALT agreements already signed represent a major contribution to strategic stability and a significant first step toward a longer term and possibly broader agreement. . . .

The agreements signed in 1972 which limited antiballistic missile [ABM] defenses and froze the level of ballistic missile forces on both sides represented the essential first step toward a less volatile strategic environment.

● By limiting antiballistic missiles to very low levels of deployment, the United States and the Soviet Union removed a potential source of instability; for one side to build an extensive defense for its cities would inevitably be interpreted by the other as a step toward a first-strike capability. Before seeking a disarming capability, a potential aggressor would want to protect his population centers from incoming nuclear weapons.

● Some have alleged that the interim agreement, which expires in October 1977, penalizes the United States by permitting the Soviet Union to deploy more strategic missile launchers, both land based and sea based, than the United States. Such a view is misleading. When the agreement was signed in May 1972, the Soviet Union *already* possessed more land-based intercontinental ballistic missiles than the United States, and given the pace of its submarine construction program, over the next few years it could have built virtually twice as many nuclear ballistic missile submarines.

The interim agreement confined a dynamic Soviet ICBM program to the then-existing level; it put a ceiling on the heaviest Soviet ICBMs [intercontinental ballistic missiles], the weapons that most concern us; and it set an upper limit on the Soviet submarine-launched ballistic missile program. No American program was abandoned or curtailed. We remained free to deploy multiple warheads. No restraints were placed on bombers—a weapons system in which we have a large advantage. Indeed, the U.S. lead in missile warheads is likely to be somewhat greater at the end of this agreement than at the time of its signature.

The SALT-I agreements were the first deliberate attempt by the nuclear superpowers to bring about strategic stability through negotiation. This very process is conducive to further restraint. For example, in the first round of SALT negotiations in 1970–72, both sides bitterly contested the number of ABM sites permitted by the agreement; two years later both sides gave up the right to build more than one site. In sum, we believed when we signed these agreements—and we believe now—that they had reduced the danger of nuclear war, that both sides had acquired some greater interest in restraint, and that the basis had been created for the present effort to reach a broader agreement.

The goal of the current negotiations is an agreement for a 10-year period. . . .

With respect to ceilings on strategic forces, we have defined our goal as essential equivalence in strategic capabilities. What constitutes equivalence involves subjective judgment. Because U.S. and Soviet forces *are* different from each other—in number and size of weapons, in technological refinement, in performance characteristics—they are difficult to compare. . . .

Numerical balance is no longer enough. To achieve stability, it will be necessary to consider as well the impact of technological change in such areas as missile throw weight, multiple reentry vehicles, and missile accuracy. The difficulty is that we are dealing not only with disparate levels of forces but with disparate capabilities, MIRV technology being a conspicuous example. The rate of increase of warheads is surging far ahead of the increase in delivery vehicles. This is why the United States considers MIRV limitation an essential component of the next phase of the SALT negotiations. If we fail, the rate of technology will outstrip our capacity to design effective limitations; constantly proliferating warheads of increasing accuracy will overwhelm fixed launchers. An arms race will be virtually inevitable.

The third area for negotiations is the pace of deployments of new or more modern systems. Neither side will remain in its present position without change for another decade. . . . Our task is to see whether the two sides can agree to slow the pace of deployment so that modernization is less likely to threaten the overall balance or trigger an excessive reaction.

Finally, a 10-year program gives us a chance to negotiate reductions. Reductions have occasionally been proposed as an alternative to ceilings; they are often seen as more desirable or at least easier to negotiate. In fact, it is a far more complicated problem. Reductions in launchers, for example, if not accompanied by restrictions on the number of warheads, will only magnify vulnerability. The fewer the aim points, the simpler it would be to calculate an attack. At the same time, reductions will have to proceed from some baseline and must therefore be preceded by agreed ceilings—if only of an interim nature. But a 10-year program should permit the negotiation of stable ceilings resulting from the start of a process of reductions.

Détente is admittedly far from a modern equivalent to the kind of stable peace that characterized most of the 19th century. But it is a long step away from the bitter and aggressive spirit that has characterized so much of the postwar period. When linked to such broad and unprecedented projects as SALT, détente takes on added meaning and opens prospects of a more stable peace. SALT agreements should be seen as steps in a process leading to progressively greater stability. It is in that light that SALT and related projects will be judged by history.

An Assessment of Detente

    . . . Major progress has been made:

● Berlin's potential as Europe's perennial flashpoint has been substantially reduced through the quadripartite agreement of 1971. The United States considers strict adherence to the agreement a major test of détente.

● We and our allies are launched on negotiations with the Warsaw Pact and other countries in the conference on European security and cooperation, a conference designed to foster East-West dialogue and cooperation.

● At the same time, NATO and the Warsaw Pact are negotiating the reduction of their forces in Central Europe.

● The honorable termination of America's direct military involvement in Indochina and the substantial lowering of regional conflict were made possible by many factors. But this achievement would have been much more difficult, if not impossible, in an era of Soviet and Chinese hostility toward the United States.

● America's principal alliances have proved their durability in a new era. Many feared that détente would undermine them. Instead, détente has helped to place our alliance ties on a more enduring basis by removing the fear that friendship with the United States involved the risk of unnecessary confrontation with the U.S.S.R.

● Many incipient crises with the Soviet Union have been contained or settled without ever reaching the point of public disagreement. . . .

● A series of bilateral cooperative agreements has turned the U.S.-Soviet relationship in a far more positive direction.

● We have achieved unprecedented agreements in arms limitation and measures to avoid accidental war.
● New possibilities for positive U.S.-Soviet cooperation have emerged on issues in which the globe is interdependent: science and technology, environment, energy.

These accomplishments do not guarantee peace. But they have served to lessen the rigidities of the past and offer hope for a better era. . . . Whether the change is temporary and tactical, or lasting and basic, our task is essentially the same: To transform that change into a permanent condition devoted to the purpose of a secure peace and mankind's aspiration for a better life. A tactical change sufficiently prolonged becomes a lasting transformation.

But the whole process can be jeopardized if it is taken for granted. As the Cold War recedes in memory, détente can come to seem so natural that it appears safe to levy progressively greater demands on it. The temptation to combine détente with increasing pressure on the Soviet Union will grow. Such an attitude would be disastrous. We would not accept it from Moscow; Moscow will not accept it from us. We will finally wind up again with the Cold War and fail to achieve either peace or any humane goal.

To be sure, the process of détente raises serious issues for many people. Let me deal with these in terms of the principles which underlie our policy.

First, if détente is to endure, both sides must benefit.

There is no question that the Soviet Union obtains benefits from détente. . . . But the essential point surely must be that détente serves American and world interests as well. If these coincide with some Soviet interests, this will only strengthen the durability of the process.

On the global scale, in terms of the conventional measures of power, influence, and position, our interests have not suffered—they have generally prospered. In many areas of the world, the influence and the respect we enjoy are greater than was the case for many years. It is also true that Soviet influence and presence are felt in many parts of the world. But this is a reality that would exist without détente. . . .

Second, building a new relationship with the Soviet Union does not entail any devaluation of traditional alliance relations.

Our approach to relations with the U.S.S.R. has always been, and will continue to be, rooted in the belief that the cohesion of our alliances, and particularly the Atlantic alliance, is a precondition to establishing a more constructive relationship with the U.S.S.R.

Crucial, indeed unique, as may be our concern with Soviet power, we do not delude ourselves that we should deal with it alone. When we speak of Europe and Japan as representing centers of power and influence, we describe not merely an observable fact but an indispensable element in the equilibrium needed to keep the world at peace. The cooperation and partnership between us transcend formal agreements; they reflect values and traditions not soon, if ever, to be shared with our adversaries.

Inevitably, a greater sense of drama accompanies our dealings with the Soviet Union, because the central issues of war and peace cannot be other than dramatic. . . . The complications attendant to adapting U.S.-European relations should not be confused with their basic character. . . . Today relations with Europe and Japan are strong and improving. We have made progress in developing common positions on security, détente, and energy. The experience of the past year has demonstrated that there is no contradiction between vigorous, organic alliance relations and a more positive relationship with adversaries; indeed, they are mutually reinforcing.

Third, the emergence of more normal relations with the Soviet Union must not undermine our resolve to maintain our national defense.

There is a tendency in democratic societies to relax as dangers seem to recede; there is an inclination to view the maintenance of strength as incompatible with relaxation of tensions rather than its precondition. But this is primarily a question of leadership. We shall attempt to be vigilant to the dangers facing America. . . .

Fourth, we must know what can and cannot be achieved in changing human conditions in the East.

The question of dealing with Communist governments has troubled the American people and the Congress since 1917. There has always been a fear that by working with a government whose internal policies differ so sharply with our own we are in some manner condoning these policies or encouraging their continuation. Some argue that until there is a genuine "liberalization"—or signs of serious progress in this direction—all elements of conciliation in Soviet policy must be regarded as temporary and tactical. In that view, demands for internal changes must be the precondition for the pursuit of a relaxation of tensions with the Soviet Union.

Our view is different. We shall insist on responsible international behavior by the Soviet Union and use it as the primary index of our relationship. Beyond this we will use our influence to the maximum to alleviate suffering and to respond to humane appeals. We know what we stand for, and we shall leave no doubt about it.

Both as a government and as a people we *have* made the attitude of the American people clear on countless occasions in ways that have produced results. I believe that both the executive and the Congress, each playing its proper role, have been effective. With respect to the specific issue of emigration:

● The education exit tax of 1971 is no longer being collected. We have been assured that it will not be reapplied.

● Hardship cases submitted to the Soviet Government have been given increased attention, and remedies have been forthcoming in many well-known instances.

● The volume of Jewish emigration has increased from a trickle to tens of thousands.

● And we are now moving toward an understanding that should significantly diminish the obstacles to emigration and ease the hardship of prospective emigrants.

We have accomplished much. But we cannot demand that the Soviet Union, in effect, suddenly reverse five decades of Soviet, and centuries of Russian, history. Such an attempt would be futile and at the same time hazard all that has already been achieved. . . . A renewal of the Cold War will hardly encourage the Soviet Union to change its emigration policies or adopt a more benevolent attitude toward dissent.

Agenda for the Future

Détente is a process, not a permanent achievement. The agenda is full and continuing. Obviously the main concern must be to reduce the sources of potential conflict. This requires efforts in several interrelated areas:

● The military competition in all its aspects must be subject to increasingly firm restraints by both sides.

● Political competition, especially in moments of crisis, must be guided by the principles of restraint set forth in the documents described earlier. . . .

● Restraint in crises must be augmented by cooperation in removing the causes of crises. . . .

● The process of negotiations and consultation must be continuous and intense. But no agreement between the nuclear superpowers can be durable if made over the heads of other nations which have a stake in the outcome. We should not seek to impose peace; we can, however, see that our own actions and conduct are conducive to peace.

In the coming months we shall strive:

● To complete the negotiations for comprehensive and equitable limitations on strategic arms until at least 1985;

● To complete the multilateral negotiations on mutual force reductions in Central Europe, so that security will be enhanced for all the countries of Europe;

● To conclude the conference on European security and cooperation in a manner that promotes both security and human aspirations;

● To continue the efforts to limit the spread of nuclear weapons to additional countries without depriving those countries of the peaceful benefits of atomic energy;

● To complete ratification of the recently negotiated treaty banning underground nuclear testing by the United States and U.S.S.R. above a certain threshold;

● To begin negotiations on the recently agreed effort to overcome the possible dangers of environmental modification techniques for military purposes; and

● To resolve the longstanding attempts to cope with the dangers of chemical weaponry.

We must never forget that the process of détente depends ultimately on habits and modes of conduct that extend beyond the letter of agreements to the spirit of relations as a whole. . . .

In cataloging the desirable, we must take care not to jeopardize what is attainable. We must consider what alternative policies are available and what their consequences would be. And the implications of alternatives must be examined not just in terms of a single issue but for how they might affect the entire range of Soviet-American relations and the prospects for world peace.

We must assess not only individual challenges to détente but also their cumulative impact: If we justify each agreement with Moscow only when we can show unilateral gain; if we strive for an elusive strategic "superiority"; if we systematically block benefits to the Soviet Union; if we try to transform the Soviet system by pressure. If in short, we look for final results before we agree to any results, then we would be reviving the doctrines of liberation and massive retaliation of the 1950s. And we would do so at a time when Soviet physical power and influence on the world are greater than a quarter century ago when those policies were devised and failed. . . .

Let there be no question, however, that Soviet actions could destroy détente as well: If the Soviet Union uses détente to strengthen its military capacity in all fields; if in crises it acts to sharpen tension; if it does not contribute to progress toward stability; if it seeks to undermine our alliances. If it is deaf to the urgent needs of the least developed and the emerging issues of interdependence, then it in turn tempts a return to the tensions and conflicts we have made such efforts to overcome. . . .

We have insisted toward the Soviet Union that we cannot have the atmosphere of détente without the substance. It is equally clear that the substance of détente will disappear in an atmosphere of hostility. . . .

We face an opportunity that was not possible 25 years, or even a decade, ago. If that opportunity is lost, its moment will not quickly come again. Indeed, it may not come at all. . . .

> *In his first major address as Secretary of State, Kissinger had told the U.N. General Assembly Sept. 24, 1973 of how detente fitted into Nixon Administration hopes for "a comprehensive, institutionalized peace encompassing all nations. . . ."*

TWO CENTURIES AGO THE PHILOSOPHER Kant predicted that perpetual peace would come eventually—either as the creation of man's moral aspirations or as the consequence of physical necessity. What seemed utopian then looms as tomorrow's reality; soon there will be no alternative. Our only choice is whether the world envisaged in the U.N. Charter will come about as the result of our vision or of a catastrophe invited by our shortsightedness.

The United States has made its choice. My country seeks true peace, not simply an armistice. We strive for a world in which the rule of law governs and fundamental human rights are the birthright of all. . . .

We start from a bedrock of solid progress. Many of the crises that haunted past General Assemblies have been put behind us. Agreement has been reached on Berlin; there is a cease-fire in the Middle East; the Vietnam war has been ended. The rigid confrontation that has dominated international life and weakened this organization for a quarter of a century has been softened.

The United States and the Soviet Union have perceived a commonality of interest in avoiding nuclear holocaust and in establishing a broad web of constructive relationships. Talks on strategic arms limitation have already produced historic accords aimed at slowing the arms race and insuring strategic stability. . . .

Two decades of estrangement between the United States and the People's Republic of China has given way to constructive dialogue and productive exchanges. President Nixon has met with the leaders of that nation; we have agreed to a historic communique that honestly sets forth both our differences and our common principles; and we have each opened a liaison office in the capital of the other.

Many other countries have seized the initiative and contributed—in substance and spirit—to the relaxation of tensions. . . .

Yet these achievement, solid as they are, have only made less precarious the dangers and divisions inherited from the postwar era. We have ended many of the confrontations of the Cold War; yet, even in this room, the vocabulary of suspicion persists. Relaxation of tensions is justified by some as merely a tactical interlude before renewed struggle. Others suspect the emergence of a two-power condominium. And as tension between the two original blocs has eased, a third grouping increasingly assumes the characteristics of a bloc of its own—the alignment of the nonaligned.

So the world is uneasily suspended between old slogans and new realities, between a view of peace as but a pause in an unending struggle and a vision of peace as a promise of global cooperation. . . .

The United States will never be satisfied with a world of uneasy truces, of offsetting blocks, of accommodations of convenience. We know that power can enforce a resigned passivity, but only a sense of justice can enlist consensus. We strive for a peace whose stability rests not merely on a balance of forces but on shared aspirations. . . .

The United States deeply believes:

That justice cannot be confined by national frontiers.

That truth is universal, and not the peculiar possession of a single people or group or ideology.

That compassion and humanity must ennoble all our endeavors.

In this spirit we ask this Assembly to move with us from détente among the big powers to cooperation among all nations, from coexistence to community.

Our journey must begin with the world as it is and with the issues now before us. The United States will spare no effort to ease tensions further and to move toward greater stability. . . .

In all these efforts the United States will be guided by fundamental principles:

We have no desire for domination. We will oppose. . .any nation that chooses this path. We have not been asked to participate in a condominium; we would reject such an appeal if it were made.

We will never abandon our allies or our friends. The strengthening of our traditional ties is essential foundation for the development of new relationships with old adversaries.

We will work for peace through the United Nations as well as through bilateral relationships. . . .

At the Pacem in Terris Conference in Washington Oct. 8, 1973, Kissinger discussed problems in détente with the U.S.S.R.

FOR A GENERATION OUR PREOCCUPATION was to prevent the Cold War from degenerating into a hot war. Today, when the danger of global conflict has diminished, we face the more profound problem of defining what we mean by peace and determining the ultimate purpose of improved international relations.

For two decades the solidarity of our alliances seemed as constant as the threats to our security. Now our allies have regained strength and self-confidence, and relations with adversaries have improved. All this has given rise to uncertainties over the sharing of burdens with friends and the impact of reduced tensions on the cohesion of alliances. . . .

The current public discussion reflects some interesting and significant shifts in perspective:

A foreign policy once considered excessively moralistic is now looked upon by some as excessively pragmatic.

The government was criticized in 1969 for holding back East-West trade with certain countries until there was progress in their foreign policies. Now we are criticized for not holding back East-West trade until there are changes in those same countries' domestic policies.

The Administration's foreign policy once decried as too Cold-War oriented is now attacked as too insensitive to the profound moral antagonism between Communism and freedom. . . .

The desirability of peace and detente is affirmed but both the inducements to progress and the penalties to confrontation are restricted by legislation.

Expressions of concern for human values in other countries are coupled with failure to support the very programs designed to help developing areas improve their economic and social conditions.

The declared objective of maintaining a responsible American international role clashes with nationalistic pressures in trade and monetary negotiations and with calls for unilateral withdrawal from alliance obligations.

It is clear that we face genuine moral dilemmas and important policy choices. But it is also clear that we need to define the framework of our dialogue more perceptively and understandingly.

Foreign policy must begin with the understanding that it involves relationships between sovereign countries. Sovereignty has been defined as a will uncontrolled by others; that is what gives foreign policy its contingent and ever incomplete character.

For disagreements among sovereign states can be settled only by negotiation or by power, by compromise or by imposition. Which of these methods prevails depends on the values, the strengths and the domestic systems of the countries involved. A nation's values define what is just; its strength determines what is possible; its domestic structure decides what policies can in fact be implemented and sustained.

Thus foreign policy involves two partially conflicting endeavors:—defining the interests, purposes and values of a society and relating them to the interests, purposes and values of others.

The policy maker, therefore, must strike a balance between what is desirable and what is possible. Progress will always be measured in partial steps and in the relative satisfaction of alternative goals.

Tension is unavoidable between values, which are invariable cast in maximum terms, and efforts to promote them, which of necessity involve compromise. Foreign policy is explained domestically in terms of justice. But what is defined as justice at home becomes the subject of negotiation abroad. It is thus no accident that many nations, including our own, view the international arena as a forum in which virtue is thwarted by the clever practice of foreigners.

In a community of sovereign states, the quest for peace involves a paradox: the attempt to impose absolute justice by one side will be seen as absolute injustice by all others; the quest for total security for some turns into total insecurity for the remainder. Stability depends on the relative satisfaction and therefore also the relative dissatisfaction of the various states. The pursuit of peace must therefore begin with the pragmatic concept of coexistence—especially in a period of ideological conflict. . . .

When policy becomes excessively moralistic it may turn quixotic or dangerous. A presumed monopoly on truth obstructs negotiation and accommodation. Good results may be given up in the quest for every elusive ideal solutions. Policy may fall prey to ineffectual posturing or adventuristic crusades. . . .

. . . The policy maker expresses his morality by implementing a sequence of imperfections and partial solutions in pursuit of his ideals. . . .

We are at one of those rare moments where through a combination of fortuitous circumstances and design man seems in a position to shape his future. What we need is the confidence to discuss issues without bitter strife, the wisdom to define together the nature of our world as well as the vision to chart together a more just future.

Nothing demonstrates this need more urgently than our relationship with the Soviet Union.

This Administration has never had any illusions about the Soviet system. We have always insisted that progress in technical fields, such as trade, had to follow—and reflect—progress toward more stable international relations. We have maintained a strong military balance and a flexible defense posture as a buttress to stability. We have insisted that disarmament had to be mutual. We have judged movement in our relations with the Soviet Union, not by atmospherics, but by how well concrete problems are resolved and by whether there is responsible international conduct. . . .

The demand that Moscow modify its domestic policy as a precondition for MFN ["most-favored-nation" treatment] or detente was never made while we were negotiating; now it is inserted after both sides have carefully shaped an overall mosaic. Thus it raises questions about our entire bilateral relationship.

Finally the issue effects not only our relationship with the Soviet Union, but also with many other countries whose internal structures we find incompatible with our own. Conditions imposed on one country could inhibit expanding relations with others, such as the People's Republic of China.

We shall never condone the suppression of fundamental liberties. We shall urge humane principles and use our influence to promote justice. But the issue comes down to the limits of such efforts. How hard can we press without provoking the Soviet leadership into returning to practices in its foreign policy that increase international tensions? . . .

For half a century we have objected to Communist efforts to alter the domestic structures of other countries. For a generation of Cold War we sought to ease the risks produced by competing ideologies. Are we now to come full circle and insist on domestic compatibility as a condition of progress? . . .

Our policy with respect to detente is clear: We shall resist aggressive foreign policies. Detente cannot survive irresponsibility in any area, including the Middle East. As for the internal policies of closed systems the United States will never forget that the antagonism between freedom and its enemies is part of the reality of the modern age. We are not neutral in that struggle. As long as we remain powerful we will use our influence to promote freedom, as we always have. But in the nuclear age we are obliged to recognize that the issue of war and peace also involves human lives and that the attainment of peace is a profound moral concern. . . .

Kissinger elaborated some of his views on detente at a year-end press conference in Washington Dec. 27, 1973.

WITH THE WAR IN VIETNAM ENDED, the major focus of our foreign policy attention could turn to the design of the structure of peace that has been the President's [Nixon's] principal goal since he came into office.

In its first phase, this meant that the United States had to reduce many of its overextended commitments and that the United States had to disengage gradually from any foreign involvement and, above all, that the United States should evoke a sense of responsibility for their own sake in many areas of the world. This was the so-called Nixon doctrine which characterized the first two or three years of the President's first term.

It was the prelude to the initiatives toward China and the détente with the Soviet Union that were to lay the basis for a fundamental realignment of the postwar period which had been based on a rigid division between opposing hostile blocs.

So, by the time the second term of the President started, we faced an international situation in which the basic assumptions of the immediate postwar period had been substantially altered. The rigid hostility between the Communist world and the non-Communist world had been altered first by the divisions within the Communist world itself and by the amelioration of relations between the Soviet Union and the United States, as well as the People's Republic of China and the United States. . . .

. . . Our policy toward both the Soviet Union and the People's Republic of China has been characterized as a policy of détente. And it is the characteristic of policies that become more or less accepted that the benefits are taken for granted and that some of the difficulties that were overlooked in the beginning become more and more apparent.

Let me explain what we understand by détente. We do not say that détente is based on the compatibility of domestic systems. We recognize that the values and ideology of both the Soviet Union and the People's Republic of China are opposed and sometimes hostile to ours. We do not say that there are no conflicting national interests. We do say that there is a fundamental change in the international environment compared to any other previous period, a change which was expressed by President Eisenhower more than 20 years ago when he said, "There is no longer any alternative to peace." Under conditions of nuclear plenty, the decision to engage in general war involves consequences of such magnitude that no responsible statesman can base his policy on the constant threat of such a holocaust and every leader with a responsibility for these weapons must set himself the task of bringing about conditions which reduce the possibility of such a war to a minimum and, indeed, over any extended period of time reduce this possibility to zero.

So we do not say that we approve of the domestic evolution of the Soviet Union or of other Communist countries with which we are attempting to coexist. Nor do we accept that détente can be used for military expansion or for threatening weaker countries or for undermining our traditional friendships. But we do make a conscious effort to set up rules of conduct and to establish a certain interconnection of interests and, above all, to establish communications between the top leaders and between officials at every level that make it possible in times of crisis to reduce the danger of accident or miscalculation.

This has been our policy with the Soviet Union, and it is the policy we have pursued as well with the People's Republic of China.

With respect to the Soviet Union, it has led us into a series of negotiations on the limitations of strategic arms, on mutual and balanced forced reductions (MBFR), on European security, on such measures as the agreement for the prevention of nuclear war—into extended exchanges between the President and General Secretary Brezhnev designed to lay the basis for a more civil discourse.

This does not preclude that this relationship can break down.

Ideology, long-established relations, as well as the internal logic of certain areas such as the Middle East, can produce tensions and indeed can produce explosions that, whether or not they are fostered by the two superpowers, may bring them into conflict with each other.

Nor is it foreordained that the behavior of the two protagonists necessarily lives up to the principles that they declare. In those cases . . . the United States will maintain its commitments and will defend its international position and the position of its friends.

But we will not be easily deflected from the course of seeking a relaxation of tension—a course which proved itself even in tension periods and a course which modern technology will impose on any administration even if we should be prevented from carrying out all the measures by different opinions about what should be the purposes of détente—such as the degree to which we should attempt to use our foreign policy to affect the domestic structure of other countries.

With respect to the People's Republic of China, we have established liaison offices in each other's capitals that are performing many of the functions that are normally carried out by embassies.

We have had two visits by myself to Peking and also a substantial expansion of economic and other exchanges.

So we believe that with respect to the two great Communist countries, we are on a course which is in the interests of all of mankind and which is essential for the long-term prospects of peace. . . .

> *In an interview published in the New York Times Oct. 13, 1974, Kissinger was asked, concerning China and the U.S.S.R., "whether . . . you have not actually chosen one over the other and in the process were playing one up against the other."*

ANY ATTEMPT TO PLAY OFF THE SOVIET Union and Communist China against each other would have a high risk that, at least for tactical reasons, they would combine against us. The rivalry and tensions between the Soviet Union and Communist China were not created by the United States. In fact, we didn't believe in their reality for much too long a time. They cannot be exploited by the United States. They can only be noted by the United States.

The correct policy for the United States is to take account of what exists and to conduct a policy of meticulous honesty with both of them so that neither believes we are trying to use one against the other. In the course of events, it may happen that one may feel that it is gaining benefit against the other as a result of dealing with us, but that cannot be our aim or purpose.

We have meticulously avoided forms of cooperation with the Soviet Union that could be construed as directed against China. We have never signed agreements whose chief purpose could be seen as directed against China, and conversely we have never participated with China in declarations that could be seen as aimed at the Soviet Union. We have developed our bilateral relationships with both and left them to sort out their relationships with each other. In fact, we have rarely talked to either of them about the other.

> *Kissinger detailed some of the achievements of the detente policy and some of its dangers in an address May 12, 1975 in St. Louis, Mo.*

ONE OF THE LEGACIES OF A SIMPLER period of American history is the conviction that we can pursue only one strand of policy at one time—either strength or conciliation, either relations with our allies or improving relations with our adversaries.

But the fact is that we do not have such a choice. In a complicated world in transition it is important to recognize that if we do not pursue all these strands, we shall not be able to pursue any of them. Our people expect their government to work for stability and peace, not to seek out confrontation. If we are faced with a crisis, the American people must know that it was forced upon us. Our alliances can be vital only if they are sustained by the conviction that their purpose is not to produce tension but to provide incentives for an ultimate settlement.

It is in this context that we must judge the contrast between the state of U.S.-Soviet relations today and 15 years ago. The world is no longer continually shaken by direct and bitter confrontations. There is a general understanding that tensions when they occur are not the result of U.S. intransigence, and this has enhanced our influence. It would be dangerous to take these achievements for granted; undoubtedly a world neatly divided between black and white was psychologically easier to handle, but it was also infinitely more dangerous.

We therefore should beware of the siren song that détente is a trap, a one-way street of American unilateral concession. In this Administration it will never be. In pursuing détente we will be guided by the following principles:

● We are not neutral in the struggle between freedom and tyranny. We know that we are dealing with countries of opposed ideology and values.

● But we owe our people and mankind an untiring effort to avoid nuclear holocaust. In the thermonuclear age, when the survival of civilization is at stake, we cannot defend peace by militant rhetoric.

● We must outgrow the notion that every setback is a Soviet gain or every problem is caused by Soviet action. In Portugal, the Middle East, even in Indochina, difficulties have resulted as much from local conditions or inadequate U.S. responses as from Soviet intervention.

● We cannot use détente as a substitute for our own effort and determination. Where a vacuum exists, it will be exploited. We have not yet reached the stage where vigilance can be relaxed.

These principles enable us to judge the state of our relations with the Soviet Union. These relations occur on many levels. The first order of business is the imperative of avoiding thermonuclear war. . . . A President has no higher responsibility than sparing our people the dangers of general nuclear war. He can have no greater goal than to put a permanent end to a spiraling arms race which, uncontrolled, can jeopardize the peace.

The agreement in principle reached last November at Vladivostok between President Ford and General Secretary [Leonid I.] Brezhnev on a long-term agreement limiting strategic offensive weapons is a major step in this direction. When this negotiation is completed later this year, a ceiling will have been placed on the qualitative as well as quantitative expansion of strategic forces for the first time in history. The momentum of military deployments will have been slowed; military planning will no longer be driven by fear of the unknown; a baseline will have been established from which reductions can be negotiated soon thereafter.

Direct communication and consultation between the United States and the Soviet Union and institutionalized cooperation in economic, scientific, and cultural fields constitute the second level of our relationship. The extent of these links is now unprecedented.

Naturally there are benefits for the Soviet Union, or else the Soviet Union would not participate in them. But they also serve our interest, or we would not conclude them. These agreements serve the additional purpose of engaging the Soviet Union at many levels in contacts with the outside world so as to provide incentives for restraint. And they occur in an environment where failure to proceed on our part only opens the door to other industrialized countries perhaps less able than we to withstand the political use of economic relationships. . . .

A third level of U.S.-Soviet relations involves the easing of tensions in areas where our vital interests impinge on each other. The Berlin Agreement of 1971 was both important and symbolic; it was a practical negotiated solution of a chronic dispute that on at least three occasions in 20 years had brought the world to the brink of war. . . .

These achievements of détente must be balanced against the record of the fourth level of U.S.-Soviet relations: the quest for stability in areas peripheral to the vital interests of the two so-called superpowers. Here the progress achieved in other fields of our relations has not been equaled. The expansion of Soviet military power and its extension around the world is a serious concern to us. The willingness of the Soviet Union to exploit strategic opportunities, even though some of these opportunities presented themselves more or less spontaneously and not as a result of Soviet action, constitutes a heavy mortgage on détente.

If détente turns into a formula for more selective exploitation of opportunities, the new trends in U.S.-Soviet relations will be in jeopardy. If our contention in peripheral areas persists, even more if it becomes exacerbated, the progress achieved in other areas of détente will ultimately be undermined. The United States is determined to maintain the hopeful new trends in U.S.-Soviet relations on the basis of realism and reciprocity. But it is equally determined to resist pressures or the exploitation of local conflict.

Our new relationship with the People's Republic of China is another priority in the design of American policy. Stability in Asia and the world requires our constructive relations with one-quarter of the human race. . . .

Before the Nixon Administration: 1968

U.S.-Soviet Cooperation Sought

The East-West Cold War that followed World War II was punctuated by efforts from both sides to bring about a relaxation of tension.

As early as 1956, not long after his emergence as the Soviet Union's most powerful figure, Nikita S. Khrushchev called for "peaceful coexistence" and asserted that the USSR's post-Stalin leaders "want to be friends with the U.S. and to cooperate with it in peace and international security." Visiting the U.S. in 1959, Khrushchev conferred with President Dwight D. Eisenhower and presented to the UN General Assembly a Soviet plan for "general and complete disarmament."

Despite serious U.S.-Soviet disagreements during the Khrushchev period, in 1963 representatives of the U.S., USSR and Britain negotiated a treaty banning nuclear weapon tests in the atmosphere, in space or under water. Agreement to set up the Washington-to-Moscow teletype "hot line" was negotiated the same year.

Halting progress in nuclear control and other improvements in U.S.-Soviet relations took place in the succeeding years. Soviet Premier Alexei N. Kosygin, in the U.S. to address the U.N. Assembly, conferred with President Lyndon B. Johnson in Glassboro, N.J. in 1967.

The efforts at detente continued during 1968, the year before Richard M. Nixon and Henry A. Kissinger assumed office.

LBJ for Soviet Peace Role. In a commencement address at Glassboro (N.J.) State College June 4, 1968, President Johnson appealed to the Soviet Union to join the U.S. and other nations, "in the spirit of Glassboro," to help achieve world peace.

Despite the strains in U.S.-Soviet relations caused by the Vietnam war, the 2 nations had shown a high degree of bilateral cooperation in other areas, Mr. Johnson pointed out. He cited the treaty outlawing armaments in outer space, the negotiation of a pact banning the spread of nuclear weapons and a civil air agreement. Although these were "steps toward peace," Mr. Johnson said, "the disagreements between the Soviet Union and the United States . . . have not been removed." In addition to Vietnam, the unsolved problems that clouded U.S.-Soviet ties were those of the Middle East, the 1962 Geneva accords on Laos and the "costly antiballistic missile race," Mr. Johnson said.

As a further move to eliminate sources of friction, Mr. Johnson proposed (a) that the Soviet Union join the U.S. and other nations in forming an International Council on the Human Environment; (b) that the Soviet Union and other East European nations join the U.S. and other countries in the global satellite communications system; (c) that the U.S. and the Soviet Union and other nations cooperate "to extend our knowledge . . . [and] develop our resources."

The President conceded that peacemaking was difficult and that "we will face reverses and setbacks." But he expressed hope that Americans would "try in the days ahead to display the fortitude, forbearance and understanding that has symbolized the Glassboro I know. . . ."

Johnson June 13 renewed his appeal for Soviet cooperation. He did so at White House ceremonies marking the exchange of the instruments of ratification of a U.S.-Soviet consular treaty. The President said the latest accord should lead to other U.S.-Soviet agreements, particularly in the field of arms control. He conceded that "we still have deep and dangerous differences with the Soviet Union. But the peace of the world is too important to let these differences prevent us from exploring every avenue to a more peaceful relationship and a more cooperative world."

Soviet Amb.-to-U.S. Anatoly F. Dobrynin, who participated in the ceremonies with State Secy. Dean Rusk, expressed hope that Soviet-American relations would someday "take a normal course." The consular pact, Dobrynin said, was evidence that both countries could reach agreements despite the differences between them.

The treaty, to take effect in 30 days, had been ratified by the Presidium of the Supreme Soviet (parliament) Apr. 26 and by the U.S. Senate Mar. 16, 1967. It granted consular officials and employes of both countries complete diplomatic and criminal immunity and guaranteed consular notification (within 3 days) and access (within 4 days) to nationals arrested or detained in the other country.

UN Approves A-Security Pledge. The UN Security Council June 19 adopted a resolution welcoming pledges by the U.S., USSR and Britain to act "immediately" through the Council in the event of a nuclear attack or threat of such an attack on non-nuclear-weapon states.

The 3-power resolution and security pledge had been submitted to the Council June 17 as a follow-up to approval of the nuclear non-proliferation treaty by the UN General Assembly June 12. The

intention of the pledge was to assure the non-nuclear-weapon states that they would not jeopardize their security by signing the treaty.

In submitting the pledge for the U.S., Amb.-to-UN Arthur J. Goldberg noted that the security guarantee "introduces a powerful element of deterrence against aggression with nuclear weapons" and "lay[s] a firm political, moral and legal basis for assuring the security of non-nuclear-weapon parties" to the non-proliferation treaty. Soviet First Deputy Foreign Min. Vasily V. Kuznetsov, submitting the Soviet pledge, said the guarantee was a "logical and natural" demand of the non-nuclear-weapon states since "there still remains in the world the possibility of unleashing a nuclear war against non-nuclear countries." Lord Caradon submitted the pledge for Britain and declared that it should be clear "to everyone" that any country considering nuclear aggression against a non-nuclear-weapon signatory of the treaty "would be deterred by these assurances." Caradon described the "common determination of East and West in this issue of supreme international concern" as a "development of the utmost significance and importance in world affairs."

East-West Détente Urged. The North Atlantic Council, holding its regularly-scheduled semi-annual meeting at the ministerial level in Reykjavik, Iceland June 24-25, appealed to the USSR and its Eastern European allies for a "mutual and balanced" reduction of forces to promote East-West *détente* in Europe.

The appeal was made in a communiqué issued June 25 at the conclusion of the meeting, which was attended by 11 foreign ministers and 4 deputies of the 15 member states.

On the *détente* issue, the council agreed that "it was desirable that a process leading to mutual force reductions should be initiated." To that end, the ministers decided "to make all necessary preparations for discussions . . . with the Soviet Union and other countries of Eastern Europe." But they said any significant reduction of the alliance's military strength must be "part of a pattern of mutual force reductions balanced in scope and timing." In a press conference before his departure from Washington June 21, U.S. State Secy. Dean Rusk had noted that the maintenance of forces was "a burden to the peoples of both sides." But, he added, "it would be a great mistake to dismantle unilaterally in any significant way the forces of NATO without corresponding reductions on the other side."

U.S. & USSR to Talk on A-Arms.

Pres. Johnson announced in Washington July 1, 1968 that the U.S. and USSR had agreed to begin talks "in the nearest future" on means of limiting and reducing their arsenals of offensive and defensive nuclear weapons. Mr. Johnson made the announcement at the White House during signing ceremonies for the nuclear non-proliferation treaty.

The President said the new talks would concern the "limitation and the reduction of both offensive strategic nuclear weapons delivery systems and systems of defense against ballistic missiles." He conceded that the discussion of this "most complex subject" would not be "easy" and that the U.S. did not underestimate the "difficulties that may lie ahead."

Mr. Johnson had proposed talks on the missile issue in Jan. 1967, and he had announced Mar. 2, 1967 that Premier Kosygin had confirmed the USSR's willingness to discuss the question. However, no further progress was reported in the following 18 months, in part because of the priority both countries had accorded to the nuclear non-proliferation negotiations in Geneva.

The President had renewed his plea in speeches at Glassboro, N.J. June 4, the United Nations June 12 and in Washington June 13. However, an article in *Izvestia*, the Soviet government newspaper, charged June 13 that the President had ignored the question of the Vietnamese war in his June 12 speech and that U.S.-Soviet cooperation was impossible as long as the war continued. *Izvestia* and *Pravda*, the Soviet CP daily, returned to this theme June 19.

The first indication of a change in the USSR's position came June 27, when Soviet Foreign Min. Andrei A. Gromyko, in a wide-ranging foreign policy address to the Supreme Soviet in Moscow, announced that the USSR was "ready for an exchange of opinion" on the question of a "mutual restriction and subsequent reduction of strategic vehicles for the delivery of nuclear weapons—offensive and defensive—including anti-missile." Gromyko declared that the Soviet Union was ready to sign

"immediately" an international convention prohibiting the use of nuclear weapons and, as in the past, to implement "a program of general and complete disarmament." He said the USSR favored immediate discontinuance of underground nuclear testing. Referring to the problem of policing such a ban, he asserted that "the necessity of some control" was "unfounded and farfetched" since "no one can explode nuclear weapons underground in secret without being detected."

In a speech in Nashville, Tenn. June 29, Pres. Johnson responded to the Gromyko announcement by noting that, with the non-proliferation treaty concluded, it was time to "turn to a task at least equally complex and difficult: to bring under control the nuclear arms race—in offensive and defensive weapons—in ways which do not endanger the security of the U.S., our allies or others."

USSR Issues Disarmament Plan.

A 9-point disarmament and arms control plan was issued in Moscow July 1 by Soviet Premier Aleksei N. Kosygin. The plan, which Kosygin disclosed had been distributed to all of the world's governments, was made public during signing ceremonies for the nuclear non-proliferation treaty.

Kosygin said the Soviet Union attached "exclusively great importance" to the proposals and felt that their "simultaneous or stage-by-stage implementation . . . would be a serious contribution to the struggle for the cessation of the arms race and for a radical solution of the disarmament problem."

The Soviet proposals:

■ The "conclusion of an international agreement banning the use of nuclear weapons."

■ An "end to the manufacture of nuclear weapons, the reduction of stockpiles and the subsequent total ban on and liquidation of nuclear weapons under appropriate international control."

■ The "mutual limitation and subsequent reduction of strategic means of delivery of nuclear weapons."

■ A ban "without delay" on "flights of bombers, carrying nuclear weapons, beyond the boundaries of national frontiers" and an "end to the patrolling by submarines, carrying nuclear missiles, within missile-striking range of the borders of the contracting sides."

■ The "banning of underground tests of nuclear weapons on the basis of using national means of detection to control this ban."

■ A study by the 18-nation UN Disarmament Committee (ENDC) of "ways and means of securing observance by all states of the Geneva protocol on a ban on the use of chemical and bacteriological weapons."

■ The urgent examination by the ENDC of the "liquidation of foreign military bases."

■ The establishment of "denuclearized zones in various parts of the world" and the "implementation of measures for regional disarmament and for the reduction of armaments in various regions of the world, including the Middle East."

■ The opening of talks by the ENDC on the "use of the sea bed beyond the limits of existing territorial waters exclusively for peaceful purposes."

Moscow-New York Air Link. The first direct airline service between the U.S. and the Soviet Union was opened July 15 with the arrival in New York of an Aeroflot flight from Moscow and the departure of 2 Pan American flights from New York to Moscow.

Each airline was to make one round trip per week, leaving Monday and returning on Tuesday.

(The direct air service came after a decade of intermittent negotiations on the plan, first mentioned in the initial U.S.-Soviet cultural agreement in 1958. The details of the arrangement were concluded in principle by 1961, but the Berlin crisis of that year delayed formal signature.. An updated agreement was signed Nov. 4, 1966; further delays were encountered due to technical problems and intermittent U.S.-Soviet tensions.)

USSR Admits Western Papers. A relaxation of curbs on the distribution of Western papers in the Soviet Union took place during 1968.

For the first time in 40 years, a U.S. newspaper, the *International Herald Tribune,* went on sale in Moscow July 9.

The London *Times, Le Monde* of Paris and the Swiss *Neue Zürcher Zeitung* had received permission earlier to be sold in limited numbers in the Soviet Union. The first of the 4 non-Communist papers to receive such permission was the international edition of the *Neue Zürcher Zeitung,* which went on sale at news stands of 4 international hotels in Moscow Apr. 13. The 3 Western European papers were kept under the counter, however, and sold only to non-Russians on request. The *Herald Tribune,* however, was placed on the counter and sold to Russians as well as to foreigners.

Sakharov Foresees Rapprochement. Prof. Andrei Dmitriyevich Sakharov, 47, a prominent Russian nuclear physicist, proposed and predicted wide-ranging collaboration between the U.S. and the Soviet Union. He stated his views in an essay that had been circulating unofficially in unpublished manuscript form in the USSR. The essay, entitled *Thoughts About Progress, Peaceful Coexistence and Intellectual Freedom,* was completed in June and was published by the *N.Y. Times* July 22, 1968.

A member of the Soviet Academy of Sciences, Sakharov called an ultimate "convergence" of the capitalist and Communist systems not only inevitable but the only solution to the dangers threatening the future of mankind. Sakharov, who had been a leader in Soviet development of thermonuclear energy, listed these dangers as the threat of thermonuclear war, famine and population crises in less-developed nations, chemical pollution of the environment, police dictatorships and infringement of intellectual freedoms. Sakharov proposed a 4-point timetable for U.S.-Soviet rapprochement by the year 2000. He held that there was actually little difference in the effectiveness of the U.S. and Soviet systems—each had moved towards the other, and each had achieved measurable economic progress.

Excerpts from Sakharov's essay, as translated by the *N.Y. Times:*

Introduction—"The division of mankind threatens it with destruction. Civilization is imperiled by: a universal thermonuclear war, catastrophic hunger for most of mankind, stupefaction from the narcotic of 'mass culture' and bureaucratized dogmatism, a spreading of mass myths that put entire peoples and continents under the power of cruel and treacherous demagogues, and destruction or degeneration from the unforeseeable consequences of swift changes in the conditions of life on our planet.

"In the face of these perils, any action increasing the division of mankind, any preaching of the incompatibility of world ideologies and nations is madness and a crime. Only universal cooperation under conditions of intellectual freedom and the lofty moral ideals of socialism and labor, accompanied by the elimination of dogmatism and pressures of the concealed interests of ruling classes, will preserve civilization. . . .

"Millions of people throughout the world are striving to put an end to poverty. They despise oppression, dogmatism and demagogy (and their more extreme manifestations—racism, fascism, Stalinism and Maoism). They believe in progress based on the use, under conditions of social justice and intellectual freedom, of all the positive experience accumulated by mankind. . . .

". . . Intellectual freedom is essential to human society—freedom to obtain and distribute information, freedom for openminded and unfearing debate and freedom from pressure by officialdom and prejudices. Such a trinity of freedom of thought is the only guarantee against an infection of people by mass myths, which, in the hands of treacherous hypocrites and demagogues, can be transformed into bloody dictatorship. Freedom of thought is the only guarantee of the feasibility of a scientific democratic approach to politics, economy and culture."

Threat of nuclear war—"3 technical aspects of thermonuclear weapons have made thermonuclear war a peril to the very existence of humanity. These aspects are: the enormous destructive power of a thermonuclear explosion, the relative cheapness of rocket-thermonuclear weapons and the practical impossibility of an effective defense against a massive rocket-nuclear attack.

"A complete destruction of cities, industry, transport and systems of education, a poisoning of fields, water and air by radioactivity, a physical destruction of the larger part of mankind, poverty, barbarism, a return to savagery and a genetic degeneracy of the survivors under the impact of radiation, a destruction of the material and information basis of civilization—this is a measure of the peril that threatens the world as a result of the estrangement of the world's two superpowers.

"Every rational creature, finding itself on the brink of a disaster, first tries to get away from the brink and only then does it think about the satisfaction of its other needs. If mankind is to get away from the brink, it must overcome its divisions. A vital step would be a review of the traditional method of international affairs, which may be termed 'empirical-competitive.' In the simplest definition, this is a method aiming at maximum improvement of one's position everywhere possible and, simultaneously, a method of causing maximum unpleasantness to opposing forces without consideration of common welfare and common interests."

Changes proposed—". . . Certain changes must be made in the conduct of international affairs, systematically subordinating all concrete aims and local tasks to the basic task of actively preventing an aggravation of the international situation, of actively pursuing and expanding peaceful coexistence to the level of cooperation, of making policy in such a way that its immediate and long-range effects will in no way sharpen international tensions and will not

create difficulties for either side that would strengthen the forces of reaction, militarism, nationalism, fascism and revanchism. . . .

"The international policies of the world's 2 leading superpowers (the United States and the Soviet Union) must be based on a universal acceptance of unified and general principles, which we initially would formulate as follows:

"(1) All peoples have the right to decide their own fate with a free expression of will. This right is guaranteed by international control over observance by all governments of the 'Declaration of the Rights of Man.' International control presupposes the use of economic sanctions as well as the use of military forces of the United Nations in defense of 'the rights of man.'

"(2) All military and military-economic forms of export of revolution and counterrevolution are illegal and are tantamount to aggression.

"(3) All countries strive toward mutual help in economic, cultural and general organizational problems with the aim of eliminating painlessly all domestic and international difficulties and preventing a sharpening of international tensions and a strengthening of the forces of reaction.

"(4) International policy does not aim at exploiting local, specific conditions to widen zones of influence and create difficulties for another country. The goal of international policy is to insure universal fulfillment of the 'Declaration of the Rights of Man' and to prevent a sharpening of international tensions and a strengthening of militarist and nationalist tendencies."

Basis for hope—"Imagine 2 skiers racing through deep snow. At the start of the race, one of them, in striped jacket, was many kilometers ahead, but now the skier in the red jacket is catching up to the leader. What can we say about their relative strength? Not very much, since each skier is racing under different conditions. The striped one broke the snow, and the red one did not have to. (The reader will understand that this ski race symbolizes the burden of research and development costs that the country leading in technology has to bear.) All one can say about the race is that there is not much difference in strength between the 2 skiers. . . .

"On the other hand, any comparison must take account of the fact that we are now catching up with the United States only in some of the old, traditional industries, which are no longer as important as they used to be for the United States (for example, coal and steel). In some of the newer fields, for example, automation, computers, petrochemicals and especially in industrial research and development, we are not only lagging behind but are also growing more slowly, so that a complete victory of our economy in the next few decades is unlikely. . . .

"The continuing economic progress being achieved under capitalism should be a fact of great theoretical significance for any non-dogmatic Marxist. It is precisely this fact that lies at the basis of peaceful coexistence, and it suggests, in principle, that if capitalism ever runs into an economic blind alley it will not necessarily have to leap into a desperate military adventure. Both capitalism and socialism are capable of long-term development, borrowing positive elements from each other and actually coming closer to each other in a number of essential aspects. . . .

"The rapprochement with the capitalist world should not be an unprincipled, antipopular plot between ruling groups, as happened in the extreme case [of the Soviet-Nazi rapprochement] of 1939-40. Such a rapprochement must rest not only on a

Socialist, but on a popular, democratic foundation, under the control of public opinion, as expressed through publicity, elections and so forth.

"Such a rapprochement implies not only wide social reforms in the capitalist countries, but also substantial changes in the structure of ownership, with a greater role played by government and cooperative ownership, and the preservation of the basic present features of ownership of the means of production in the Socialist countries."

4-Stage plan for cooperation—"(1) In the first stage, a growing ideological struggle in the Socialist countries between Stalinist and Maoist forces, on the one hand, and the realistic forces of leftist Leninist Communists (and leftist Westerners), on the other, will lead to a deep ideological split on an international, national and intraparty scale. In the Soviet Union and other Socialist countries, this process will lead first to a multiparty system (here and there) and to acute ideological struggle and discussions, and then to the ideological victory of the realists, affirming the policy of increasing peaceful coexistence, strengthening democracy and expanding economic reforms (1960–80). The dates reflect the most optimistic unrolling of events.

"(2) In the 2d stage, persistent demands for social progress and peaceful coexistence in the United States and other capitalist countries, and pressure exerted by the example of the Socialist countries and by internal progressive forces (the working class and the intelligentsia) will lead to the victory of the leftist reformist wing of the bourgeoisie, which will begin to implement a program of rapprochement (convergence) with socialism, *i.e.*, social progress, peaceful coexistence and collaboration with socialism on a world scale and changes in the structure of ownership. This phase includes an expanded role for the intelligentsia and an attack on the forces of racism and militarism (1972–85). (The various stages overlap.)

"(3) In the 3d stage, the Soviet Union and the United States, having overcome their alienation, solve the problem of saving the poorer half of the world. The above-mentioned 20% tax on the national income of developed countries is applied. Gigantic fertilizer factories and irrigations systems using atomic power will be built [in the developing countries], the resources of the sea will be used to a vastly greater extent, indigenous personnel will be trained, and industrialization will be carried out. ... At the same time disarmament will proceed (1972–90).

"(4) In the 4th stage, the Socialist convergence will reduce differences in social structure, promote intellectual freedom, science and economic progress and lead to creation of a world government and the smoothing of national contradictions (1980–2000). ...

"The foregoing program presumes: (a) worldwide interest in overcoming the present divisions; (b) the expectation that modifications in both the Socialist and capitalist countries will tend to reduce contradictions and differences; (c) worldwide interest of the intelligentsia, the working class and other progressive forces in a scientific democratic approach to politics, economics and culture; (d) the absence of unsurmountable obstacles to economic development in both world economic systems that might otherwise lead inevitably into a blind alley, despair and adventurism."

Cheprakov Rejects 'Convergence' Theory. The Soviet government newspaper *Izvestia* Aug. 11 published an in-

direct rebuttal to the Sakharov essay. In an article entitled *Problems of the Last 3d of the Century,* a Soviet economist, Dr. Viktor A. Cheprakov, predicted that instead of collaboration and ultimate convergence of capitalism and communism over the next 3 decades, an intensification of the struggle between them would ensue with communism emerging as the victor.

Cheprakov's article did not mention Sakharov or his essay, but it dealt specifically with some of Sakharov's theories. In direct opposition to Sakharov's prediction, Cheprakov said: "Socialism and capitalism, the 2 fundamentally different world systems, are developing in diametrically opposed directions;" the "struggle" between the 2 forces, not a convergence of them, would permeate the last 3d of the century.

Cheprakov agreed with Sakharov that nuclear war, famine and overpopulation were threatening problems. But he disagreed with Sakharov's solution and said: "Only communism can solve the basic problems of society and rid mankind of oppression and exploitation of hunger and poverty, of militarism and wars, and insure on earth a genuine democracy, peace and friendship among nations, and a flowering of civilization." Capitalism not only was no solution to these dangers, but by "its very existence and by the reactionary, antipopular actions of its ruling classes, the capitalist system is raising obstacles in the way of a solution." The strongholds of capitalism were actually the sources of military danger and the main obstacles on the road of progress for mankind." The problems were also complicated by Communist China and Mao Tse-tung's policies.

Czechoslovakia Invaded, East-West Relations Hurt

Red Forces Occupy Country. Armed forces of the Soviet Union, East Germany, Poland, Hungary and Bulgaria invaded Czechoslovakia in a swift military move during the night of Aug. 20–21, 1968. The Warsaw-Pact action, ordered by the Soviet Union to halt Czechoslovakia's movement toward a democratization of communism, had a chilling effect on East-West negotiations for arms limitation.

The invaders quickly occupied the country and seized several leading liberal members of the government, the National Assembly and the Czechoslovak Communist Party, including CP First Secy. Alexander Dubček, and flew them to Moscow.

The invasion was carried out by about 10 divisions of Soviet troops, supported by units from 4 other Warsaw Pact countries.

By early Aug. 21 the 4-pronged pincer movement, comprising armored and artillery divisions, had taken control of the whole of Czechoslovakia.

Occupiers Uphold Invasion. In a statement justifying the invasion, the Soviet government claimed Aug. 21 that the armed forces of 5 Warsaw Pact nations had acted after Czechoslovak "party and government leaders" had requested "urgent assistance" to repulse the threat "emanating from the counter-revolutionary forces" within Czechoslovakia. The statement, distributed by Tass, the Soviet news agency, said: "The further aggravation of the situation in Czechoslovakia affects the vital interest of the Soviet Union and other Socialist states, the interests of the security of the states of the Socialist community. The threat to the Socialist system in Czechoslovakia constitutes at the same time a threat to the mainstays of European peace."

U.S. Reaction. Pres. Johnson summoned the National Security Council in Washington into emergency session Aug. 20 to discuss the invasion. The meeting was called immediately after the President had received an aide-memoire in which Soviet Amb.-to-U.S. Anatoly Dobrynin informed him of the Communists' action.

In his first public comment on the crisis, Mr. Johnson said in a brief TV address Aug. 21: "The Soviet Union and its allies have invaded a defenseless country to stamp out a resurgence of ordinary human freedom. It is a sad commentary on the Communist mind that a sign of liberty is deemed a fundamental threat to the security of the Soviet system."

(It was reported in Washington Aug. 22 that the U.S. and Soviet Union had reached agreement just prior to the Soviet invasion of Czechoslovakia on the details of the opening of bilateral talks on missile disarmament. Discussion of the arrangements had been in progress for more than 6 weeks, but announcement of the agreement reportedly was being delayed because of the Czechoslovak crisis. Soviet diplomats had expressed hope to U.S. officials that U.S.-Soviet "state relations" would not be adversely affected by the invasion.)

Following a cabinet discussion of the situation Aug. 22, State Secy. Rusk confirmed that the U.S. was not planning any "retaliatory actions or sanctions" against the Soviet Union. Rusk called on the Soviet Union and its Warsaw Pact allies "not to engage in punitive or excessive measures" against the Czechoslovaks and "to bring about a prompt withdrawal of their forces."

A State Department statement Aug. 23 denounced reports that Soviet intervention in Czechoslovakia had been made possible through a tacit understanding on the U.S.' and USSR's respective "spheres of influence." The statement said: "The U.S. has never entered into any sphere-of-influence agreements or undertakings with anyone anywhere in the world"; suggestions to that effect were "malicious and totally without foundation."

The State Department announced Aug. 30 that the entire U.S. cultural and educational exchange program with the Soviet Union had been placed "under review" because of the occupation of Czechoslovakia. The State Department subsequently announced the cancellation of these East-West projects: a tour of the Soviet Union by the Univeristy of Minnesota symphonic band (Sept. 5), the 2d inaugural flight of the USSR Aeroflot air line from Moscow to New York (Sept. 5), the U.S.-Polish semi-official cultural exchange program (Sept. 6) and the American exhibit at the September trade fair in Bulgaria (Sept. 10).

U.S. Sees Power Balance Shift. A statement issued by the U.S. State Department Aug. 31 asserted that the East-West balance-of-power system had been upset by the movement of Warsaw Pact forces into Czechoslovakia. As a consequence, the statement said, the U.S. and its NATO allies were reviewing their military posture in Western Europe.

The Soviet Union reacted to the U.S. assessment Sept. 3 by asserting that it was the West, not the Communist bloc, that was seeking to alter the balance of power.

U.S. State Secretary Dean Rusk, in the UN General Assembly's general debate Oct. 2, again denounced the invasion.

Rusk asked whether the Soviets would ignore the UN Charter whenever it conflicted with the laws of the "class struggle." Speaking of U.S.-Soviet relations, Rusk said: "Let us say very plainly and simply to the Soviet Union: The road to *détente* is the road of the Charter."

U.S. Backs Tito. U.S. State Undersecy. Nickolas deB. Katzenbach visited Belgrade Oct. 17–18 to demonstrate U.S. concern over the increasing Soviet pressure on Yugoslavia due to Yugoslavia's opposition to the Soviet-led invasion. Observers said that the talks centered largely on Yugoslavia's economic and security position in the wake of the Czechoslovak invasion.

The official Yugoslav news agency, Tanyug, described a 90-minute conference of Pres. Tito with Katzenbach Oct. 18 as a "prolonged and friendly meeting." Yugoslav officials regarded Katzenbach's visit as a follow-up to an Oct. 15 White House statement in which Pres. Johnson had declared his "very clear and continuing interest in Yugoslavia's independence, sovereignty and economic development."

Nixon Plans Administration

Election Campaign. Republican candidate Richard M. Nixon was elected U.S. President Nov. 5, 1968 after a campaign in which he promised to shift from confrontation with the USSR to negotiation.

In an address before the International Platform Association July 25, Nixon had said that the long-term U.S. foreign-policy goal should be to switch "from a relationship of conflict to one of cooperation with the Soviet Union. If elected President, he said, he would strive to ease world tensions by rebuilding the Atlantic alliance, encouraging Asian regionalism to promote economic progress and political stability and by opening a dialogue with Communist China. Within this context, "we can talk with the Soviet leaders with new purposefulness and hope about a basic settlement." Steps must be taken to "insulate the 'third world'" from conflicts among great powers, Nixon said. "We must make clear to Soviet leaders that the willful exploitation of local tensions, as in the Middle East in 1967, produces unacceptable risks of conflict."

At the Republican National Convention Aug. 6, Nixon had said at a press conference on foreign affairs that his view of the Communist world had changed since 1960, when he had advocated a U.S. foreign policy based fundamentally on resistance to Communist expansion. The Communist world had been "monolithic" in 1960, he said, but today it was "a split world, schizophrenic, with very great diversity," especially in Eastern Europe. He asserted that the "era of confrontation" was past and had been succeeded by "an era of negotiations with the Soviet Union" and eventually with Communist China.

In his speech accepting the Presidential nomination, Nixon Aug. 8 promised "action" on "a new policy for peace abroad, a new policy for peace and progress and justice at home."

Nixon called for "a new internationalism" with respect to America's allies and said it was time for "an era of negotiations" with leaders of the Communist world. He pledged to "restore the strength of America so that we shall always negotiate from strength and never from weakness."

Nixon urged that America's goals "be made clear" in such negotiations. He held that the Communists should be told that the U.S. did "not seek domination over any other country" and would "never be belligerent" but would be "as firm in defending our system as they are in expanding theirs."

Nixon said he would "extend the hand of friendship to all people," and specifically the Russian and Chinese peoples.

On a statewide TV program in Los Angeles Sept. 17, Nixon said although the Soviet Union sought "expansion" and the U.S. sought "peace," an attempt at negotiations would have "to start with a policy of strength." This was "not a belligerent position," he maintained, but "one the Soviets will understand. They will appreciate strength and firmness, a non-belligerent firm policy, and I believe that's why, in a series of summit meetings, we can find those areas where we can agree."

Suggesting a series of summit conferences with the Soviet leaders on the Middle East, Western Europe and other problems, Nixon declared in a TV discussion in Detroit Sept. 30: "I think . . . the Soviet Union's interest in avoiding a world war is greater than their interest in expanding communism. We've got to make it very clear to them that if they continue to probe into areas like the Mideast, or if they should move into Western Europe, the possibilities of world war are very great. . . . I don't mean that in a threatening way. Only by sitting across the table with them, I think this will come across, and then I think we can have a meaningful dialogue."

Nixon charged Oct. 24 that the Democratic Administrations of Presidents Kennedy and Johnson had fostered "a gravely serious security gap." Since 1960, he said, the U.S. had followed "policies which now threaten to make America 2d best both in numbers and quality of major weapons." "The Soviets have vigorously advanced their military effort as we put ours in 2d gear," he declared.

Nixon made these charges in a nationwide radio address (CBS). Claiming that "the present state of our defenses is too close to peril point, and our future prospects are in some respects downright alarming," Nixon pledged if elected to restore "clear-cut" military superiority over the Soviet Union.

On a TV panel show broadcast over an 8-state area and the District of Columbia Oct. 25, Nixon said he was not advocating a weapon-by-weapon arms race with the Soviet Union. He favored improving the "over-all strength" of the U.S. on a short-term basis in order to provide "the kind of superiority which will enable us to convince them [the USSR and Communist China] that the time has now come for the great powers —on a controlled, inspected basis—to reduce this tremendous expenditure for armaments. The major objective of my Administration will be to initiate that kind of negotiations."

In a nationwide radio address Oct. 26, Nixon then pledged, if elected, to seek "meaningful arms control agreements with our adversaries." Nixon said: "The vast resources of the industrialized nations must be diverted from the nonproductive and wasteful channels of war-making capabilities and harnessed to a full-scale attack on the age-old problems of hunger, disease and poverty." He would seek ratification of the treaty to halt the spread of nuclear weapons. "We must move away from confrontation in this nuclear age into a new era—the era of negotiation."

Kissinger Gets Security Job. Pres.-elect Nixon announced in New York Dec. 2 that he had chosen German-born Prof. Henry Alfred Kissinger, 45, a Harvard specialist in international and defense studies, to be his special assistant for national security affairs. Mr. Nixon said that Kissinger would begin immediately on plans to reorganize "the entire White House security planning machinery."

(At a 2-day conference of the American Foreign Service Association, held in Washington Nov. 14–15, Kissinger had called the Soviet leadership "inconclusive, incompetent" and said that this type of leadership might bring a greater danger to the world than Stalin had. He added that the USSR possessed "more than 1,100" nuclear-tipped intercontinental ballistic missiles.)

Relations With China

U.S.-China Talks. Closed meetings between U.S. and Communist Chinese ambassadors had been initiated in Geneva in 1955 and were later transferred to Warsaw. By the end of 1967, 133 of these meetings had taken place, but they had started to become increasingly infrequent. There were only five meetings annually in 1964 and 1965, three in 1966, two in 1967 and one in 1968.

The single 1968 meeting, the 134th in the series, took place in Warsaw Jan. 8, when U.S. Ambassador John A. Gronouski conferred for 2½ hours with Chinese Chargé d'Affaires Chen Tung.

Although the talks were normally held at the ambassadorial level for both sides, the U.S. agreed to meet with the Chinese chargé in view of the absence of Chinese Amb.-to-Poland Wang Kuo-chuan, who was still in Peking after having been called home in the summer of 1967.

State Undersecy. Nicholas deB. Katzenbach and Eugene V. Rostow, under secretary for political affairs, urged in separate speeches May 21 that Communist China reconsider its policy of isolation and accept U.S. offers of new contacts and exchanges. Rostow said: "We have made clear our willingness to welcome Chinese scientists, scholars and journalists to the United States and have encouraged our own academics to establish contacts with their counterparts on the mainland of China." Katzenbach hinted that the U.S. was ready to reconsider its policy of no trade with China. Leonard H. Marks, director of the U.S. Information Agency, had invited Communist China May 2 to send journalists to cover the 1968 U.S. Presidential election. Speaking at a convention of the American Women in Radio and TV, Marks stated: "The Voice of America will make prime listening time available daily to these journalists for broadcasts to their homeland." "We stand ready to discuss such exchanges on a broad, general basis or on specific points."

Contact With Nixon Aides Asked. Direct communication between Red China and the U.S. appeared to have lapsed in November due to another postponement of the Warsaw meetings between the 2 governments and the closing of a telephone-radio link across the Pacific. However, China proposed that its representatives meet Nixon Administration officials in February 1969.

"Regretfully" concluding that the Chinese Communists were not interested in continuing contacts with the outgoing Johnson Administration, U.S. officials suggested Nov. 1 that the 135th regular Warsaw meeting be rescheduled for February 1969. The U.S. had proposed a meeting for Nov. 20, but the Chinese had failed to answer the request.

Peking Nov. 26 proposed that its representatives meet with those of the Nixon Administration Feb. 20, 1969 in Warsaw. The statement, issued by the Foreign Ministry, called on the U.S. to join "an agreement on the 5 principles of peaceful coexistence" and "to immediately withdraw all its armed forces from China's Taiwan Province and the Taiwan Straits and dismantle all its military installations in Taiwan Province."

According to the *N.Y. Times* Nov. 27, there was no previous record of a "public" call by China for a peaceful coexistence agreement with the U.S. The "5 principles of peaceful coexistence," one of the public tenets of Chinese foreign policy in the mid-1950's, were: mutual respect for territorial integrity and sovereignty, mutual nonagression, mutual noninterference in internal policy, equality and mutual benefit and peaceful coexistence.

It was reported Nov. 29 that the U.S. had decided to accept Peking's proposal that their ambassadors meet in Warsaw Feb. 20, 1969 and review the suspended U.S.-Communist Chinese ambassadorial talks. Members of the Johnson Administration and representatives of Pres.-elect Nixon had cleared the decision in accordance with the agreement to coordinate foreign policy before the transfer of power to the future Nixon Administration.

(The Soviet news agency Tass asserted Dec. 14 that "inside China people who believe in the anti-imperialist demagogy of the Maoists should react to the offer of peaceful coexistence with the U.S as to an 'alliance of the great helmsman with the devil himself.' " The report noted that the Chinese proposal had not included earlier demands that Taiwan be returned to Mainland China and that the U.S. end military aid to Nationalist China.)

The *Wall Street Journal* reported Nov. 20 that China had cut the only remaining telephone cable to the U.S. The cable, which linked Oakland, Calif. and Shanghai, handled about 20 calls per year. Opened in 1937, the circuit had operated continuously except during World War II.

Sino-Soviet Relations Worsen. Following the Warsaw Pact invasion of Czechoslovakia, China intensified its diplomatic and propaganda criticism of the Soviet Union, centering on the USSR's "revisionism" and its alleged collusion with the U.S. in world affairs.

Peking radio said Aug. 27, 1968 that China had delivered a protest to the Soviet ambassador in Peking charging the USSR had "threatened the security of the Chinese embassy in Prague." The broadcast, monitored in Tokyo and reported by AP, said that Soviet troops had infringed on the territory of the embassy Aug. 25 and fired shots over it Aug. 26.

Another note, delivered to the Soviet chargé d'affaires Sept. 5, charged that Soviet troops in Prague had distributed anti-Chinese literature outside the embassy, threatened the safety of its members, and intercepted its foreign visitors.

China charged formally Sept. 16 that Soviet aircraft had violated its northeastern borders. A note presented to the Soviet chargé d'affaires in Peking, Y. N. Razdukhov, listed 29 intrusions over Heilungkiang Province Aug. 9–29 and 119 intrusions during the past year. The protest was the first publicized complaint against the alleged border violations; it accused Moscow of engineering "reconnaissance, harassment and provocation" flights to support its "aggression against Czechoslovakia."

The Soviet government newspaper *Izvestia* Nov. 2 denied the Chinese allegations and asserted that Soviet aircraft were prohibited from flying in certain border areas.

Nixon Policy Takes Shape: 1969

Nixon in Office

Richard M. Nixon became the 37th President of the U.S. Jan. 20, 1969. During his early days in office Nixon indicated that he welcomed opportunities to negotiate with the Soviet Union and China but that he did not intend to make one-sided bargains with them and that he intended to deal with them from a position of strength.

Inauguration. Nixon was sworn in as President Jan. 20, minutes after Spiro T. Agnew had taken the oath of office as Vice President.

The new President's inaugural address, cast for the most part in general terms, was solemn and restrained. It stressed the importance of international peace and America's need for reconciliation of black and white. It made no specific references to the war in Vietnam, nor did it chart the new Administration's policy on such issues as the nuclear nonproliferation treaty or U.S.-Soviet talks on arms limitation.

Nixon said in the address:

I ask you to share with me today the majesty of this moment. In the orderly transfer of power, we celebrate the unity that keeps us free.

Each moment in history is a fleeting time, precious and unique. But some stand out as moments of beginning, in which courses are set that shape decades or centuries.

This can be such a moment. Forces now are converging that make possible for the first time the hope that many of man's deepest aspirations can at last be realized.

The spiraling pace of change allows us to contemplate, within our own lifetime, advances that once would have taken centuries.

In throwing wide the horizons of space, we have discovered new horizons on earth.

For the first time, because the people of the world want peace and the leaders of the world are afraid of war, the times are on the side of peace.

Eight years from now America will celebrate its 200th anniversary as a nation. And within the lifetime of most people now living, mankind will celebrate that great new year which comes only once in a thousand years—the beginning of the third millennium.

What kind of a nation we will be, what kind of a world we will live in, whether we shape the future in the image of our hopes, is ours to determine by our actions and our choices.

The greatest honor history can bestow is the title of peacemaker. This honor now beckons America—the chance to help lead the world at last out of the valley of turmoil and on to that high ground of peace that man has dreamed of since the dawn of civilization.

If we succeed, generations to come will say of us now living that we mastered our moment, that we helped make the world safe for mankind.

This is our summons to greatness.

And I believe the American people are ready to answer this call. . . .

As we learn to go forward together at home, let us also seek to go forward together with all mankind.

Let us take as our goal: where peace is unknown, make it welcome; where peace is fragile, make it strong; where peace is temporary, make it permanent.

After a period of confrontation, we are entering an era of negotiation. Let all nations know that during this Administration our lines of communication will be open.

We seek an open world—open to ideas, open to the exchange of goods and people, a world in which no people, great or small, will live in angry isolation.

We cannot expect to make everyone our friend, but we can try to make no one our enemy.

Those who would be our adversaries, we invite to a peaceful competition—not in conquering territory or extending dominion, but in enriching the life of man.

As we explore the reaches of space, let us go to the new worlds together—not as new worlds to be conquered, but as a new adventure to be shared.

And with those who are willing to join, let us cooperate to reduce the burden or arms, to strengthen the structure of peace, to lift up the poor and the hungry.

But to all those who would be tempted by weakness, let us leave no doubt that we will be as strong as we need to be for as long as we need to be.

Over the past 20 years, since I first came to this Capitol as a freshman Congressman, I have visited most of the nations of the world.

I have come to know the leaders of the world, the great forces, the hatreds, the fears that divide the world.

I know that peace does not come through wishing for it—that there is no substitute for days and even years of patient and prolonged diplomacy.

I also know the people of the world.

I have seen the hunger of a homeless child, the pain of a man wounded in battle, the grief of a mother who has lost her son. I know these have no ideology, no race. . . .

I have taken an oath today in the presence of God and my conscience: To uphold and defend the Constitution of the United States. And to that oath, I now add this sacred commitment: I shall consecrate my office, my energies and all the wisdom I can summon, to the cause of peace among nations.

Let this message be heard by strong and weak alike.

The peace we seek—the peace we seek to win—is not victory over any other people, but the peace that comes with healing in its wings; with compassion for those who have suffered; with understanding for those who have opposed us; with the opportunity for all the peoples of this earth to choose their own destiny.

First News Conference. Problems of foreign affairs dominated his first week in office, Richard M. Nixon told newsmen Jan. 27 at his first news conference as President. At the conference itself, Mr. Nixon responded to questions on Vietnam, Communist China, arms control and nuclear-weapon strength and the Middle East.

Among Nixon's comments:

Arms control & missile policy—"I favor the nonproliferation treaty" and "will urge its ratification [by the Senate] at an appropriate time and I would hope an early time." He favored strategic arms talks with the Soviet Union, and "the context of those talks" was "vitally important." "What I want to do is to see to it that we have strategic arms talks in a way and at a time that will promote, if possible, progress on outstanding political problems at the same time, for example, on the problem of the Mideast, on other outstanding problems in which the United States and the Soviet Union acting together can serve the cause of peace."

Mr. Nixon was asked about "the need for superiority over the Soviet Union" in nuclear weapons, a point "stressed, quite hard" by Mr. Nixon and Defense Secretary Melvin R. Laird. He was asked to "distinguish between the validity of that stance and the argument of Dr. Kissinger for what he calls 'sufficiency.'" Mr. Nixon replied: Kissinger's "suggestion of sufficiency" "would meet, certainly, my guideline—and I think Secretary Laird's guideline—with regard to superiority." "I think sufficiency is a better term, actually, than either superiority or parity." Parity opened the possibility for each side to believe "it has a chance to win" a war and, "therefore, parity does not necessarily assure that a war may not occur." Superiority "may have a detrimental effect on the other side, in putting it in an inferior position and, therefore, giving great impetus to its own arms race."

(Asserting that the "arms race is the greatest single danger facing humanity," outgoing Vice President Hubert Humphrey Jan. 17 had urged the new President to move immediately to begin missile talks with the U.S.S.R. Humphrey condemned the U.S. Senate's "unpardonable delay" in ratification of the nuclear nonproliferation treaty, and he advocated negotiations to head off construction of costly anti-ballistic missile systems by the two nuclear super-powers.)

Communist China—"The policy of this country and this Administration at this time will be to continue to oppose Communist China's admission to the United Nations." But his Administration looked forward to the scheduled Feb. 20 meeting with Peking's negotiators in Warsaw, and "we will be interested to see what the Chinese Communist representatives may have to say at that meeting, whether any changes of attitude on their part on major substantive issues may have occurred. Until some changes occur on their side, however, I see no immediate prospect of any change in our policy."

Trip to Europe. Nixon visited five European nations Feb. 23–March 2. He met with West European leaders in Brussels, London, Bonn, West Berlin, Rome, Paris and the Vatican as well as with NATO officials and with the U.S. negotiating team at the Vietnam peace talks in Paris.

The President was accompanied by 18 top government officials, including Secretary of State William P. Rogers, Presidential adviser Henry A. Kissinger, officials of the State and Defense Departments and members of the National Security Council. In a statement issued Feb. 21, Mr. Nixon had emphasized that the trip was intended to create a "new spirit of consultation" and "confidence" between the U.S. and its European allies and to strengthen relations among the NATO countries. Stating that his purpose was to create an atmosphere of cooperation, and not to resolve specific issues, he said: "We are going there to listen to them, to exchange views, to get their best information and their best advice as to how their problems should be solved and how world problems should be solved. We need their advice and we are going there very honestly trying to seek it." He cautioned the public not to expect "spectacular news from this trip."

After his return to Washington Nixon reported to the American people March 4 on his trip to Western Europe. The setting was an evening news conference televised from the White House.

On the major world problems—the war in Vietnam, the Berlin situation, the Israeli-Arab conflict and limitation of strategic arms—the President stressed the vital role of the Soviet Union and indicated the need for a Soviet-U.S. accommodation on these issues. Mr. Nixon again called his trip "a condition precedent to an East-West summit."

Among the President's remarks:

His European trip—There were "no illusions about the limits of personal diplomacy in settling great differences and great general difficulties." But "there is an intangible factor [of trust] which does affect the relations between nations. . . . When there is trust between men who are leaders of nations, there is a better chance to settle differences than when there is not trust. . . . One of the accomplishments of this trip is that we have established between the United States of America and the major nations of Europe—and I trust other nations of Europe, as well—a new relationship of trust and confidence that did not exist before."

Mr. Nixon found great concern among Europeans about "the possibility of a U.S.-Soviet condominium, in which at the highest level the two superpowers would make decisions affecting their future without consulting them. . . . The fact about the United States and the Soviet Union making decisions will not happen as a result of this trip."

Berlin—"I believe that the Soviet Union does not want to have the situation in West Berlin heated up to the point that it would jeopardize some, what they consider to be, more important negotiations at the highest level with the United States, and because those negotiations, in effect, are in the wings, I think I could predict that the Soviet Union will use its influence to cool off the West Berlin situation, rather than to heat it up."

Middle East—A "tangible" result "of this trip was substantial progress on the Middle East. . . . As a result of the consultations . . . , the positions of our European friends—the British and the French—are now closer to ours than was the case before."

The U.S. had "encouraging talks with the Soviet ambassador . . . with regard to the Mideast. We will continue these bilateral consultations; and if they continue at their present rate of progress, it seems likely that there will be four-power discussions in the United Nations on the Mideast." Although the four powers (U.S.S.R., U.S., Great Britain, France) "cannot dictate a settlement in the Middle East." They "can indicate those areas where they believe the parties directly involved . . . could have profitable discussions."

Soviet role—He had formed "a cautious conclusion" that "the Soviet Union will play possibly a peace-making role in the Mideast and even possibly in Vietnam. . . . I base this only on talks that have taken place up to this time, but we are going to explore that road all the way that we can, because, let's face it, without the Soviet Union's cooperation, the Mideast is going to continue to be a terribly dangerous area if you continue to pour fuel on those fires of hatred that exist on the borders of Israel. And without the Soviet Union's cooperation, it may be difficult to move as fast as we would like in settling the war in Vietnam."

The Soviet Union was "in a very delicate and sensitive position" in regard to Vietnam. Although it aided North Vietnam and was "vying for power in the Communist world" against Communist China, "I believe at this time that the Soviet Union shares the concern of many other nations in the world about the extension of the war in Vietnam . . . . They recognize that if it continues over a long period of time, the possibility of escalation increases. And I believe the Soviet Union would like to use what influence it could appropriately to help bring the war to a conclusion."

Strategic arms limitation—His Administration had indicated that the interests of the Soviet Union and the U.S. "would not be served by simply going down the road on strategic-arms talks without at the same time making progress on resolving these political differences that could explode." All European leaders he had talked to on his trip "recognize that most wars have come, not from arms races . . . but . . . from political explosions. Therefore, they want progress, for example, on Berlin; they want progress in the Mideast; they want progress on Vietnam, at the same time that they want progress on strategic arms talks.

"So our attitude toward the Soviet is not a highhanded one of trying to tell them that you do this or we won't talk. Our attitude is very conciliatory, and . . . in our talks with the Soviet ambassador, I think that they are thinking along this line now, too. If they are, we can make progress on several roads toward a mutual objective."

NATO's 20th Anniversary. The foreign and defense ministers of the 15 North Atlantic Treaty nations met in Washington April 10–11 to commemorate the 20th anniversary of the alliance. The main themes of the two-day ministerial meeting of the NATO Council were political, rather than military.

At formal ceremonies opening the anniversary meeting, President Nixon

addressed the Council in the Departmental Auditorium on Constitution Avenue. Nixon asserted that a new detente with the Soviet bloc was possible, depending on the actions of East European nations. He declared: "Living in the real world of today means unfreezing our old concepts of East versus West, while never losing sight of great ideological differences." The President called on the West to be prepared to change the alliance's fist "into a hand of friendship" toward the Soviet-bloc nations. But the President cautioned that talk about a detente must reflect "some change of mind about political purpose." Recalling that the past 20 years of tension "were not caused by superficial misunderstandings," he said: "It is not enough to talk of European security in the abstract; we must know the elements of insecurity and how to remove them. Conferences are useful if they deal with concrete issues, which means they must be carefully prepared. It is not enough to talk of detente, unless at the same time, we anticipate the need for giving it the genuine political content that would prevent detente from becoming delusions."

Arms & Nuclear Control

Soviets Urge Talks. The Soviet government declared Jan. 20, 1969 that it was General Assembly in 1968 and affirmed: prepared to begin talks with the U.S. on control of nuclear-armed missiles. The statement, read to a news conference at the Foreign Ministry in Moscow by Leonid M. Zamyatin, ministry press chief, and Kirill V. Novikov, director of the ministry's International Organizations Department, reviewed the Soviet disarmament plan presented by Foreign Minister Andrei A. Gromyko at the UN General Assembly Oct. 2, 1968 and said: "The problem of limiting the nuclear arms race is, in the opinion of the Soviet government, a practically realizable, though not an easy, undertaking." Questioned about the coincidence of the Soviet statement with the inaugural of Richard M. Nixon, Zamyatin denied that it was deliberate.

Highlights of the Soviet statement:

"Of great importance for strengthening

peace and international security is the treaty on the nonproliferation of nuclear weapons, the entry into force of which would create favorable prerequisites for further efforts to stop the arms race."

"The Soviet Government has proposed that all nuclear powers immediately enter into negotiations on the cessation of nuclear weapon production, and the reduction of nuclear stockpiles followed by complete prohibition and elimination of nuclear weapons. The Soviet government has also proposed that agreement be reached on a mutual limitation and subsequent reduction of strategic means of delivery of nuclear weapons."

"European and international security cannot be safeguarded through the arms race or inflated war preparations—they can be safeguarded on the basis of peaceful cooperation, a genuine relaxation of tensions and the solution of existing international problems by peaceful means at the table of negotiations."

Missile Defense Plan. Nixon announced March 14 his decision to proceed with a revised ABM (antiballistic missile) defense system dubbed Safeguard.

The ABM debate had enveloped Senate consideration of the nuclear nonproliferation treaty. The Senate had approved the treaty March 13 by 83–15 vote (49 D & 34 R vs. 8 R & 7 D), and chairman J. W. Fulbright (D, Ark.) of the Senate Foreign Relations Committee, a leading opponent of ABM proposals, had told the Senate just before it acted: "I can't believe that the President of the United States, in the face of this vote, would go ahead with the deployment of the ABM."

The ABM system recommended by Mr. Nixon would consist of 12 sites emplaced to defend the nation's missile retaliatory capacity. Each site would be equipped with both long- and short-range missiles. The system, to be operative in the mid-1970s, would cost an estimated $6–$7 billion.

Mr. Nixon stressed that his plan was flexible and would be reviewed at every phase "to insure that we are doing as much as necessary but no more than that required by the threat existing at that time." He called his proposed system

"truly a 'Safeguard' system, a defensive system only." He said: "It safeguards our deterrent and under those circumstances can in no way . . . delay the progress which I hope will continue to be made toward arms talks. . . ." "The imperative that our nuclear deterrent remain secure beyond any possible doubt requires that the U.S. must take steps now to insure that our strategic retaliatory forces will not become vulnerable to a Soviet attack." The modified ABM plan would safeguard against "any attack by the Chinese Communists that we can foresee over the next 10 years" and against "any irrational or accidental attack" from the Soviet Union.

Mr. Nixon discounted arguments that initiation of a U.S. ABM system would escalate the arms race or jeopardize arms-control talks with the Soviet Union. His program was "not provocative," he said, and "the Soviet retaliatory capacity is not affected by our decision. The capability for surprise attack against our strategic forces is reduced. In other words, our program provides an incentive for a responsible Soviet weapons policy and for the avoidance of spiraling U.S. and Soviet strategic arms budgets."

As for arms talks, Mr. Nixon pointed out that the Soviet Union had agreed to talks only four days after the Johnson Administration decision to deploy a Sentinel ABM system. Under his own plan, Mr. Nixon said, the Soviet Union would have "even less reason to view our defense effort as an obstacle to talks."

The President said at his news conference April 18: "I'm going to fight as hard as I can for it [Safeguard] because I believe it is absolutely essential for the security of the country." Intelligence estimates of the Soviet Union's nuclear strength had risen 60% over estimates at the time of the Johnson Administration decision to deploy an ABM system to protect urban centers. The U.S.S.R. seemed determined to proceed with the SS-9 and its 25-megaton warhead and to augment its nuclear submarine fleet by almost two-thirds.

Nixon also predicted that an inferior arms position would impair the U.S.' "diplomatic credibility" in the event of a crisis. He held that diplomatic credibility would suffer unless "we could protect our country against a Chinese attack aimed at our cities." Mr. Nixon said it was essential "to avoid putting an American President . . . in a position where the United States would be second rather than first or at least equal to any potential enemy."

Both members of the losing Democratic Presidential ticket in 1968 opposed the Safeguard decision. Ex-Vice President Hubert H. Humphrey, in an editorial in the Saturday Review (released March 30), discussed the Administration's intimations that the U.S.S.R. intended to build a nuclear force capable of destroying the U.S. before it could retaliate. "If there is anything to this view," he declared, "the President should lay it before the country with all the detail and gravity that a change of this magnitude commands. But if the view is not solidly grounded in new facts and estimates, raising this specter is the height of irresponsibility—a destabilizing factor of the first magnitude and, quite possibly, the political trigger for a new round in the arms race which might well dwarf any possible effect of ABM deployment."

In a speech April 3, Humphrey urged the Administration to avoid "raising specters of massive Soviet strategic commitments until we have determined through direct talks their willingness or unwillingness to decelerate the arms race." "Then we will not have to speculate on such critical matters," he stated. "We will know."

Sen. Edmund S. Muskie (D., Maine) told an interviewer April 3 that if President Nixon thought the Soviet Union was seeking a first-strike capability, he should have said so at the time of his decision to proceed with Safeguard. "The debate [over Safeguard] sort of floats along from disclosure to disclosure by the Defense Department in a way that makes it difficult for the American people to focus on the essential elements of a decision." On the Senate floor April 3, Muskie deplored the apparent intention of the Administration to deploy Safeguard "as a blunt challenge to the Soviets to come to the bargaining table and negotiate over strategic weapons or else the United States will heat up the arms race, counting on our superior technology to protect us if negotiations

fail." "I cannot believe that this kind of bluster would have any rational justification," he declared, "and I must caution the Senate and the country that such diplomacy is the very essence of provocation."

U.S.-Soviet Talks on Peaceful Uses. Representatives of the U.S. and the Soviet Union met April 14 in Vienna to exchange information on peaceful uses of nuclear explosions. The talks, which were the outgrowth of the 1968 agreement on a nuclear non-proliferation treaty, were held in Vienna, which was headquarters site for the International Atomic Energy Agency (IAEA).

The U.S. delegation was led by Gerald F. Tape, member of the Atomic Energy Commission. Yevgeny K. Federov, a member of the Soviet Academy of Sciences, led the Soviet delegation.

After three days of closed door sessions, the delegates issued a joint statement April 16 that held out hope for the peaceful uses of atomic blasts: "The parties were of the view that underground nuclear explosions may be successfully used in the not so far off future to stimulate oil and gas production and to create underground cavities. It may also be technically feasible to use them in earthmoving works for the construction of water reservoirs in arid areas, to dig canals and in removing the upper earth layer in surface mining etc."

Missile Moratorium Hinted. President Nixon said June 19 his Administration was considering the possibility of offering a moratorium on tests of multiple-warhead missiles as part of an arms control agreement with the Soviet Union. The President, addressing a news conference, said the U.S. would not agree to unilaterally suspend such tests.

Mr. Nixon reiterated his support for the Safeguard antiballistic missile (ABM) system, saying it was "even more important" than ever. He cited recent intelligence data that indicated progress by the Soviet Union in the development of multiple-warhead missiles and the targeting of these missiles "to fall in somewhat the precise area" in which the U.S. Minuteman missile silos were located.

The President said 80% of the Minuteman force would be "in danger" from such Soviet missiles by 1973, and "ABM is needed particularly in order to meet that eventuality."

Both subjects—multiple-warhead missiles and ABM systems—would be on the agenda at forthcoming arms control talks with the Soviet Union, Mr. Nixon said.

Bundy on Opportunities. In an article in the October issue of Foreign Affairs (published Sept. 17), McGeorge Bundy, former special assistant to the President for national security affairs, said the next year or two would provide the U.S.S.R. and the U.S. the best opportunity to limit the strategic arms contest. Bundy said: "The neglected truth about the present strategic arms race between the U.S. and the Soviet Union is that in terms of international political behavior that race has now become almost completely irrelevant. The new weapons systems being developed by each of the two great powers will provide neither protection nor opportunity in any serious political sense. Politically the strategic nuclear arms race is in a stalemate."

The article, entitled "To Cap the Volcano," argued that in political terms, as distinct from technical, the idea of nuclear "superiority" was totally incorrect. Bundy said: "In sane politics . . . there is no level of superiority which will make a strategic first strike between the two great states anything but an act of folly. . . . Sufficiency is what we both have now, in ample measure, and no superiority worth having can be achieved." Bundy praised President Nixon for recognizing the need was for "sufficiency" not "superiority," and said that "if the President is hesitant about arms limitation, it is . . . because he does not yet see any solid political base, here at home, for relatively low-keyed, low-cost parity."

Krylov Sees U.S. Nuclear Threat. Marshal Nikolai I. Krylov charged Aug. 30 that the U.S. was preparing a surprise nuclear attack on the U.S.S.R. In an article in the Russian (RSFSR) newspaper Sovetskaya Rossiya, Krylov, commander of the Soviet strategic missile forces and deputy defense minister, said: "Preparing for a surprise attack on the Soviet Union and other Socialist countries, . . . the U.S. some time ago created a special 'department of strategic planning' which is working out plans for a massive nuclear-rocket blow against targets on the territory of our country and other Socialist countries." Krylov implied that it was necessary to maintain a powerful Soviet nuclear arsenal to deter the U.S.

The article had been written to commemorate the 30th anniversary of World War II Sept. 1.

Soviet & East European Developments

May Day Celebrations. With the exception of East Germany, Soviet bloc countries celebrated May Day (International Labor Day) with peace-oriented civilian celebrations. In Moscow, where the traditional May Day military parade had not even been scheduled, Communist Party General Secretary Leonid I. Brezhnev's 20-minute speech emphasized the U.S.S.R.'s desire for peace and willingness for negotiations with the West. His address, like the speeches of other East European leaders, omitted the usual denunciations of the U.S., Israel and West Germany.

Liberation Day Celebrations. The 24th anniversary of the defeat of Nazi Germany was celebrated in Czechoslovakia and the Soviet Union May 9. In an article in the Czechoslovak Communist Party newspaper Rude Pravo, First Secretary Gustav Husak said the Soviet liberation of the country in 1945 had set the line for its future political development. "We realized," he said, "that the free future of our country was based only on the most friendly relations with the Soviet Union. . . . [May 9] did not arrive for us as the start of a new way without preconditions."

(A large, pro-American demonstration took place in Plzen May 5, the 24th anniversary of the city's liberation by the U.S. Army. A reported 5,000 demonstrators, some chanting "U.S.A., U.S.A.," clashed with the police.)

In Moscow, Soviet military leaders warned that the U.S.-West German alliance could touch off a third world war. Defense Minister Andrei A. Grechko also expressed concern over Communist China's foreign policy. He wrote in Pravda: "The adventurist policy of the Mao Tse-tung group, which proclaims its chauvanistic-hegemonistic desires and makes anti-Sovietism the official line of its policy, cannot but give rise to concern."

Inquirers in Moscow who sought more details on Brezhnev's comments were referred to an article by Vikenty Matveyev published May 28 in the Soviet government newspaper Izvestia. Matveyev discussed the possibility that a power vacuum would be created in Asia by Britain's withdrawals from Far Eastern, Indian Ocean and Persian Gulf bases, and by the eventual withdrawal of the U.S. from South Vietnam. In this connection, wrote Matveyev, "Mao and his henchmen entertain quite definite designs on a number of countries in this part of the world." However, Matveyev said, the dismantling of foreign bases would pave the way for a collective security system in which newly-independent countries—specifically, India, Pakistan, Afghanistan, Burma, Cambodia and Singapore—could pool their efforts. The article said Russia would continue to insure peace and security in Asia through "mutual assistance" but did not indicate direct Soviet involvement in the area.

Chinese Premier Chou En-Lai July 13 denounced Russia's Asian security proposal as a step toward an anti-Chinese military alliance and a concealed attempt at aggression against Asian countries, the Yugoslav news agency Tanyug reported.

Brezhnev Plan for Asia. Speaking at the world Communist conference held in Moscow June 5–17, Soviet Communist Party General Secretary Leonid I. Brezhnev expressed "the opinion that the course of events is ... putting on the agenda the task of creating a system of collective security in Asia."

U.S.S.R. Foreign Policy. Soviet Foreign Minister Andrei A. Gromyko delivered a wide-ranging foreign policy address before the Supreme Soviet in Moscow July 10. The speech was highlighted by a bid for friendly relations with the U.S. and expressions of concern over Communist China. Major points of the Gromyko speech:

U.S. Relations. Gromyko said friendly relations with the U.S. would correspond to the interests of both the Soviet and American peoples." In the first public Soviet acknowledgement of the plea President Nixon had made (in his inaugural address in January) for good relations with the U.S.S.R. (and other Communist nations), Gromyko noted Nixon's statement that "after a period of confrontation, the era of negotiations has arrived." Gromyko admitted that "deep class differences" existed between the two powers, but declared: ". . . when it comes to problems of safeguarding peace, the Soviet Union and the United States can find a common language." In what observers viewed as a comparatively mild reference to the Vietnam war, Gromyko said: "The earlier the United States makes the correct conclusions and recognizes the need for ending the Vietnam War and for withdrawing all American troops from Vietnam, the better—and the better also for the United States." In a specific proposal for improved relations, Gromyko suggested an exchange of delegations from the Supreme Soviet and the U.S. Congress.

Disarmament. Gromyko stressed that halting the strategic arms race was "one of the most acute problems facing humanity." He said Moscow was prepared for strategic arms negotiations with Washington and he indicated interest in Nixon's proposal of a "well-prepared" summit meeting.

Agreements to stop the production of nuclear weapons could be reached only if all nuclear powers participated, Gromyko said. He called on the Western powers not to complicate the issue of a total nuclear test ban with "unjustified conditions which extend beyond the framework of the tasks of banning nuclear weapons tests." A nuclear arms-free zone covering the Mediterranean was "more vital today than ever before," Gromyko said.

(Secretary of State William P. Rogers July 11 praised the "positive tone" of Gromyko's speech, but he asserted that the U.S. was still awaiting word from Moscow on the time and place of the talks.)

Chinese Relations. Gromyko charged that China had "done everything to break" good relations between the two Communist powers. He noted that (1) Sino-Soviet trade had dropped to less than half of its 1959 level; (2) scientific, technical and cultural exchanges had stopped almost completely; and (3) economic agreements had been annulled or suspended. Gromyko condemned the "anti-Soviet statements of the Chinese leaders that show hostile intentions against our country." He said the Soviet Union would "rebuff all the attempts to speak with the Soviet Union in terms of threats or, moreover, weapons." Gromyko charged China with obstructing the Khabarovsk border navigation talks by its attitude at the negotiating table and by its recent provocation on the Amur River.

Relations With Socialist Countries. Gromyko stressed that the Warsaw Treaty Organization would never permit any encroachment on the "gains of socialism" made by its member states—an apparent reference to the Soviet invasion of Czechoslovakia in August 1968. Gromyko denounced as slander Western interpretations of the so-called "Brezhnev doctrine of limited sovereignty." He rejected the idea that "Socialist countries come out not for complete sovereignty of states but for some limited sovereignty." He added: "Nothing can attach fuller content to the concept of sovereignty than the right of people to defend to the end the chosen road . . . Nobody can deprive such people of the right to rely on the help of friends loyal to their internationalist duty and the treaty obligations."

Western Europe. Gromyko repeated past Soviet proposals for a European Security Conference. He also proposed "an exchange of opinions" on West Berlin between the Allied Big Four—the U.S., Britain, France and Russia—in order to "prevent complications" that could bring a new Berlin crisis. Moscow also sought improved relations with West Germany, Gromyko said.

Nixon & Other Americans Abroad

Nixon's World Tour. Nixon, accompanied by his wife, toured eight countries in Europe and Asia July 26–Aug. 3, 1969. The countries he visited were the Philippines, Indonesia, Thailand, South Vietnam, India, Pakistan, Rumania and Britain.

The President said on his arrival in Manila July 26 that "if peace is to come from Asia—and I emphasize this point—the United States will play its part and provide its fair share." "But," he continued, "peace in Asia cannot come from the United States. It must come from Asia. The people of Asia, the governments of Asia, they are the ones who must lead the way to peace in Asia."

The crux of Mr. Nixon's message to Philippine leaders, according to Presidential aides, was that the responsibility for Asian security must be borne primarily by Asians themselves. While the U.S. realized the importance of Asia and was determined to honor its treaty commitments, it would shun future wars of the Vietnam type and reduce its Asian military commitments.

The President's views were given to Philippine President Ferdinand E. Marcos and other officials at a conference July 26 in Manila's Malacanang Palace. Mr. Nixon and Marcos met privately while their aides conferred in a nearby room. The U.S. delegation included Secretary of State William P. Rogers; Henry A. Kissinger, the President's chief foreign policy adviser; Assistant Secretary of State Marshal Green; State Department counselor Richard F. Pedersen; and Pres-

idential Press Secretary Ronald L. Ziegler.

Mr. Nixon met later July 26 with leaders of the Philippine opposition Liberal Party. He reportedly stressed to them the pressures in the U.S. for troop withdrawals from Vietnam and for avoidance of expensive and entangling commitments abroad.

In a toast to Marcos at a state dinner that evening Mr. Nixon spoke of their mutual realization "that if war is to come it is most likely to come again from the Pacific and from Asia in the last third of this century, but. . .if peace is to come, it must come primarily from the initiatives of those who live in Asia."

President Nixon had outlined his Asian policy during an informal news conference (no direct quotation permitted) July 25 on Guam, a stopover point on his way to Manila. It followed the lines of his message to Manila leaders: the U.S. would not become involved in more wars like that in Vietnam; it would reduce its military commitments throughout Asia; it would keep its treaty commitments and watch Asian developments.

The President opposed military involvements (such as the Vietnam war) that tended to generate emotional and economic discord at home. As for the problem of military defense, except for the threat of a major power involving nuclear weapons, the Asian nations themselves would have to deal with internal subversion or external aggression, Mr. Nixon said.

Mr. Nixon reportedly expressed doubt that non-Communist Asian nations would soon be able to form collective security arrangements, but he was optimistic about signs of economic progress in these nations and the apparent decline in their vulnerability to Communist ideology.

The highlights of the President's trip were his unannounced visit to South Vietnam and his stop in Rumania. Mr. Nixon said that the enthusiastic reception given him by the Rumanian public was "the most moving experience I have had in traveling to over 60 countries." He made the comment on his return to Washington Aug. 3. He told the 3,000 persons gathered for his homecoming at Andrews Air Force Base that "America has millions of friends in this world." His trip, he said, had been a "quest for peace." He said his Rumanian reception showed "that deep political differences cannot permanently divide peoples of the world."

Among details of the trip:

Thailand—In an extemporaneous speech shortly after his arrival July 28 in Bangkok, where he and Mrs. Nixon were greeted by King Phumiphol Aduldet and Queen Sirikit, Mr. Nixon spoke of the U.S. "obligations" to Thailand under SEATO (Southeast Asia Treaty Organization) and said the U.S. "will stand proudly with Thailand against those who might threaten it from abroad or from within."

The statement seemed to contradict the President's statement on Asian policy July 25, which stressed that defense problems would be handled primarily by Asian nations themselves. But his Bangkok remark generally was interpreted as public reassurance to an ally deeply involved in the Vietnam war.

White House Press Secretary Ronald L. Ziegler noted later July 28 that "Thailand has not asked for any troops and the President is not talking about sending troops here." An "additional [Presidential] statement" also was released later, although it had been prepared before the extemporaneous remarks. It said the U.S. determination to honor its commitments was "fully consistent with our conviction that the nations of Asia can and must increasingly shoulder the responsibility for achieving peace and progress in the area." "If domination by the aggressor can destroy the freedom of a nation," it said, "too much dependence on a protector can erode its dignity."

The President and Kissinger met July 29 with Premier Thanom Kittikachorn and Foreign Minister Thanat Khoman. Presidential aides later issued a statement saying that Thai leaders had authorized announcement of complete agreement with Mr. Nixon's view that they and other threatened Asian countries must combat subversion with their own forces and had not requested commitment of U.S. ground forces to a counterinsurgency effort.

Rumania—The largest and most enthusiastic crowds encountered during the tour greeted Mr. and Mrs. Nixon in Rumania Aug. 2–3. Estimates of the size of the crowds lining Bucharest's streets on their arrival ranged from a quarter of a million to 900,000. Many waved American and Rumanian flags (distributed by authorities prior to the Nixons' arrival). The first American president in nearly a quarter of a century to visit a Communist nation, Mr. Nixon expressed the belief Aug. 2 that "nations can have widely different internal orders and live in peace." While the U.S. believed that "the rights of all nations must be equal," he said, ". . . we do not believe that the character of all nations must be the same." If international amity were to prevail, he said, the nations of the world must be prepared "to see the world as it is—a world of different races, of different nations, of different social systems—a real world, where many interests divide men and many interests unite them."

Rumanian President Nicolae Ceausescu responded "that in the complex conditions of international affairs today, the development of relations between states on the basis of the principles of peaceful coexistence and respect for independence, sovereignty, equal rights and non-interference in the internal affairs, represents the safe way toward promoting a climate of confidence and understanding among peoples and of peace and security in the world."

It was announced Aug. 3 that the two leaders had agreed to reopen formal negotiations on a consular convention and hoped that negotiations for a civil air agreement could be resumed "at an appropriate opportunity." A U.S. library was to be opened in Rumania and a Rumanian library in the U.S. In a joint statement, the two leaders further asserted agreement to "look for new ways" of increasing economic exchanges between the two countries.

(A scheduled trip by Soviet leaders to Rumania just prior to the Nixon visit—in mid-July to sign a 20-year friendship tready—had been postponed until fall. The postponement was attributed to the President's visit.)

Congress Leaders Briefed On Trip. President Nixon reported on his trip to the Far East and Rumania at a White House meeting Aug. 4 with Vice President Spiro T. Agnew and 22 Congressional leaders of both parties.

According to White House Press Secretary Ronald L. Ziegler, the President told the group that the new U.S. policy on Asia he enunciated during the trip had been accepted by all the Asian leaders with whom he had conferred. The President also reported, according to Ziegler, that all the Asian leaders consulted had inquired about the U.S. position on the collective security arrangement for Asia proposed by Leonid I. Brezhnev. Nixon's response, Ziegler said, was that the U.S. would not support any sort of condominium in Asia.

Ziegler also said Nixon had told Rumanian officials that the U.S. could move to open trade with Eastern Europe after the end of the Vietnam war. Mr. Nixon's position at the White House meeting was that the U.S. should not furnish strategic materials to countries supplying arms to North Vietnam.

Several key Administration officials went abroad early in August on missions related to Mr. Nixon's world tour. Secretary of State William P. Rogers visited six Asian countries July 28–Aug. 8. Kissinger reported to French leaders in Paris Aug. 4 and to the NATO Permanent Council in Brussels Aug. 5. Sisco, who had accompanied the President to Rumania, went to Belgrade Aug. 4 to confer with Yugoslav officials.

During his tour, Rogers expressed the desire of the U.S. to renew diplomatic talks with Communist China.

In Canberra, Australia Aug. 8, Rogers said the U.S. would "soon be making another approach to see if a dialogue with Peking can be resumed. This could take place in Warsaw or at another mutually acceptable site." "We intend to disregard Peking's denunciations of United States efforts to negotiate with the Soviet Union," he said. "and we intend to disregard Soviet nervousness at steps we take to re-establish contacts between us and the Chinese Communists."

He said the goals of the new U.S. policy in Asia were to obtain peace in Vietnam, to reaffirm America's role as a Pacific power and its determination to meet treaty obligations in the area, to encourage Asian leaders "to meet their own internal security needs while providing material assistance when required," to promote economic development "with emphasis on increasing regional cooperation," to "stand unaligned in the Sino-Soviet conflict while persisting in efforts to engage in a constructive dialogue with both," and "to play a full supporting role in the general evolution of a secure and progressive Pacific community."

In his public remarks in Seoul and Taipei Aug. 1, Rogers had pledged that the U.S. would stand by its treaty obligations to its allies, specifically South Korea and Nationalist China.

In Japan, Rogers participated in a three-day cabinet-level conference on Okinawa, trade and other economic matters July 29–31. He stressed U.S. willingness to improve relations with both Communist China and the Soviet Union. He said July 29 the U.S. was preparing a new approach to the Soviet Union on the Berlin problem. "There is some evidence from Moscow of at least a flickering sense of mutual interest with the United States and other nations in moving toward a somewhat less dangerous and less hostile state of international relations," he said.

HHH in Yugoslavia & U.S.S.R. Former Vice President Hubert H. Humphrey visited the Soviet Union and Yugoslavia as a private citizen in July. His Russian trip was at the invitation of the Soviet government to hunt wild boar.

Arriving in Russia July 9, Humphrey toured major Soviet cities, and was received in Moscow July 17 by government officials, including First Deputy Foreign Minister Vasily Kuznetsov and the editors of Pravda and Izvestia, the official party and government newspapers.

Humphrey conferred with Premier Aleksei N. Kosygin July 21. At a news conference following their two-hour meeting, Humphrey reported that Kosygin had asked him to convey to President Nixon the Soviet Union's desire to cooperate with the U.S. in "the cause of peace." Although a variety of topics was discussed, Humphrey indicated the issue of strategic missile talks dominated the meeting.

Humphrey arrived in Belgrade July 21, and met with President Tito the next day for private talks at Brioni Island.

Borman in U.S.S.R. Col. Frank Borman, 41, U.S. astronaut who had commanded Apollo 8 in the first manned orbiting of the moon, visited the U.S.S.R. July 2–10 on a trip during which he stressed the desirability of U.S.-Soviet cooperation in space projects. Borman, accompanied by his wife, Susan, and his sons, Frederick, 17, and Edwin, 15, was a guest of the Soviet-American Relations Institute. Although his visit was unofficial, Borman conferred with Soviet President Nikolai V. Podgorny in the Kremlin July 9 and later said that the meeting "was very encouraging and beneficial when we think of cooperation in space."

Borman, the first U.S. astronaut to visit the U.S.S.R., was greeted on his arrival in Moscow July 2 by three Soviet cosmonauts—Lt. Col. Gherman S. Titov, Maj. Gen. Georgi T. Beregovoi and scientist Konstantin Feoktistov.

Visiting Leningrad July 3, Borman said at a press conference: "I am now working on a program under which, in the mid-1970s, we hope to launch a big orbiting space station or manned laboratory. . . . I hope and can foresee a time in that program when U.S. and Soviet spacemen will fly together."

Borman July 5 visited Vzyozdnigorodok (Star Town), the cosmonaut community 20 miles northeast of Moscow, an area normally closed to foreigners. He and his family, guided by Titov, flew July 6 to Simferopol in the Crimea, where he became the first American (and the third foreigner of any nationality) to tour the Yevpatoria space tracking station. They flew July 8 to Novosibirsk, in Siberia, where Borman visited Academgorodok (Academic Town) and talked to the elite Soviet scientists stationed there. Dr. Feoktistov, who accompanied them, helped describe scientific and technological achievements of the center. They then flew back to Moscow late July 8.

After meetings with Podgorny and leading Soviet scientists in Moscow July 9, Borman left the U.S.S.R. with his family July 10 to return to the U.S.

SALT Preliminaries

U.S., U.S.S.R. Agree to Preliminary Arms Talks. The U.S. and the U.S.S.R. jointly announced Oct. 25 that both countries had agreed to send representatives to Helsinki, Finland Nov. 17 for "preliminary discussion" on curbing the strategic arms race. The negotiations were generally referred to by the acronym SALT (for strategic arms limitation talks).

At a White House briefing, Presidential Press Secretary Ronald L. Ziegler said that Soviet Ambassador to the U.S. Anatoly F. Dobrynin had proposed the place and date of the meeting to President Nixon in an unreported meeting Oct. 20 and Mr. Nixon had accepted immediately. The President then asked Dobrynin to work out the details with Secretary of State William P. Rogers. This he did Oct. 22.

The U.S. and the U.S.S.R. reportedly had reached an agreement on strategic arms talks in the summer of 1968, but progress toward talks was interrupted by the Czechoslovak invasion.

Podgorny's Cautious View on SALT. Soviet President Nikolai V. Podgorny said Nov. 6 in a Bolshevik anniversary address, "A positive outcome of these talks would undoubtedly help improve Soviet-U.S. relations and preserve and strengthen the peace. The Soviet Union is striving to achieve precisely such results." Referring to U.S. intentions to proceed with missile developments, Podgorny warned, however, that "We have never allowed and will not allow anybody to talk to the Soviet Union from a position of strength."

Rogers on U.S. View. Secretary of State William P. Rogers urged the Soviet Union Nov. 13 to recognize that both countries would benefit from a limitation on the arms race despite certain risks.

Declaring that both sides could effectively destroy the other side no matter who struck first, Rogers said, "The risks in seeking an agreement seem to be manageable, insurable and reasonable ones to run. They seem less dangerous than the risks of open-ended arms competition—risks about which we perhaps have become somewhat callous." Without mentioning any specific proposals that the Administration might make at SALT, Rogers asserted that "competitive accumulation of more sophisticated weapons would not add to the basic security of either side." He listed three U.S. objectives at the Helsinki talks: (1) to raise international security "by maintaining a stable U.S.-Soviet strategic relationship through limitations on the deployment of strategic armaments"; (2) to "halt the upward spiral" of the arms race and thus avoid uncertainties, tensions and costs; and (3) to decrease the risk of nuclear war "through a dialogue about issues arising from the strategic situation."

Preliminaries Start. The U.S. and USSR formally opened preliminary SALT talks in Helsinki Nov. 17. Each side pledged to avoid any agreement that would put the other at a military disadvantage.

Deputy Foreign Minister Vladimir S. Semyonov, chief of the Soviet delegation, said the U.S.S.R. attached great significance to curbing the arms race. He declared: "Given genuine desire on both sides to seek mutually acceptable agreement without prejudice to the security of our states and all other countries, it is possible and imperative to overcome obvious complexities and obstacles and to bring about reasonable solutions."

Gerard C. Smith, chief of the U.S. delegation, read a statement by President Nixon who asserted that the U.S. would be guided by the principle of maintaining "sufficiency in the forces required to protect ourselves and our allies." Mr. Nixon said he recognized that the Soviet Union had similar defense responsibilities but he affirmed: "I believe it is possible, however, that we can carry out our respective responsibilities under a mutually acceptable limitation and eventual reduction of our strategic arsenals." The President

continued: "We are prepared to discuss limitations on all offensive and defensive systems, and to reach agreements in which both sides can have confidence . . . We seek no unilateral advantage. Nor do we seek arrangements which could be prejudicial to the interests of third parties. We are prepared to engage in bona fide negotiations on concrete issues, avoiding polemics and extraneous matters."

In his welcoming address, Finnish Foreign Minister Ahti Karjalainen emphasized the urgency for negotiations on the arms race. Calling the meeting "a historic occasion," Karjalainen said: "By starting these discussions, the two powers which are in control of the major part of the nuclear arsenal of the world have on their part acknowledged their supreme responsibility for the peace and security."

■Communist China accused the U.S. and the Soviet Union Nov. 5 of using the Helsinki talks to maintain their "nuclear collusion." Peking said the two countries were cooperating with each other "in their big conspiracy to further the nuclear military alliance between the two countries so as to maintain their already bankrupt nuclear monopoly . . ."

■U.S. officials in Washington disclosed Nov. 14 that Undersecretary of State Elliot L. Richardson had proposed at a NATO meeting in Brussels Nov. 5 that NATO invite Warsaw Pact members to negotiations on reducing conventional forces in Europe. The NATO-Warsaw Pact talks, according to the sources, could begin after the preliminary talks in Helsinki were completed.

China & Its Adversaries

Nixon Under Attack. The Peking government launched personal attacks on **Richard M. Nixon in two Communist Party publications Jan. 27, 1968. The** article, which appeared in Jenmin Jih Pao (People's Daily) and Hung Chi (Red **Flag, party ideological journal), char-** acterized Nixon as a frightened man taking over the reigns of a government threatened by economic catastrophe and revolt. **The Chinese article denounced his inaugural address as "utter non-** sense" and asked: "How can his ramblings block the victorious advance of Marxism, Leninism, Mao Tse-tung's thought, throughout the world?" The article also assailed the Soviet Union for its expressions of good will to the new President and added that the Soviet leaders hoped to gain support from the new "American imperialist chieftain" in a "futile effort to divide the world through U.S.-Soviet collusion." The article was signed "Commentator," a nom de plume used for authoritative pronouncements by the Peking regime.

Peking Cancels Talks with U.S. The Communist Chinese government informed the U.S. Feb. 18 that it had canceled their bi-lateral meeting scheduled to begin in Warsaw Feb. 20. In a note delivered to the U.S. ambassador to Poland, Walter J. Stoessel, Peking said that the defection of its charge d'affaires at The Hague, Liao Ho-shu, was the reason for the cancellation.

The note said Liao "was incited to betray his country and [was] carried off to the U.S. by the Central Intelligence Agency," and it further charged that the Nixon Administration had "inherited the mantle of the preceding U.S. government in flagrantly making itself the enemy of the 700 million Chinese people."

Officials in Washington said that Peking had used the defection of Liao as a pretext for its action and that the two countries were still too far apart in their attitudes for meaningful talks. Liao, who had defected Jan. 24, had arrived in Washington Feb. 4 and had requested political asylum.

Communist China had protested Liao's defection and had demanded that the U.S. return him to Peking. A Chinese broadcast had said that the affair showed that Presidents Nixon and Johnson "are jackals of the same lair" and that the defection was "another towering crime committed by the U.S. government."

In a statement distributed Feb. 18 by the State Department, Secretary of State William P. Rogers implied that the U.S. was prepared to accept a Chinese recommendation that the two countries agree to principles of peaceful coexistence. He indicated that the Nixon Administration

intended to extend previous offers for cultural and scientific exchanges.

New Sino-Soviet Border Fighting. Soviet and Chinese border forces fought two heavy skirmishes March 2 and 15 on the Manchurian border 250 miles north of Vladivostok. The fighting, over a disputed island in the frozen Ussuri River, involved thousands of men, tanks and artillery; its severity was indicated by the fact that 31 Soviet border guards were reported killed in the first clash. Unlike earlier border clashes between the two countries, the latest were immediately publicized by both governments.

(Sovereignty over the islands in the Ussuri River had long been disputed by both countries. Peking had contended that the 1860 Sino-Russian [Peking] treaty, which established the frontier, in effect had been imposed on China to seize vast tracts of its territory. Under the treaty, China had ceded to Russia all of its territory east of the Ussuri River. The New China News Agency [NCNA] claimed March 3 that "Chenpao Island is indisputable Chinese territory and it always has been under Chinese jurisdiction and patrolled by Chinese frontier guards since long ago." The NCNA also reported that "between November 1967 and Jan. 5, 1968, the Soviet revisionist renegade clique sent Soviet frontier guards on 18 occasions to intrude into the area of Chibiching Island, north of Chenpao Island . . . disrupting Chinese people's production and on many occasions killing and wounding Chinese people who were engaged in productive labor." Moscow, on the other hand, had argued that Peking was attempting to regain roughly 500,000 square miles of Far Eastern territory from the Soviet Union.)

(The Washington Post reported March 4 that about 800,000 Chinese troops—about one-third of China's armed forces—were believed to be positioned along the 6,000-mile Soviet-Chinese border, from Manchuria to Central Asia. Western intelligence analysts, according to the New York Times March 3, would not reveal their estimates of the number of Soviet troops along the border; however, they did say that the U.S.S.R. had gradually built up its Far East defenses under a "large-scale program" under way for some time. The analysts also said that the build-up had continued even at the expense of Soviet troop commitments in Central Europe. Soviet troop strength in East Germany alone was estimated at 200,000 men.)

The Soviet embassy in Peking was besieged March 3 by an estimated 10,000 demonstrators protesting the border incident. Two Soviet correspondents were manhandled by the crowd, but managed to enter the embassy compound. Posters throughout the city denounced "Soviet aggression" and "imperialism." A second protest note was delivered to Soviet officials by Deputy Foreign Minister Chi Peng-Fei, who warned that "decisive measures" would be taken if Moscow continued to "provoke incidents." The note was officially rejected by Moscow.

A joint editorial published March 4 by Jenmin Jih Pao (People's Daily) and Chiehfang Chun Pao, the Communist Party and army newspapers, attacked Soviet leaders as "imperialists and prototype tsars." The editorial, entitled "Down with the New Tsar," accused the Moscow government of having been "all along . . . hostile to the Chinese people. Particularly since the beginning of the cultural revolution . . . the Soviet revisionist clique, with hatred and fear, has intensified its efforts in anti-China activities. In addition . . . it has massed troops along the Sino-Mongolian and the Sino-Soviet border regions and made repeated intrusions into our territory and air space, creating border incidents and posing a military threat to our country." The editorial accused the Soviet Union of having collaborated with the U.S. "in the hope of rigging up an anti-China encirclement." It asserted that by their occupation of Czechoslovakia and their conversion of the "Mongolian People's Republic into their colony," Soviet leaders had shown that "they are more greedy than the Tsar."

A new aspect was added to the conflict March 5 and 6 when China accused the Soviet Union of collusion against it with the Nationalist Chinese regime on Taiwan, the U.S. and Japan. A reported 50,000 demonstrators in Wenchow, Chekiang Province, denounced Moscow March 5 for "currying favor with the Nixon Administration and collaborating with bandit Chiang [Kai Shek] to wage anti-China activities and conduct acts of social imperialism and social fascism."

Further clashes reported—Sources in Moscow reported May 10 that Chinese and Soviet troops had clashed several times along the border separating Soviet Kazakhstan and China's Sinkiang region during the week. Casualties were reported on both sides, but there was no official confirmation. The U.S.S.R. reportedly was holding military exercises along its Far Eastern and Siberian borders.

Chinese Party Congress. The long-awaited Ninth Congress of the Chinese Communist Party opened in Peking April 1. The congress was the first one held since 1956, and it began without advance announcement. The meeting, which lasted until April 24, adopted a new party constitution naming Lin Piao as successor to Chairman Mao Tse-tung.

In a report to the Congress, Lin sharply attacked "U.S. imperialism" and Soviet "revisionism." Claiming that the two countries had colluded and attempted to divide and control the world, Lin said that China had to make preparations for the possibility that either the U.S. or the U.S.S.R. might "at an early date" launch a conventional or nuclear war. Quoting a hitherto unpublicized statement of Mao, Lin said: "With regard to the question of world war, there are but two possibilities: One is that the war will give rise to revolution and the other is that revolution will prevent war." Lin assailed the U.S. "occupation" of Taiwan and added that the Chinese army was "determined to liberate the sacred territory of Taiwan."

Terming the U.S.S.R.'s leadership a "revisionist, renegade clique," Lin attacked the Soviet doctrines of "limited sovereignty," "international dictatorship" and "socialist community." He said: "What does all this [the doctrines] mean? It means that your sovereignty is 'limited' while his is unlimited. You won't obey him? He will exercise 'international dictatorship' over you—dictatorship over the people of other countries to form the 'socialist communist' rule by the new czar. . . ." Lin also disclosed that Soviet Premier Aleksei N. Kosygin had "asked to communicate with our leaders by telephone March 22" on the recent Ussuri River border clashes but that the Chinese had replied the next day that discussions by telephone were "unsuitable." He said that Peking was still considering a reply to the Soviet offer March 29 to resume the two countries' 1964 border negotiations.

Lin pledged Peking's support for national revolutionary movements everywhere, but in particular he cited Albania's "struggle against imperialism and revisionism," the Vietnamese people's "war of resistance against U.S. aggression," and "the people of Czechoslovakia and other countries in their just struggle against Soviet revisionist social imperialism." In stressing Chinese support of wars of national liberation, Lin said: "Our proletarian foreign policy is not based on expediency; it is a policy in which we have long persisted. This is what we did in the past, and we will persist in doing the same in the future."

(Western observers noted that of the nearly 4,000 words devoted to foreign policy in Lin's address, 45% were focused on a denunciation of the U.S.S.R. and only 7.5% were devoted to attacks on the U.S.)

Kennedy for New China Policy. Sen. Edward M. Kennedy (D, Mass.) urged the Nixon Administration March 20 to seize its opportunity "to rectify the errors of the past" and engage in "new initiatives" toward better relations between the U.S. and Communist China. Peking should be offered a "clear and attractive alternative to the existing impasse in our relations," he said.

Kennedy made the remarks in New York at a conference sponsored by the National Committee on United States-China Relations.

Kennedy urged the elimination of U.S. military bases in Taiwan and announcement by the U.S. of its "willingness to re-establish the consular offices we maintained in the People's Republic during the earliest period of Communist rule." The "demilitarization of Taiwan could take place at no cost to our treaty commitments, or to the security of the island," he said.

Kennedy said the Administration's recent decision to deploy an antiballistic missile defense system would "likely . . . be seen in Peking as a new [U.S.] military provocation." He asserted that "virtually no experts on China expect Peking to commit aggression, in the conventional sense of forcibly occupying the territory of another country, as the Soviet Union recently occupied Czechoslovakia. Such action is in accord with neither past Chinese actions nor present Chinese capabilities."

Speakers at the concluding session of the conference March 21 viewed the current frontier conflict between China and the Soviet Union as an opportunity for the U.S. to improve its relations with both countries.

The conference chairman was Harvard Prof. Edwin O. Reischauer, former ambassador to Japan. The committee, a private educational organization, was headed by Columbia Prof. A. Doak Barnett. Among those participating in the conference were Arthur J. Goldberg, former chief U.S. representative at the U.N., and Theodore C. Sorensen, former aide to the late President John F. Kennedy. Sorensen held that "we should no longer continue our policy of making a greater effort toward understanding and friendly relations with the Soviet Union than we do with Communist China."

China Curbs Eased. The Nixon Administration July 21, 1969 announced steps to relax travel and trade restrictions that had been applied to Communist China since 1950. Beginning July 23, U.S. citizens traveling abroad would be allowed to bring back $100 worth of goods produced in Communist China, the State Department announced. The agency also announced that certain categories of U.S. citizens would be allowed to travel to China, although a general travel ban would remain in effect.

State Department spokesman Robert J. McCloskey said the steps were designed to "relax tensions and facilitate the development of peaceful contacts" between citizens of the two countries. He emphasized that the decisions had been made unilaterally and the department did not expect a favorable response from

China. Department officials said the measures had beeen chosen because they required no reciprocal action from Peking.

The eased restrictions on Chinese goods would apply only to noncommercial purchases made by travelers abroad. It was expected to especially affect U.S. tourists visiting Hong Kong and Singapore. Certificates of origin had been required for goods brought back from these ports to prove the products had not come from mainland China.

Six categories of citizens were to be automatically cleared for travel to China by the State Department: congressmen, journalists, teachers, scholars with postgraduate degrees and undergraduates enrolled in a college or university, scientists, and medical doctors and American Red Cross representatives. Department officials noted, however, that travelers would still have to obtain entry visas from Peking. Although more than 40 journalists had been cleared by the State Department for travel to Communist China since 1957, officials said they knew of only two cases of visas being granted by the Chinese.

McCloskey Dec. 13 made public three new changes liberalizing U.S. trade relations with Communist China. The changes, effective Dec. 22, were (1) affiliates and subsidiaries of U.S. companies abroad would be allowed to sell nonstrategic goods to China and to purchase items from China for resale on foreign markets; (2) Affiliates and subsidiaries would no longer be required to obtain certificates of "non-Chinese origin" on products shipped to "third" countries; the certificate would still be necessary for export to the U.S. (3) The $100 ceiling on purchases of Chinese goods by Americans for non-commercial use was eliminated; the items, however, could not be for resale.

In describing the partial lifting of the 19-year embargo, McCloskey said the changes were "a small step forward, not a great leap forward." He emphasized the trade relaxations were "strictly unilateral and are not related to recent Warsaw contacts with Communist Chinese representatives."

U.S. Sino-Soviet Policy Outlined. Undersecretary of State Elliott L. Richardson, addressing the 65th annual meeting of the American Political Science Association (APSA) in New York City Sept. 5, expressed the Nixon Administration's concern that an intensification in the border tensions between the Soviet Union and Communist China might escalate the dispute "into a massive breach of international peace and security." Richardson said the Administration did not seek to "exploit" the hostilities "for our own advantage" but would try "to pursue a long-term course of progressively developing better relations" with both nations.

Rejecting the alternative of isolating Communist China, Richardson said that "Soviet apprehensions" would not prevent the U.S. "from attempting to bring China out of its angry, alienated shell." He said the Administration believed that "ideological differences between the two Communist giants are not our affair" and that "our national security would in the long run be prejudiced by associating ourselves with either side against the other."

Diplomatic Recognition. The Senate, by a 77–3 vote Sept. 25, passed a sense-of-the-Senate resolution (S Res 205) stating that U.S. recognition of a foreign government and exchange of diplomatic representatives with it did not "of itself" imply approval by the U.S. "of the form, ideology, or policy of that foreign government."

The resolution, endorsed by the State Department, was sponsored by Sens. Alan Cranston (D, Calif.) and George D. Aiken (R, Vt.), ranking Republican on the Foreign Relations Committee. The committee noted that the resolution was not designed to effect recognition of mainland China. Nevertheless, the resolution was generally considered a new approach to the China problem in that it would eliminate the conncept of "democratic legitimacy" associated with extension of diplomatic recognition ever since the Wilson Administration. Cranston had said that the resolution would not settle the question of U.S. recognition of Communist China, but would remove a barrier in the event "a time comes when recognition would otherwise be negotiable and would clearly serve our national interest."

It should be made clear, he said, that "recognition of a foreign government is done not to confer a compliment but to secure a convenience and is intended not as an ineffective stamp of moral approval but as a step designed to serve our national interest."

U.S. & U.S.S.R. Again Accused. Communist China celebrated its 20th National Day Oct. 1 with a massive rally in Peking's Tienanmen Square. Communist Party Chairman Mao Tse-tung and Vice-Chairman Lin Piao presided over the rally.

In the keynote address, Lin's main theme was the necessity for preparing China against the possibility of war. He said: "U.S. imperialism and social-imperialism [i.e., the Soviet Union] are colluding and at the same time contending with each other, carrying out arms expansion and war preparations and widely attempting to engineer a war of aggression against our country and flagrantly resorting to nuclear blackmail against us." In order for the Chinese to protect themselves, Lin said, "The people of the whole country must heighten their vigilance, strengthen preparedness against war and be ready at all times to wipe out all the enemies who dare invade us." Lin concluded his speech with an appeal to the people of the world to "unite and oppose the war of aggression . . . especially one in which atom bombs are used as weapons." (At a dinner reception in Peking Sept. 30, Lin had said: "We develop nuclear weapons solely for defense and for breaking the nuclear monopoly, and our ultimate aim is to eliminate nuclear weapons.")

(The highest-ranking Soviet official at a reception Oct. 1 at the Chinese embassy in Moscow was Deputy Foreign Minister Nikolai P. Firyubin.)

The 25th anniversary of the establishment of Communist rule in Albania was celebrated Nov. 28. In a speech, Communist Party First Secretary Enver Hoxha praised the aid given unconditionally by Peking to Albania and he denounced the "Soviet revisionist renegades," whose "so-called aid . . . is poison and a snare to enslave people." Hoxha assailed the 1968 Czechoslovak invasion and occupation, which he described as "the starting point for yet bigger adventures against the freedom and independence of other peoples," notably Yugoslavia, Rumania and Albania, and he decried Soviet "armed provocations" on the frontiers of China. He also termed the appeal for a European security conference a "diabolical trap" of the U.S. and U.S.S.R. to preserve their "colonial privileges."

Soviet bloc delegations walked out of a National Day reception Nov. 29 after an Albanian ambassador had declared: "The sharp battle of principle that the Albanian party and people have unfailingly waged against the Khrushchevian line of Soviet revisionism, the Brezhnev-Kosygin clique of today, and the other revisionists, is a great battle."

At a dinner at the Albanian embassy in Peking Nov. 30, Communist Chinese Premier Chou En-lai made a speech exhorting the people of the world to "use revolutionary warfare" against the U.S.S.R. and the U.S. if the two countries should join in aggression. Referring to an agreement concluded Nov. 21 for the U.S. to give Okinawa back to Japan in 1972, the Chinese premier charged that the pact was "entirely a fraud" and showed the "intensified military collusion" between the two nations. He then charged, without naming the Soviet Union directly, that "Socialist imperialist" forces had joined the U.S. and its allies to oppose China and to suppress world revolutionary movements.

Progress Toward Detente: 1970-71

China Policy Evolves

U.S. policy continued to shift slowly during 1970 toward greater acceptance of more-normal relations with the People's Republic of China, both bilaterally and in world affairs. Although the Chinese made little observable change in their traditional harsh denunciations of the U.S., some Western sources noted signs that China was also seeking acceptable ways to relax Sino-U.S. tensions.

New Year's message. A 1970 New Year's Day message to the Chinese people predicted that the next 50–100 years would be a "great era of radical change." The message, entitled "Usher in the Great 1970s," was published jointly by the Communist Party newspaper Jenmin Jih Pao (People's Daily), the party ideological journal Hung Chi (Red Flag) and the official army publication Chiehfang Chun Pao, and transmitted in English by the New China News Agency Jan. 1.

The message declared that during the 1960s "the revolutionary movement of the proletariat and the broad masses of the people has swept the world with the momentum of an avalanche and the force of a thunderbolt." In the strongest denunciation of the U.S.S.R. since Sino-Soviet border talks began in Oct. 1969, it asserted: "The Soviet revisionist rene-

gade clique—the center of modern revisionism—is heading for total bankruptcy at an accelerated tempo. Khrushchev, the clown, who swaggered like a conquering hero not long ago, is now a heap of dirt beneath the contempt of mankind. His successors Brezhnev and company are faring even worse, and their conditions deteriorating year after year; they are saddled with crisis both at home and abroad. They are enforcing fascist dictatorship at home and carrying out aggression and expansion abroad."

The editorial denounced the U.S. for engaging in "arms expansion and war preparations" and said that "The rapid decline of U.S. imperialism strikingly demonstrates that the capitalist system is already in the grip of a new and most acute general crisis." Predicting that the 1970s would witness rising "storms of the peoples' revolution" and the hastening "collapse of imperialism," the editorial contended that "U.S. imperialism and Soviet revisionism can never escape their doom no matter how they collide with each other and contend for spheres of influence, no matter how many schemes and tricks they resort to and what kind of wars of aggression they launch." In contrast to the "doom" forecast for the two superpowers, it hailed developments in China under the leadership of Chairman Mao Tsetung, stating that the country had become "even more consolidated, prosperous, powerful and vigorous."

Quoting a recent statement of Mao to "unite and oppose the war of aggression launched by any imperialism or social-imperialism, especially one in which atom bombs are used as weapons," the editorial exhorted people to make stronger preparations for war. Nevertheless, the editorial concluded by proposing the development of diplomatic relations "with all countries on the basis of the five principles of peaceful coexistence."

Agnew on China. U.S. Vice President Spiro T. Agnew discussed the evolving U.S. policy on Asia during a trip to the Far East during December 1969–January 1970.

En route to Taiwan, Agnew Jan. 2 told newsmen that Red China, "a country of over 800 million people, . . . can't be ignored." The U.S., he said, "should not sit still in a stance of armed preparedness" but should seek "meaningful dialogue" with mainland China. He favored "initiatives to develop an atmosphere that will allow us to reduce the amount of military spending and use some of our money in some of the programs so desperately needed in the areas of the environment, the cities and the like at home."

After his arrival in Taipei and a private conference Jan. 3 with President Chiang Kai-shek of Nationalist China, Agnew reported that while Chiang was "not sympathetic" with the U.S. diplomatic and trade overtures to the mainland, he had shown "understanding that this is a changing world and we must all work toward a lessening" of its tensions. Agnew cited U.S. determination to uphold its treaty commitment to Nationalist China.

On the flight from Taiwan to Bangkok Jan. 3, Agnew told newsmen he had discerned from his talks with Asian leaders so far that "they are very concerned about a movement of Chinese Communists." "What is presently on their minds is total attack," he said. "I wouldn't say nuclear attack, but an unmistakable attack by another power that amounts to an act of war." The U.S. had pledged protection against "aggressions

from the outside while they're intended to take care of the local insurrections," he said. Asian leaders "are frightened and they want reassurance that the American presence will continue," he said.

Nixon foresees A-blackmail. At a press conference Jan. 30, Nixon indicated that the U.S. must be prepared to maintain a flexible defense program for the Pacific. The President predicted that within 10 years Communist China would have made significant strides in its nuclear delivery capabilities, and that the U.S. must be ready to block any attempts by China of "nuclear blackmail" against the U.S. or its Pacific allies. The President also said the U.S. would seek to make "some normalization of our relationships with Communist China."

U.S. & China resume meetings. The U.S. State Department announced Jan. 8 that the U.S. and Communist China had agreed to resume ambassadorial talks in Warsaw Jan. 20. The agreement to renew talks came after a two-hour meeting between U.S. Ambassador to Poland Walter J. Stoessel Jr. and Chinese Charge d'Affaires Lei Yang, who would represent their respective countries at the talks.

(The Soviet newspaper Izvestia Jan. 9 published the news of the renewed talks adjacent to a strong attack on the "anti-Soviet slander" of "Maoists." The juxtaposition of the articles, according to correspondents, appeared to indicate a new warning against possible U.S.-Chinese "collusion" against the U.S.S.R. The Chinese were charged with creating a "war psychosis" against the Soviet Union and with "glorifying militarism and chauvinism.")

Two meetings were held—the 135th in the series took place in the Chinese embassy Jan. 20, and the 136th was held in the U.S. embassy Feb. 20. As usual, no details were disclosed.

(The Soviet weekly foreign affairs journal Za Rubezhom claimed Feb. 21 that by "continuing to deliberately create tension in their relations with the Soviet Union and other countries of the Socialist community, the Maoists are speeding up their reconciliation with the American imperialists.")

Chinese cancel talks—Communist China May 18 announced cancellation of the scheduled May 20 session of the U.S.-Chinese ambassadorial talks in Warsaw. The information was delivered orally by two Chinese liaison officers, Ch'ien Yung-nien and Yeh Wei-lan, to their American counterpart in the Polish capital, Thomas W. Simons, Jr.

The Communist Chinese news agency Hsinhua explained May 19 that the cancellation had been done "in view of the increasingly grave situation created by the United States government, which has brazenly sent troops to invade Cambodia and expanded the war in Indochina." For this reason, the dispatch said, "the Chinese government deems it no longer suitable for the 137th meeting of the Sino-U.S. ambassadorial talks to be held on May 20 as originally scheduled."

The holding of future talks, according to Hsinhua, was to be "decided upon later through consultation by the liaison personnel of the two sides." State Department spokesman Robert J. McCloskey said May 18 that the "postponement" had not been "entirely unanticipated" and that the Chinese diplomats announcing the decision in Warsaw had "indicated" their government would probably be willing to set a new date for the talks in "several weeks."

Chou appears on French TV. Communist Chinese Premier Chou En-lai, in an interview broadcast July 27 on French television, endorsed Sino-French relations and opposed efforts by "superpowers" to determine world affairs.

Urging that U.S. troops be withdrawn from Indochina, South Korea and Taiwan, Chou said: "In a broader sense, all the U.S. armed forces and the armed forces of other countries should be withdrawn from all the territories they are occupying and go home so that the people of all countries may enjoy the right to solve their problems on their own, without any menace or interference from outside. . . . There exists in the world one or two superpowers that constantly seek to oppress the others by force, and

to treat the weak and the small badly while fighting among themselves for world hegemony. The time when the great powers could decide the fate of the world has gone forever. We must smash the myth that creates fear of the great powers."

Chou's remarks had been made July 14 in a Peking interview with representatives of the French film group Agence Francaise des Images.

U.S.-Soviet Relations Improve

U.S.S.R. favors U.S. at conference. Leonid M. Zamyatin, head of the press department of the Soviet Foreign Ministry, said at a press conference in Moscow Jan. 13, 1970 that the U.S.S.R. favored U.S. participation in an all-Europe security conference that East European nations had been proposing.

U.S. State Department spokesman Robert J. McCloskey confirmed Jan. 13 that the U.S. had been informed of the U.S.S.R. attitude.

Journal studies U.S. A new Soviet journal devoted to the study of U.S. politics and culture was issued Jan. 31. The monthly journal, called SSShA: Ekonomika, Politika, Ideologiya (U.S.A: Economics, Politics, Ideology), was published by the Institute on the U.S. of the Soviet Academy of Sciences. The first scholarly journal devoted entirely to the U.S., the issue included a 7-page article by Premier Aleksei N. Kosygin's daughter, Mrs. Lyudmila A. Gvishiani, on U.S. attitudes towards the U.S.S.R. in 1919; an article by Gus Hall, general secretary of the Communist Party of the U.S.; and the first part of a serialization of Theodore H. White's book "The Making of the President: 1968."

Foreign affairs message. President Nixon submitted to Congress Feb. 18 a foreign policy message outlining, and entitled, "United States Foreign Policy for the 1970's: A New Strategy for Peace." The President referred to it as the first "annual report" by an American president on the state of the world.

Among statements Nixon made in the message:

The Soviet Union—U.S. policy was "not to employ negotiations as a forum for cold-war invective or ideological debate" but to "regard our Communist adversaries first and foremost as nations pursuing their own interests as they perceive these interests." Negotiations should consist of "authentic give-and-take" on the issues, and there should be an appreciation of the "interrelationship of international events."

Among the lessons of the past two decades for the Soviet Union and the U.S. were the limitations of great power and "the worldwide decline in the appeal of ideology."

The overall relationship with the U.S.S.R. "remains far from satisfactory." Soviet leaders had failed to exert a helpful influence on the North Vietnamese in Paris and continued to supply North Vietnam with war material. In the Middle East, "we have not seen on the Soviet side that practical and constructive flexibility" necessary for successful negotiations and "we see evidence, moreover, that the Soviet Union seeks a position in the area as a whole which would make great-power rivalry more likely."

Eastern Europe—The U.S. did not intend "to undermine the legitimate security interests of the Soviet Union" and "the time is certainly past . . . when any power would seek to exploit Eastern Europe to obtain strategic advantage against the Soviet Union." The U.S. pursuit of negotiation and detente was meant to reduce existing tensions.

But the U.S. viewed these countries "as sovereign, not as parts of a monolith" and would not accept any doctrine "that abridges their right to seek reciprocal improvement of relations with us or others." It was prepared to enter into negotiations with these nations, "looking to a gradual normalization of relations," and was willing to adjust "to whatever pace and extent of normalization these countries are willing to sustain."

Communist China—"The Chinese are a great and vital people who should not remain isolated from the international community." The U.S. would seek to "define a new relationship" and move toward "improved practical relations with Peking." But it would "not ignore hostile acts" and intended to maintain its treaty commitment for the defense of Nationalist China.

"Our desire for improved relations is not a tactical means of exploiting the clash between China and the Soviet Union. We see no benefit to us in the intensification of that conflict, and we have no intention of taking sides. Nor is the United States interested in joining any condominium or hostile coalition of great powers against either of the large Communist countries. Our attitude is clear-cut—a lasting peace will be impossible so long as some nations consider themselves the permanent enemies of others."

Arms control—The preliminary strategic-arms-limitation-talks (SALT) with the Soviet Union were "serious and businesslike" and the U.S. would make "a determined effort throughout these negotiations to reach agreements that will not only protect our national security but actually enhance it."

The U.S. also was ready to discuss practical arrangements to curb the sale of weapons to regions in conflict. "We must not be drawn into conflicts by local rivalries. The great powers should try to damp down rather than fan local passions by showing restraint in their sale of arms to regions in conflict."

America also would seek "closer cooperation in potential crises" and "find a way to share more information with our adversaries to head off conflict without affecting either our own security interests or those of our friends."

Trade curbs lifted. The U.S. April 29 lifted restrictions on 222 items for export to almost all Communist countries, although licenses would still be necessary before the goods could be exported to Communist China, Cuba, North Vietnam and North Korea. The Associated Press reported the action April 29. Included on the list were textile fabrics, chemicals, iron and steel products, office machines, telephone and telegraph equipment, agricultural machines, some radio and television equipment, hand and power tool parts and electrical apparatus.

∎The Wall Street Journal March 23 reported substantial increases of Soviet purchases in Western markets during the first part of 1970. Flour, wheat, butter, rubber, copper, tin, cocoa, beef and mutton were being purchased in exchange for Soviet shipments of diamonds, furs, nickel and sugar.

Ford refuses offer—The Ford Motor Co. May 13 refused a Soviet government request to build a big truck factory near Kazan in the eastern part of European Russia. The U.S.S.R. had wanted the plant to be ready in 1974 with a capacity of 150,000 general-duty trucks capable of handling payloads of up to 40 tons. Henry Ford II said May 14, however, that the company was still considering other joint projects suggested by the Soviets.

Ford added: "We accepted the Soviet invitation because it is the express policy of the U.S. government to encourage increased trade with East European nations." His remarks were considered a response to Defense Secretary Melvin R. Laird, who had said in a magazine interview reported May 14: "Before giving away the technology to construct trucks in the Soviet Union, and establishing plants for them, there should be some indication on the part of the Soviet Union that they're not going to continue sending the trucks to North Vietnam by shiploads for use on the Ho Chi Minh trail."

Ford's reversal on the project was generally attributed to criticism by Laird and other government officials.

Supreme Soviet elections. The Communist Party newspaper Pravda reported June 17 the results of elections to the Supreme Soviet held June 14. The paper said a total of 153,172,213 voters, 99.96% of those on the lists, had elected 1,517 unopposed candidates to the bicameral parliament. In elections to the Soviet of the Union 99.74% of the electorate voted; only 396,343 were reported to have cast ballots against the single-list candidates of the party. In elections to the Soviet of Nationalities 99.79% voted; 320,633 cast opposing ballots.

In pre-election speeches June 10–12, the three principal Soviet leaders had addressed the voters of their Moscow constituencies on matters of domestic and foreign policy.

Speaking in the Kremlin's Palace of Congresses June 12, CP General Secretary Leonid I. Brezhnev assessed progress in the country since the last Supreme Soviet election in June 1966.

Reiterating Soviet policy on the Middle East and Indochina, he warned: "Let no one in Washington have doubts about our firmness and let them know that the Soviet Union will give resolute rebuffs to the efforts of aggressive circles and will support the peoples subjected to aggression." Of relations with the U.S., Brezhnev observed: "The differences between the U.S.S.R. and the U.S. are really deep. They reflect the struggle between two systems on the world scene which are directly opposite in class, but this does not rule out a settlement of international issues by peaceful means. Precisely for this reason, we believe it necessary to work for such a development of Soviet-American relations that would facilitate the cause of peace and international security.

President Nikolai V. Podgorny said in a speech June 11 at the Bolshoi Theater that Soviet relations with the U.S. were "in a frozen state."

Soviets deny Cuban base report. The Soviet Union Sept. 30 discounted a warning received from the Nixon Administration Sept. 25 against Soviet construction of a submarine-missile base in Cuba.

The Communist party newspaper Pravda called the warning an attempt to stir up a "war psychosis" and said: "It is clear to anyone that the furor about preparations in Cuba that supposedly threaten U.S. security has been raised for a definite purpose."

According to the New York Times Oct. 3, the Soviet Union had been reguarly operating missile-carrying submarines off the east coast of the U.S. and possibly in the Caribbean since April.

U.S.-Soviet space plans. An official of the U.S. National Aeronautics & Space Administration (NASA) announced Oct. 12 that five NASA engineers would attend a two-day conference in Moscow Oct. 26–27 to discuss ways of achieving joint docking operations for Soviet and American spacecraft.

Arrangements for the discussions, considered a major cooperative effort and expected also to focus on space rescue operations, grew out of correspondence begun in 1969 between former NASA Administrator Dr. Thomas O. Paine and Prof. Mstislav V. Keldysh, president of the Soviet Academy of Sciences.

The five U.S. space officials met in Moscow Oct. 26–27 with a delegation of Soviet space experts for the first of a planned series of talks on U.S.-Soviet cooperation in space rescue and possibly other space matters.

The discussions were confined almost completely to such technical matters as linking vehicles (docking) in space and transferring crew members between space ships

The conference produced an agreement providing for future meetings by three committees of space technicians from the two countries. The agreement was signed in Moscow Oct. 28 by Robert S. Gilruth, head of the U.S. delegation and director of the U.S. Manned Spacecraft Center, and by Boris N. Petrov, head of the Soviet delegation' and chairman of the Soviet Council for International Cooperation in the Exploration & Use of Space.

Members of the U.S. delegation were taken on a tour of Svezdny Gorodok (Stellar Town, or Star City), the carefully guarded cosmonaut and space scientist community near Moscow, where they were shown spacecraft and other Soviet space hardware. They were reported to be the first foreigners invited to see the lunar soil brought back to earth by the unmanned Soviet lunar probe Luna 16.

The Moscow meeting took place shortly after two Soviet cosmonauts, Maj. Gen. Andrian G. Nikolayev and Vitali I. Sevastyanov, had arrived in New York Oct. 18 for a 10-day U.S. visit. The two cosmonauts toured the Manned Spacecraft Center in Houston, where they spoke Oct. 22 at the concluding session of the four-day seventh annual meeting of the American Institute of Aeronautics & Astronautics.

Moon-soil exchange—American and Soviet scientific delegations agreed in Moscow Jan. 21, 1971 to exchange about three grams of lunar surface material. The agreement was signed by Acting NASA Administrator George M. Low and the U.S.S,R.'s Prof. Keldysh. Low had arrived in Moscow Jan. 16 with a six-man U.S. delegation to discuss U.S.-Soviet space science cooperation following successful negotiations on space rescue and standardizing docking devices. The American delegation left Moscow Jan. 21 after agreeing to the formation of international working groups on synchronizing research.

In another demonstration of U.S.-Soviet space cooperation, Dr. Aleksandr P. Vinogradov, vice president of the Soviet Academy of Sciences, attended the second annual Lunar Science Conference, held by NASA in Houston, Tex. Jan. 11–14. The U.S.-Soviet lunar-soil exchange was endorsed by Vinogradov at the Houston meeting Jan. 14.

Data exchange—NASA and the Soviet Academy of Sciences agreed to exchange information on the biological effects of space flight, it was reported Dec. 31, 1971.

A NASA announcement said that meetings of experts from both nations' space programs, to take place at least once a year, would include "the exchange of pre-, post- and inflight data in sufficient detail to assure a full understanding of the flight experience of each country from a psysiological and medical viewpoint."

The agreement had been reached at meetings in Moscow earlier in December by a joint U.S.-Soviet working committee. General agreement to exchange information had been reached in 1970.

Nixon, Gromyko confer. President Nixon and Soviet Foreign Minister Andrei A. Gromyko held a cordial and lengthy conference in Washington Oct. 22, 1970. The meeting, Nixon's first with a Soviet leader since taking office, was portrayed afterwards by both sides in positive terms.

"The meeting was conducted in a friendly atmosphere," according to White House Press Secretary Ronald

L. Ziegler, who said "it is felt the meeting was helpful for laying the basis for improved relations" between the two countries. Gromyko, in a statement distributed by the Soviet embassy, called the discussions "interesting" and expressed hope the meeting and talks "will be of positive significance for the development and improvement of Soviet-American relations."

The agenda for the meeting, according to Ziegler, included the general problems of European security, such as Berlin, the Strategic Arms Limitation Talks (SALT), the Middle East and Vietnam. The subject of Cuba, Ziegler said, was "not on the agenda."

The meeting was one of the longest the President had had with a visiting statesman. It lasted two hours 35 minutes and included a private, 10-minute discussion without aides or interpreters. Among the aides attending the larger meeting were Secretary of State William Rogers, Dr. Henry Kissinger, the President's national security adviser, and Anatoly Dobrynin, Soviet ambassador to the U.S.

Arms & Nuclear Energy

U.S.-Soviet talks on blast uses. In talks in Moscow Feb. 12–17, 1970, U.S. and Soviet delegations agreed that greater possibilities existed for peaceful use of nuclear explosions. A joint statement issued after the talks said there had been "an identity of views" on the use of nuclear explosions for such projects as oil and gas extraction and the excavation of reservoirs and canals. (The New York Times reported March 5 that Soviet delegates to the talks had disclosed that the U.S.S.R.'s program for peaceful use of nuclear explosions was more extensive than the corresponding U.S. Atomic Energy Commission Plowshare Program. The Soviet program reportedly had included 13 experiments with nuclear explosives for a wide range of projects. The U.S. had conducted 10 such experiments and eight other tests.)

The Moscow talks were a continuation of those held in April 1969 in Vienna.

Nuclear treaty in effect. The nuclear nonproliferation treaty became effective March 5 with ceremonies in Washington, London and Moscow, after more than 43 nations had deposited instruments of ratification.

In Washington, President Nixon called the treaty "one of the first and major steps in that process in which the nations of the world moved from a period of confrontation to a period of negotiation and a period of lasting peace." He said that the Soviet-American strategic arms limitation talks (SALT) were the next step.

In Moscow, Soviet Prime Minister Aleksei N. Kosygin expressed "profound gratification" at the treaty, but he noted that it "does not eliminate nuclear armaments as such." He asserted that the Soviet government "attaches great importance to the dialogue with the United States which began at the end of last year on questions of restraining the strategic arms race."

U.S.S.R. sees nuclear parity. In a major article published March 7 by the Communist Party newspaper Pravda, the Soviet Union asserted that virtual nuclear parity existed between itself and the U.S. and that it was not seeking supremacy in nuclear arms. The article was signed "Observer," a traditional pen name for a high government official.

The article asserted that possibilities existed for agreement at the SALT talks due to resume in Vienna April 16, but it questioned whether America sincerely wanted such an accord. Particular emphasis was given to Defense Secretary Melvin R. Laird's recent arguments for speeded deployment of the Safeguard antimissile system in order to meet the threat of Russian SS-9 missiles.

Western diplomats in Moscow felt the statement reflected Soviet fears that deployment of the Safeguard system would give the U.S. a stronger bargaining position at the SALT talks. They reasoned

U.S. proposal at SALT. Gerard C. Smith, chief U.S. negotiator at the strategic arms limitation talks (SALT) in Vienna, formally presented a U.S. package proposal on the limitation of strategic weapons July 24. (Delegates to the talks had met July 14 and 21. A meeting scheduled for July 17 was omitted, at the request of American representatives; in order to give both sides time for "stock-taking.")

The Smith proposal conformed in its main outline to reports published previously of an emerging agreement to limit the number of intercontinental ballistic missile (ICBM) launchers and to restrict antiballistic missile (ABM) systems to a low level. The proposal also specifically mentioned the Soviet SS-9 missiles as subject to a numerical limitation on launching systems.

A New York Times report July 24 said the proposal had not mentioned either multiple warheads or launching systems directed at European targets or based there.

In a related development, Henry A. Kissinger, White House adviser on national security, told a secret meeting of 10 congressmen July 23 that the U.S. must proceed with deployment of the Nixon-proposed Safeguard ABM system in order to insure progress at the SALT talks. Sen. Hugh Scott (R, Penn.) said Kissinger had discussed the "interrelationship" between SALT and Safeguard, but gave no other details of the briefing.

The Vienna phase of the SALT talks were concluded Aug. 14, 1970, and the talks were resumed in Helsinki, Finland Nov. 2, 1970.

There were no reported changes in the composition of the delegations, which were headed by Smith and Vladimir S. Semyonov.

At ceremonies in the Finnish State Banquet Hall Nov. 2 to mark the opening of the talks, Semyonov expressed the hope that the discussions would "eventually produce positive results." He said the Soviet Union had "consistently come out in favor of the relaxation of tension in the world, the stopping of the arms race fanned up by certain imperialist circles, and the strengthening of international security."

Smith said: "It is the profound hope of my government that in this current session of our talks significant progress will be made in fashioning the contribution which the U.S. and the Soviet Union can make" toward limiting the world's

capacity for self-destruction. He continued: "A SALT agreement would be a momentous contribution to international peace and well-being. . . . With hard work and a mutual recognition of the legitimate security interests of each side, we should be able to make a start in the limitation of arms and a redirection to more constructive ends of some of the resources and energies of our societies."

Nuclear crisis seen in U.S. bases. A Senate report Dec. 20 said the ring of U.S. nuclear bases around the Soviet Union and Communist China could lead to a nuclear crisis if either country tried to "break out of the nuclear ring" by deploying their nuclear weapons in similar fashion. "We could face an international crisis comparable to that of the Cuban missile crisis of 1962," the report said.

The U.S., it said, "went to the brink of nuclear war when faced with the possibility that the Soviet Union was putting missiles in a country 90 miles from the United States" and "we must assume that the Soviets, as they view our placement of tactical nuclear weapons in countries far closer to their borders than Cuba is to ours, will seek to break out of the nuclear ring that has been drawn around them."

The report was prepared by the Foreign Relations Subcommittee on Security Agreements and Commitments Abroad after a two-year study of the U.S. military and political commitments in 13 countries and the North Atlantic Treaty Organization. The subcommittee's chairman was Sen. Stuart Symington (D, Mo.), who appended a statement to the report expressing hope that the panel's hearing testimony would provide the basis for "a continuing analysis and discussion" by Congress and the public toward "a new foreign-military policy and overseas base structure."

The report called for a "thorough inquiry on the part of Congress" into "cases where nuclear warheads should properly be withdrawn from countries where their use may now have been overtaken by technology, or where political dangers involved could well make it desirable that the weapons be removed."

The study found that "in most countries over the past few years the overall level or number of the warheads maintained has increased" despite the fact that "often the original missions of the weapons have been changed."

■ Mikhail A. Suslov, member of the Soviet Communist party Political Bureau, said at a Kremlin rally Nov. 6 that U.S. military bases around the world were directed "first of all" against the Soviet Union. Suslov said his government was equipping its military forces with "the most modern" weapons in order to give "a crushing rebuff to those who would try to encroach" on Soviet borders.

U.S. Policy Views

Laird, Rogers discuss world affairs. Secretary of Defense Melvin R. Laird and Secretary of State William P. Rogers, appearing together on the radio and TV news program "Issues and Answers" Oct. 11, 1970, discussed the state of the world and what they termed were attempts by the Soviet Union to tip the precarious balance of power.

They said the Nixon Administration regarded as bad faith recent Soviet activities ranging from a speedup in the arms race to Moscow's denunciation of President Nixon's peace plan for Indochina.

Laird said that unless the Soviet Union agreed to accords limiting strategic arms and negotiated with Washington to ease other world tensions, the U.S. might have to undertake a "tremendous increase" in defense spending. The defense secretary assailed Moscow for what he said was its recent weapons buildup. He said the U.S. had monitored missile-firing, nuclear-powered Soviet submarines "on station off the coast of the U.S. which are capable of reaching our shores."

Laird said that unless the strategic arms limitations talks (SALT) with the Russians succeeded in limiting the arms race, "we are going to have to face up to some hard, tough decision here which could require a tremendous increase as far as defense expenditures are concerned."

Laird warned that the U.S. would not let a Soviet arms buildup go unchallenged. He said that the U.S. had delayed the start of a new nuclear submarine program pending the outcome of the SALT talks but that the Administration would not wait much longer for a breakthrough in the negotiations. "I don't believe from the standpoint of a defense planner," Laird said, "we can delay those decisions more than 12 months."

Nixon urges peaceful rivalry. In a speech at the U.N. in New York Oct. 23, 1970 during a commemorative session in honor of the world body's 25th anniversary, Nixon appealed to the U.S.S.R. to join the U.S. in keeping the U.S.-Soviet rivalry peaceful despite "very profound and fundamental differences."

Nixon conceded that "power has a role in our relations," but he asserted that "our mutual obligation is to discipline that power."

The President singled out "four great factors that provide a basis for a common interest in working together to contain and reduce" the differences between the two great powers: (1) "neither of us wants a nuclear exchange"; (2) both would "certainly welcome the opportunity to reduce the burden" of "the enormous cost of arms"; (3) both are "major industrial powers" which could greatly benefit from increased trade and commerce; and (4) both could contribute to the "global challenge of economic and social development."

Nixon deplored the "traditional game of international relations" and invited the leaders of the Soviet Union "to join in a peaceful competition, not in the accumulation of arms but in the dissemination of progress; not in the building of missiles but in waging a winning war against hunger and disease and human misery in our own countries and around the globe."

U.S. "two-China" policy hinted. A Nixon Administration official hinted Oct. 25 that the U.S. might be willing to accept U.N. membership for both the Republic of China (Taiwan) and the Communist Peoples Republic of China.

In response to questioning Oct. 25, White House Press Secretary Ronald L. Ziegler said: "The U.S. opposes the admission of the Peking regime into the U.N. at the expense of the expulsion of the Republic of China." According to the New York Times Nov. 6, this deliberate phrasing was designed to indicate a softening of the U.S. position, said to contrast "sharply with the attitude expressed by President Nixon when he took office."

In what was seen as a shift away from the traditional U.S. policy of total opposition to the seating of Communist China in the United Nations, the U.S. Nov. 12 argued against expulsion of Chiang Kaishek's Nationalist Chinese regime from the world body. The statement of the U.S. delegation, delivered by Deputy Permanent Representative Christopher H. Phillips, came on the first day of the annual China debate in the General Assembly.

The debate opened with the introduction by Algeria of the traditional Albanian resolution calling for the admission of Communist China and the expulsion of the Taiwan regime from the U.N. The resolution was sponsored by 118 countries.

Philippine Ambassador Privado Jimenez then introduced a second resolution, also sponsored by 118 member nations including the U.S. That resolution would declare the matter of Chinese representation an important question requiring a two-thirds vote for any change in seating.

The U.S. appeal in the debate was free of the hostile language against the Peking regime common in other years. Phillips reviewed attempts by the Nixon Administration to extend U.S. contacts with Communist China, citing the recent talks between representatives of the two nations in Warsaw.

"The U.S. is as interested as any in this room to see the People's Republic of China play a constructive role among the family of nations," Phillips asserted. "All of us are mindful of the industry, talents and achievements of the great people who live in that ancient cradle of civilization."

It was also considered significant that Phillips had referred to Communist China by its desired name; in the past, U.S. delegates had indicated references to Communist China without naming it in full.

The basic argument advanced in the U.S. brief, however, was the contention that Peking did not have the right to insist on the expulsion of Nationalist China as a condition for its own seating in the world organization. Phillips also maintained that such expulsion by a simple majority would "set a most dangerous precedent." He further argued that the Taiwan regime, which had been one of the founders of the U.N. Charter, had not offended the charter or given any grounds for expulsion.

Observers saw the U.S. statement as a shift toward endorsement of a so-called two-China policy. Although the notion of two sovereign Chinese regimes had been unacceptable to both Chinese capitals in the past, it was thought that a new German-type formula might be negotiated. The formula, advanced by West German Chancellor Willy Brandt, would acknowledge two German states within a single German nation. It was thought that the U.S. might be moving toward support of such a formula with regard to China in the U.N.

The Soviet Union, in a statement issued in Moscow Nov. 12, declared that any U.S. moves toward a two-China policy in the U.N. were "untenable . . . and had no chance of success."

The Albanian delegation Nov. 13 denounced what it termed U.S. support for the two-China policy as "a plot of American imperialism."

In Washington Nov. 13, White House Press Secretary Ronald L. Ziegler declared that the U.S. had not altered its policy of opposition to the admission of Communist China into the U.N. Ziegler said the speculation that had followed Phillips' statement in the General Assembly could have been "a matter of semantics." Ziegler said Peking "must demonstrate they have a desire to be a responsible member of the international community" before gaining a seat in the U.N. But he added that the U.S. sought to "open channels of communication" with Communist China and opposed its U.N. admission "at the expense of the expulsion of Nationalist China."

Nixon maintains policy. Nixon indicated at a press conference Dec. 10, 1970 that he intended to press forward with his policy of seeking accommodation with the Soviet Union and the People's Republic of China. Among his statements on the issues:

U.S.-Soviet relations—These would continue "to be difficult, but the significant thing is that we are negotiating and not confronting. . . . We are two great powers that are going to continue to be competitive for our lifetime. But I believe that we must continue on the path of negotiation."

He did not think U.S. security was threatened by Soviet military activity in the Caribbean.

U.S.-China relations—"We have no plans to change our policy with regard to the admission of Red China to the United Nations at this time. . . . We are going to continue the initiative" of relaxing trade and travel curbs and trying to open channels of communication with China.

Arms, Middle East & Cuba. In a TV talk Jan. 4, 1971, Nixon discussed foreign policy developments after his first two years in office. Among his remarks:

Soviet relations—". . . in terms of arms control we have some overwhelming forces that are going to bring about an agreement eventually, and it's simply this—the Soviet Union and the United States have a common interest in avoiding the escalating burden of arms."

"In the Mideast, it's true we're far apart, but we are having discussions. On Berlin, we're far apart, but we are negotiating. And, finally, with regard to the rhetoric . . . the rhetoric, while it has been firm, has generally been noninflammatory on our part and on theirs."

Cuba—"President Kennedy worked out an understanding in 1962 that the Russians would not put any offensive missiles into Cuba. That understanding was expanded on Oct. 11 [actually Oct. 13, 1970] . . . by the Russians when they said that it would include a military base in Cuba and a military naval base. They in effect, said that they would not put a military naval base into Cuba on October the 11th. Now, in the event that nuclear submarines were serviced either in Cuba or from Cuba, that would be a violation of the understanding. . . . We expect them [the Soviet Union] to abide by the understanding. I believe they will."

State-of-the-World message. Nixon Feb. 25, 1971 sent to Congress a 65,000-word annual State-of-the-World message in which he expanded on his views on U.S.-Soviet and Sino-U.S. relations and on detente in general.

U.S.-Soviet relations—"An assessment of U.S.-Soviet relations at this point in my Administration has to be mixed," Nixon said. He cited encouraging developments—"a serious dialogue" in the strategic arms limitation talks (SALT), a treaty signed to bar nuclear weapons from the seabeds, ratification of a nuclear nonproliferation treaty, Berlin negotiations begun and a first step toward practical cooperation in outer space.

However, Nixon said, "certain Soviet actions" in the Middle East, Berlin and Cuba were "not encouraging" and "taken against a background of intensive and unrestrained anti-American propaganda, . . . inevitably suggest that intransigence remains a cardinal feature of the Soviet system." The U.S.S.R. also had added "significantly" to its strategic force capability over the past year, the President said. While the U.S. had not increased the number of its operational ICBMs from 1,054 during 1970 or the number of submarine-launched ballistic missiles (SLBMs) from 656, the U.S.S.R. had increased its ICBMs from 1,109 to 1,440 and its SLBMs from 240 to 350.

On the other hand, he said, the Soviet Union "in the past few months appears to have slowed the deployment of land-based strategic missile launchers."

Arms control—The President said one of the differences with the Soviet Union was in definition of strategic offensive weapons—the U.S.S.R. included any that could "reach the other side's territory," such as those on U.S. aircraft carriers, but excluded its own theater nuclear forces with medium or intermediate-range missiles; the U.S. included ICBMs, SLBMs and heavy strategic bombers.

The U.S. also wanted an agreement covering both offensive and defensive systems, in contrast with the Soviet proposal for defensive limitations first. There were also "certain differences" on the issue of verification.

"We shall strive for an initial agreement which is as broad and comprehensive as possible," Nixon said, but "it must deal with the interrelationship between offensive and defensive limitations."

The President also stressed the need to clarify the relationship between negotiations and "actions taken during the talks and even after an initial agreement." It was clear, he said, "that restraint is essential. If the Soviet leaders extend their strategic capability especially in ways that increase the threat to our forces, we would face new decisions in the strategic field."

Defense—The President said it was necessary to have the option to make a selective nuclear response to a provocation. "We must insure that we have the forces and procedures that provide us with alternatives appropriate to the nature and level of the provocation. This means having the plans and command-and-control capabilities necessary to enable us to select and carry out the appropriate response without necessarily having to resort to mass destruction."

China—Nixon said the U.S. favored "drawing the People's Republic of China into a constructive relationship with the world community" and was "prepared to establish a dialogue with Peking." However, he asserted, the dialogue would not be "at the expense of the U.S. Asian allies. . . . Our present commitment to the security of the Republic of China" was exclusively defensive and should not constitute an obstacle to a move toward normal relations between the U.S. and the People's Republic of China. The U.S. felt that the differences between the two Chinas "must be resolved by peaceful means."

The question of a U.N. seat for Communist China was not one merely of participation but also one "of whether Peking should be permitted to dictate to the world the terms of its participation." The U.S. would continue to oppose attempts to deprive Nationalist China of its membership in the U.N.

Europe—"We and our allies seek a European detente," Nixon said, but he added: "We must improve NATO's conventional deterrent, especially correcting qualitative deficiencies in present allied forces," and maintaining a complementary tactical and strategic nuclear deterrent. The U.S. would continue to consult on "defining the precise role of tactical nuclear weapons."

The U.S. would maintain and improve its forces in Europe and "not reduce them without reciprocal action by our adversaries."

As for detente, it meant "negotiating the concrete conditions of mutual security that will allow for expanded intra-European contact and cooperation without jeopardizing the security of any country. Soviet policies and doctrine, however, too often interpret detente in terms of Western ratification of the status quo and acknowledgement of continuing Soviet hegemony over Eastern Europe. Beyond this, Soviet policy has been tempted to offer a relaxation of tension selectively to some allies but not to others, and only on limited issues of primary interest to the U.S.S.R. In view of this fundamental difference . . . our principal objective should be to harmonize our policies and insure that our efforts for detente are complementary. . . . East-West detente and Western cohesion can be mutually supporting. . . ."

The U.S. opposed the U.S.S.R. proposal for a general conference on European security unless "a political basis for improving relations" was created through specific current negotiations. "Any lasting relaxation of tension in Europe must include progress in resolving the issues related to the division of Germany," Nixon said. While this basically was a question for the German people, the "reshaping of German relations with the East inevitably affects the interests of all European states as well as the relationship between the U.S. and the Soviet Union. . . . It is clearly established that allied responsibilities and rights are not affected by the terms" of the new treaties West Germany negotiated with the U.S.S.R. and Poland. The U.S. supported West Germany's objective of normalizing relations with its eastern neighbors.

As for Eastern Europe, trade with Rumania and Yugoslavia, both countries Nixon had visited, had increased substantially and Congress would be asked to extend guarantees to American private investment in both countries.

China & arms talks. At a nationally televised news conference March 4, 1971, Nixon answered questions about arms talks and relations with China.

On relations with Communist China, the President said the U.S. attitude would be governed by that nation's "attitude toward us." "We would like to normalize relations with all nations," he said, but there had been "no receptivity on the part of Communist China." As for Nationalist China, the U.S. would stand by its defense commitments to Taiwan, Nixon said, and Taiwan "could not and would not be expelled from the United Nations as long as we had anything to say about it." The question of seating Communist China in the U.N. was "moot," he said, since Communist China refused to discuss the matter and would not "until Taiwan gets out, and we will not start with that kind of a proposition."

On the arms talks, Nixon said he was optimistic about "eventual success" since the superpowers "now have nuclear parity" and "neither can gain an advantage over the other if the other desires to see to it that that does not occur." He said it was in the interests of both powers to negotiate some kind of limitation on offensive and defensive weapons. He rejected negotiation for a separate agreement on defensive weapons alone.

Arms & Nuclear Control

Jackson reports new Soviet ICBM. Sen. Henry M. Jackson (D, Wash.) claimed March 7, 1971 that the U.S.S.R. was deploying a new version of its SS-9 intercontinental ballistic missile.

Appearing on the CBS television program "Face the Nation," Jackson declared: "The Russians are now in the process of deploying a new generation, an advanced generation, of offensive systems. Contrary to the position earlier indicated, with the so-called leveling off of the number of new SS-9 sites, we now find that the new developments are ominous indeed." In a telephone interview

after the program, Jackson told a New York Times reporter that the new missiles were bigger than the SS-9 and that "there are different characteristics that I can't get into."

Pentagon spokesman Jerry W. Friedheim confirmed that the U.S. had "detected some new ICBM construction in the Soviet Union" but added: "We are not sure exactly what it is or what the Soviets' intentions are." According to the New York Times March 7, what had been observed was the construction of missile silos and related equipment but not the missiles themselves.

The Washington Post March 9 reported that Jackson's remarks had been inspired by a Congressional briefing given by CIA Director Richard Helms and that "the senator's statement was said to have been more specific than the available information." The Post remarked that the new Soviet silos, of approximately the size needed to house SS-9s, did not necessarily indicate deployment of a new type of missile.

New U.S. deterrent strategy. U.S. Defense Secretary Melvin R. Laird presented to Congress March 9 a "defense posture" statement outlining a "strategy of realistic deterrence." In an unclassified public version of a report given in closed session to the House Armed Services Committee, Laird said his "new" policy, based on "adequate strength, true partnership and meaningful negotiations," would steer "a prudent middle course between two policy extremes—world policeman or new isolationism."

The U.S. nuclear deterrent would remain the core of defense policy, but new emphasis was placed on modernizing the defense forces of U.S. allies, coordinating them with U.S. forces, and on utilizing diplomacy to merge them into "regional security agreements." Stress was also placed on the value of negotiations—such as the arms talks and on the Middle East—to lessen chances of major confrontations.

Increased emphasis would be placed on research in weaponry to guard against technological surprise by adversaries. Weapons reserves were to be studied in relation to a unified allied effort. For example, the U.S. would continue to build nuclear-powered attack submarines but would encourage its allies to supply less expensive boats and acquire anti-submarine aircraft.

The overall strategy was based on providing enough force to fight one major and one minor war, or a $1\frac{1}{2}$-war strategy, compared with the $2\frac{1}{2}$-war strategy under the two previous administrations. The new concept would eliminate maintenance of large U.S. ground combat forces in Asia, where reliance would be put on strong air, naval and support capabilities and mobilization, in case of emergencies, for transport to the affected area, of non-NATO-committed forces or the NATO reserve forces based in the U.S.

In reporting missile strength, Laird said the Soviet Union had more intercontinental ballistic missiles (ICBMs) than the U.S. and warned that the "missile gap" might increase. But he said the U.S. led the Soviet Union in the number of H-bombs that could be fired in a war, 4,000–1,800 and, by mid-year, probably 4,600–2,000. He said the Soviet missile submarine force was the "fastest growing element" of the Soviet threat but that the trend of Soviet ICBM development was not clear. There was evidence, he said, of several new Soviet missile "holes" larger than those for the multiple-warhead SS-9 missiles but no indication whether the trend was toward a new missile or a modified SS-9.

Laird said China "may have" deployed its first medium-range missiles and switched focus to development of an intermediate-range missile. Again the evidence was not definitive but suggested a test of a missile at a 2,000-mile range and potentially capable of a greater range.

Laird estimated Soviet and Chinese military aid to their allies at about $15 billion for 1955–70, with the Soviets supplying 70%.

As part of the U.S. missile defense stance, Laird favored proceeding toward a full 12-site Safeguard system, better Minuteman missile silos to guard against attack, development of a new strategic bomber and a new missile submarine. He suggested development of a system to protect against a small-scale missile attack in the event an arms agreement prohibited the 12-site Safeguard system.

A decision on plans for expansion of Safeguard, however, was being delayed by President Nixon pending the next round of the arms control talks with the U.S.S.R.

Laird reports Soviet ABM work—Laird said April 27 that construction had resumed on at least one of four antiballistic missile (ABM) sites around Moscow after being halted in 1968. Laird also declared that the Soviet Union was deploying multiple warheads on its SS-9 missles.

Laird had cited the multiple warhead deployment April 21 in a New York speech to a group of publishers when he remarked that the Soviet Union was "involved in a new—and apparently extensive—ICBM [intercontinental ballistic missile] construction program." He said the construction, "coupled with additional momentum in the strategic defense area, all clearly planned months ago, must be of major concern" and might require "additional offsetting U.S. action" beyond what had already been budgeted. Laird warned that the U.S. was in danger of slipping into a "second-rate strategic position."

In a related development, the Soviet Defense Ministry newspaper Krasnaya Zvezda commented June 1 on the need to maintain defense preparedness while negotiating arms limits. The author of the article remarked: "The desire for peace of the Socialist countries does not free their peoples from the necessary development of military affairs and of strengthening their defense. . . . Our preparedness to support real measures for disarmament must match and does match our preparedness for any turn in the development of events."

SALT meetings resume. The fourth round of the U.S.-Soviet strategic arms limitations talks (SALT) took place in Vienna March 15–May 28, 1971.

The U.S. and U.S.S.R. announced May 20 that they had decided to have the SALT negotiators discuss an agreement on defensive nuclear weapons.

The disclosure was made simultaneously in each nation—in the Soviet Union by Moscow Radio and in the U.S. by President Nixon in a brief televised address.

Nixon began his brief address by saying he was announcing "a significant development" in the SALT talks, "deadlocked for over a year." The President then said that the U.S. and the Soviet Union had "agreed to concentrate this year on working out an agreement for the limitation of the deployment of antiballistic missile systems—ABMs." Nixon also said that "together with" the agreement on ABM limitation, the two states "will agree on certain measures with respect to the limitation of offensive strategic weapons." The President added: "Intensive negotiations . . . will be required to translate this understanding into a concrete agreement. . . . If we succeed, this joint statement that has been issued today may well be remembered as the beginning of a new era in which all nations will devote more of their energies and their resources not to the weapons of war but to the works of peace."

Armaments specialists considered that the effect of the U.S.-Soviet understanding was to relieve SALT delegates temporarily of the need to consider land-based ICBMs, an area of Soviet strength, and missiles delivered by submarine and by bombers, an area of U.S. dominance.

U.S.S.R. proposes nuclear parley. The Soviet Union June 15 formally proposed a five-nation conference to discuss nuclear disarmament. The U.S. indicated tentative acceptance of the offer June 29.

The Soviet proposal, first contained in a March address by Communist Party General Secretary Leonid I. Brezhnev, was delivered to the White House June 15 by Soviet Ambassador Anatoly F. Dobrynin. It consisted of the suggestion that the five nuclear powers—France, Great Britain, the U.S., the Soviet Union and Communist China—meet as soon as possible at a convenient place to discuss disarmament.

State Department spokesman Robert J. McCloskey said June 15 that "if you desire to have meaningful disarmament throughout the world, at some point the Chinese will have to participate."

Although it was not known when Communist China was approached about the projected conference, the New York Times said June 23 that an unnamed

Chinese embassy official in Moscow had expressed reservations about the proposal when he complained that the "nuclear superpowers" were "trying to dominate the world and disarm China." The Washington Post said July 3 that China had rejected the Soviet proposal but had repeated the previous day its call for "a conference of all nations, big and small," to discuss a nuclear ban.

U.S.-Soviet Relations

Brezhnev's report. An analysis of U.S.-Soviet relations was made by Soviet Communist Party General Secretary Leonid Brezhnev March 30, 1971 in his report at the 24th Soviet Communist Party Congress.

Relations with the U.S. were made uneasy by "frequent zig-zags in U.S. foreign policy, which are apparently connected with some kind of domestic political moves from short-term considerations," Brezhnev asserted. He remarked that in "the recent period the U.S. Administration has taken a more rigid stance on a number of international issues, including some which have a bearing on the interests of the Soviet Union." Nevertheless, he said, "we proceed from the assumption that it is possible to improve relations between the U.S.S.R. and the U.S."

As to Communist China, Brezhnev observed that the Soviet Union "has resolutely opposed the attempts to distort the Marxist-Leninist teaching and to split the international Communist movement and the ranks of the fighters against imperialism. . . . We resolutely reject the slanderous inventions concerning the policy of our party and our state which are being spread from Peking and instilled into the minds of the Chinese people."

The congress formally adopted a Soviet policy of "peaceful coexistence" with the U.S.

Trade developments. In a reversal of a long-standing policy, the U.S. disclosed June 3, 1971 that it had decided to grant licenses for exporting to the Soviet Union more than $50 million worth of equipment for the manufacture of light trucks. Two orders publicly disclosed June 3 were a $22.5 million agreement with the Gleason works of Rochester, N.Y., and $2 million worth of equipment for the manufacture of truck radiators, to be supplied by Scheuer & Co. of New York City. The Cross Company of Fraser, Mich., announced June 7 it had received government permission to sell $31 million worth of automated machine tools to the Soviet Union.

Mack Trucks, Inc., a subsidiary of Signal Companies, Inc., of Allentown, Pa., made public June 17 a preliminary agreement (signed May 18) to design and supply machine tools and trucks to the Soviet Union's Kama River truck plant. In 1970 the Ford Motor Co. had declined an offer to help build the plant, reportedly because of Defense Department objections.

The Kama River plant agreement entailed shipment to the Soviet Union of at least $750 million in tools and equipment and the purchase by the Soviet Union of 100 Mack trucks, valued at approximately $22 million, to be used in mining.

The U.S. Commerce Department announced Aug. 9 that two unidentified U.S. firms had been granted licenses for the export of $162 million worth of "foundry equipment for the manufacture of automotive castings" at the plant. A third license was granted to the Swindell-Dressler Co. of Pittsburgh to seek a Soviet contract to design the plant's foundry. The Swindell-Dressler contract was signed Dec. 22; in reporting the deal, the Soviet news agency Tass said that in addition to the design work the contract "envisages U.S. sales of equipment for the Soviet foundry."

In a related development, Soviet Minister of Agriculture Vladimir V. Matskevich said Dec. 9 in Washington that his country wanted to buy agricultural machinery and licenses from the U.S. for production in the U.S.S.R. of tractors, combines and other equipment "by the millions." He had begun an 11-day visit to the U.S. the previous day at the invitation of the Agriculture Department.

■ Commerce Secretary Maurice H. Stans arrived in Moscow Nov. 20 for talks with Premier Aleksei N. Kosygin and other officials on improving trade between the two countries. Kosygin remarked after meeting with Stans: "We don't expect this one visit to yield momentous decisions, but feel that we can reach an understanding in preparation for future important decisions." Stans' departure for the Soviet Union coincided with a Commerce Department announcement Nov. 18 that it had approved the licensing of $528 million worth of equipment and technical data for sale to the Kama River plant.

■ Nixon Administration officials revealed Nov. 5 the impending sale of $136 million worth of grain to the Soviet Union for livestock feed. The sale, to be made by Continental Grain Company and Cargill, Inc., had been facilitated by the waiver of U.S. maritime unions of their demand that 50% of grain shipments to the Soviet Union be carried in U.S. ships.

U.S.-Soviet accords signed. Soviet Foreign Minister Andrei A. Gromyko and U.S. Secretary of State William P. Rogers signed in Washington Sept. 30, 1971 two agreements for prevention of nuclear accidents and for modernizing the Washington-Moscow "hot line" for emergency messages.

The first pact obliged each party to notify the other "in the event of detection by missile warning system of unidentified objects" or "an accidental, unauthorized or any other unexplained incident involving a possible detonation of a nuclear weapon which could create a risk of outbreak of nuclear war." Each party agreed to notify the other "in advance of any planned missile launches if such launches will extend beyond its national territory in the direction of the other party."

The "hot line" accord was to replace the existing line with a satellite that would provide instantaneous voice and teletype communication. It required the U.S. to build and operate on its territory a station for the Soviet Molniya II system while the U.S.S.R. was to do the same for the U.S. Intelsat system.

After the signing, Rogers commented that although "considerable progress" had been made toward disarmament, "much remains to be done." Gromyko declared: "The agreements signed today do not yet solve in any way the substance of the problem of limiting strategic armaments. This task is still outstanding ..."

Relations With China

McGovern for recognizing China. Sen. George S. McGovern (S.D.), campaigning Jan. 24, 1971 for the Democratic Presidential nomination, urged a new U.S. policy toward China.

McGovern urged the U.S. to give diplomatic recognition to mainland China. He said Communist China should be admitted to the United Nations and its Security Council as a permanent member, with Nationalist China relinquishing its Security Council seat while remaining in the General Assembly.

Science exchange offered. Secretary of State William P. Rogers told a House committee Jan. 26 that it was U.S. policy to seek exchanges of technical and scientific data with all nations, even those with which the U.S. did not maintain diplomatic relations.

Following Rogers' appearance before the House Science and Astronautics Committee, his science aide said the secretary had Communist China in mind.

Rogers told the committee that the U.S. could benefit from an exchange program. "Scientific and technological cooperation is not a one-way street," he said. "We have as much to gain as anybody from cooperation." Regardless of the state of diplomatic relations between the U.S. and any other nation, Rogers said it was the Administration's policy to permit exchange of "unclassified scientific and technical information with the scientists and institutions of any country."

Rogers' science aide, Herman Pollock, said the U.S. had been sending scientific data to Cuba, Albania, East Germany and Communist China despite the absence of normal diplomatic ties. The exchange between the U.S. and Red China had slowed to a virtual stop over the past five years. Pollack said the data most often dealt with agricultural, oceanographic and weather information.

U.S. ends travel ban. The U.S. March 15, 1971 discontinued the requirement that its citizens obtain specially validated passports for travel to Communist China.

In announcing the policy change, Charles W. Bray 3d, a State Department spokesman, said the action was in conformity with a resolve expressed by President Nixon in February, when he delivered his State-of-the-World message, to "carefully examine what further steps we might take to create broader opportunities for contacts between the Chinese and American peoples."

Bray also announced that the U.S. was seeking through private channels to bring about a resumption of the U.S.-Chinese ambassadorial talks in Warsaw.

China & the U.S.S.R. After nearly nine months, Soviet and Communist China propaganda hostilities resumed March 17, 1971 on the eve of the 24th Soviet Communist party Congress. In an article transmitted by the official news agency Hsinhua and attributed to major Peking publications, Communist China March 17 accused the Soviet Union of asking liberation movements "to reduce revolutionary violence to the minimum" while itself using "the most savage and brutal means to deal with revolutionary people."

The article, commemorating the Paris Commune of 1871, said political power came "invariably by the power of the gun" and not by "elections and parliaments."

The author of a foreign policy work published by the Soviet Academy of Sciences warned Communist China March 17 against playing a "dangerous game" by trying to improve relations with the U.S. According to an Associated Press report, the volume claimed Communist China had "reached an understanding" to stay out of Vietnam as long as U.S. ground forces stayed out of North Vietnam.

The official Soviet press agency Tass denounced Communist China March 21 for its "rude attacks and slander" the previous week. Tass said the Chinese article had contained "a distortion of Marxist-Leninist teaching and of the principles of the Paris commune" and that "anti-Communists especially appreciated Peking's new attacks against the international Communist movement, against its cohesion and against the Socialist community."

Communist Chinese Premier Chou En-lai met in Peking March 21 with Vasily S. Tolstikov, the Soviet ambassador, and Leonid F. Ilyichev, Soviet delegate to the Chinese border talks. No details were revealed.

At a March 23 news conference, Vladimir S. Alkhimov, Soviet deputy foreign trade minister, reported that Sino-Soviet trade in 1970 had dropped to approximately $46 million, but said a recent agreement envisioned a tripling of the trade volume in 1971.

U.S.-Chinese Breakthrough: 1971-72

Ping-Pong Diplomacy

By April 1971 the U.S. and Peking were ready for some sort of breakthrough in normalizing relations with each other. The signal to the world was a Communist Chinese invitation to a U.S. table-tennis team to visit the mainland. In China, where table tennis was much more a major sport than it was in the U.S., the American team was greeted with enthusiastic friendliness. Three months later President Nixon announced that he planned to visit mainland China, and he did so in February 1972. In the meantime, the U.S. withdrew its objections to Communist Chinese membership in the U.N., and the Peking government was admitted to the world body in October 1971.

Table-tennis team's visit. The invitation to the U.S. team was tendered April 6 at the world table tennis championships in Nagoya, Japan and accepted there the following day by Graham B. Steenhoven, president of the U.S. Table Tennis Association.

Sung Chung, a spokesman for the Chinese team, said the invitation to nine U.S. players, four officials and two wives had been made "so that we can learn from each other and elevate our standards of play. We have also extended the invitation for the sake of promoting friendship between the peoples of China and the U.S." (Glenn Cowan, a member of the U.S. team, said on arrival in Communist China April 10 that a Chinese player at Nagoya may have sparked the invitation by making the first move in an exchange of gifts with Cowan. Other sources reported U.S. players sought the invitation.)

Following several days of travel through China, the U.S. players were defeated in exhibition matches in Peking April 13. They were received April 14 by Premier Chou En-lai, who also received teams from Britain, Canada, Nigeria and Colombia which had been invited at Nagoya.

Chou told the U.S. team that "with your acceptance of our invitation, you have opened a new page in the relations of the Chinese and American people."

The Chinese premier informed all five visiting groups that Chinese teams would accept invitations to their countries. Steenhoven reportedly told correspondents later that the Chinese had been invited to play in the U.S.

Western newsmen admitted—Reversing a policy maintained since 1949, Communist China April 10 granted visas to seven Western newsmen to cover the U.S. team's visit.

Those affected were John Roderick of the Associated Press; John Rich and Jack Reynolds of the National Broadcasting Company (NBC); Hiromasa Yamanaka and Masaaki Shiihara, Japanese television technicians employed by NBC; and English correspondent John Saar, and cameraman Frank Fischbeck, both of Life magazine.

Tillman Durdin, chief of the New York Times Hong Kong bureau, and Mark Gayn, a Canadian correspondent, were authorized to enter Communist China April 13. No known restrictions were made on the length of their stay.

(At the Peking reception April 14, Chou said U.S. newsmen would be allowed to enter China "but they cannot all come at one time, they will have to come in batches." He then said to Roderick: "Mr. Roderick, you have opened the door.")

20-year trade embargo relaxed. President Nixon April 14 took another step aimed at easing U.S. relations with Communist China by relaxing a 20-year embargo on trade with the country.

The President's decision was understood to have been made several weeks before the invitation to the table-tennis team.

Nixon's announcement said he was asking the National Security Council for "a list of items of a nonstrategic nature which can be placed under general license for direct export to the People's Republic of China. Following my review and my approval of specific items on this list, direct imports of designated items from China will then also be authorized."

The statement also said that U.S. firms would be allowed to trade with China in dollars and that the U.S. was "prepared to expedite visas" for visitors or groups of visitors from China.

U.S. oil companies were to be allowed to supply fuel to ships or planes proceeding to or from mainland China with the exception of Chinese-owned or Chinese-chartered carriers going to or from North Vietnam, North Korea or Cuba. U.S. carriers were to be allowed to transport Chinese cargos between non-Chinese ports, and U.S.-owned carriers under foreign flags could call at Chinese ports.

According to the New York Times April 14, the President's order on currency transactions would not free some $100 million of mainland Chinese dollar assets frozen in 1950.

Nixon trip to China hinted. The possibility of Richard M. Nixon visiting China was brought up before the end of April 1971.

The mainland Chinese leader, Chairman Mao Tsetung, said in the April 30 issue of Life magazine that President Nixon would be welcome in China either in his official capacity or as a tourist. Mao's remarks were made in an interview with Edgar Snow, the U.S. writer.

U.S. Secretary of State William P. Rogers had declared in an interview taped for British television April 28 that a visit to China by Nixon "might well be possible" if relations between the two countries continued to improve. Rogers also described himself as "very much in favor" of an exchange of journalists, students and professional people with mainland China in the near future.

Reaction. The Soviet foreign affairs weekly New Times accused Peking April 21 of playing a "diplomatic game" with the U.S. The journal asserted that China's foreign policy was designed to "win a place for China as a world power capable of imposing its decisions on other states." New Times added: "The political practices of the Maoists have shown that they can easily betray friends and quickly come to terms with those whom they had just called enemies, and that they can repudiate the principles they once proclaimed if they consider it in the great-power nationalistic interests of Peking." (The same periodical had charged the U.S. March 26 with conducting a "diplomacy of smiles" toward Communist China.)

The Soviet Union May 5 accused the Nixon Administration of pursuing "anti-Soviet objectives" in allowing the table-tennis team to make its visit to mainland China. The accusation, expressed in the foreign affairs weekly Za Rubezhom, held that the present U.S. government, "true to its rabid anti-Communist policy," had "long been trying to weaken the positions of the Socialist camp, striving to set Socialist countries against each other, and first of all against the Soviet Union."

At a Washington news conference April 23, Secretary of State William P. Rogers said he hoped recent events signaled "the beginning of new relations" between the U.S. and Communist China. Rogers declared: "I think it was the prime minister of the People's Republic of China who said that it was a new page in our [Sino-U.S.] relations. We would hope that it becomes a new chapter, that there would be several pages to follow." Rogers said a review of U.S. policy on the admission of Communist China to the U.N. was "actively underway" and was being discussed with "many other governments."

The thaw in U.S.-Chinese relations was discussed at the annual conference of the Southeast Asia Treaty Organization (SEATO), held in London April 27-28. Rogers, representing the U.S. in London, called the visits of the Americans to China "a very small but significant step." He noted speculation that the Chinese gesture was either "part of a general diplomatic campaign for international recognition" or "a reaction to Peking's differences with the Soviet Union." "Whatever the motive, we welcome the Chinese overture," Rogers said.

Australian Foreign Minister Leslie Bury expressed reservations about Peking's latest stance. He said "there is yet little to inspire confidence that Peking has in fact abandoned those policies which have prevented her from being regarded as a responsible member of the family of nations."

Generalissimo Chiang Kai-shek, head of the Nationalist Chinese government on Taiwan, commented on the U.S. table tennis team's recent visit to mainland China in an interview telecast April 27 but filmed the previous week. Chiang said: "Such Chinese tactics of external infiltration and subversion have borne their first fruit. If all of us are aware of this, I think there should be no substantial change in the relationship between the U.S. and the Chinese Communists." The interview was conducted on Taiwan by representatives of the CBS-TV program "60 Minutes."

According to the New York Times April 27, Administration officials disclosed that day that Rumania was acting as intermediary in communications between the U.S. and Communist China.

The Times said Gogu Radulescu, the Rumanian deputy premier, had transmitted U.S. hopes for improved relations during meetings with Premier Chou En-lai in Peking in November 1970 and again March 22, 1971.

The '2-China' Problem & U.N. Membership

U.S. plans Red membership. The U.S. disclosed in April 1971 that it was prepared to accept U.N. membership for the Peking government.

A special Presidential commission headed by Henry Cabot Lodge, former chief U.S. delegate to the U.N., recommended in a 100-page report April 26 that the U.S. try to obtain the admission of Communist China to the U.N. without the expulsion of Nationalist China from the U.N. The report said: "However difficult the People's Republic of China's membership in the U.N. might become, the commission believes there is more hope for peace in its interaction in the organization than in its continued isolation from the U.N. and from the U.S." The commission emphasized that admission of Peking and retention of Nationalist China were "equally important" and that "under no circumstances" should Taiwan be expelled. "This is not a question of dual representation for one China, but the provision of two seats for two governments," it said.

Nixon's view. President Nixon discussed the China issue at a press conference April 29. Concerning the recent moves in trade with Communist China, "what we've done is broken the ice," he said. "Now we have to test the water to see how deep it is." He had not made a decision concerning a "two-China" or "one-China" policy and would not speculate on it. He considered a proposal of direct negotiations between Nationalist and Communist governments for China "completely unrealistic." "Nothing could be further from the truth" than speculation that the goal of normalizing relations with Communist China was in some way to "irritate the Soviet Union." "We are seeking good relations with Communist China and the interests of world peace require good relations between the Soviet Union and Communist China," he said.

Taking a "long-term" view, he expected to visit mainland China "sometime in some capacity—I don't know what capacity," and he hoped to contribute to a policy for a "new relationship" with mainland China, Nixon said.

Dispute over '2-China' policy. Peking and the U.S. differed over what the Chinese regarded as the U.S. espousal of a "two-China" policy.

Charles W. Bray, a State Department spokesman, said April 28 that it might be possible to resolve the status of Taiwan by negotiation between Nationalist China and Communist China. Bray, who denied he was articulating a new policy, said that the U.S. "must deal with the practical situation as we find it." There was on the one hand "a treaty commitment to the defense of Taiwan and the Pescadores Islands" but on the other hand "mainland China has been controlled and administered by the People's Republic of China for 21 years and for some time we have been dealing with that government on matters affecting our mutual interest."

Peking, in a statement published in the Communist Party newspaper Jenmin Jih Pao May 4, denounced Bray's statement as "brazen interference" in China's internal affairs. Jenmin Jih Pao spoke of continued friendship between the Chinese and American people but said President Nixon's expressed desire for better relations with Peking became "fraudulent" in light of Bray's remarks.

Peking also criticized the Lodge commission for recommending U.N. membership for both Nationalist and Communist China.

Barriers Continue to Fall

China dollar curbs lifted. U.S. Treasury Secretary John B. Connally announced May 7 a general license for the use of dollars in transactions with the People's Republic of China.

U.S. scientists in China. Two biologists, Dr. Arthur W. Galston of Yale University and Dr. Ethan Signer of the Massachusetts Institute of Technology, were guests of mainland China's scientific community May 13-25.

The two men met Premier Chou Enlai May 19. They told newsmen May 23 that China had developed "a lot of important scientific information of which we are unaware."

The biologists reported that the National Academy of Sciences in Peking, closed at the start of the Cultural Revolution in 1966, was again in operation and that its members would welcome invitations to international scientific conferences which were not attended by representatives of Nationalist China.

Galston and Signer, who stressed that more contacts between Chinese and U.S. scientists would be "of mutual benefit," also remarked that "Chinese scientists admire us as the world leaders in science and they would be glad to accept advice and help if given in the right way. They would benefit from our technology tremendously."

Exports to China eased. President Nixon June 10 released a list of 47 categories of items made exportable to mainland China, and he announced that Communist Chinese exports to the U.S. would be treated in the same manner as items from other Communist countries.

The President's list included such nonstrategic goods as farm products, household appliances, automobiles and basic metals. Among items omitted were locomotives, trucks, high-grade computers, petroleum products and commerical aircraft. The announcement said, however, that "consistent with the requirements of national security" such items could be deemed exportable under special licenses following a review by the Commerce Department and other government agencies.

Ronald L. Ziegler, White House press secretary, said Nixon would "later consider the possibility of further steps" to "re-establish a broader relationship" with mainland China, whose total imports in 1970 were valued at $2 billion, of which 75% came from non-Communist countries.

In a related development, Nixon also lifted a requirement by which 50% of grain shipments to China, the Soviet Union and other Eastern European countries were to be carried in U.S. ships.

Chinese press continue attacks. Despite the improvement in U.S. relations with Peking, Communist Chinese press attacks on the U.S. continued without apparent change.

An editorial published in major Peking newspapers May 20, the first anniversary of a foreign policy address by Mao Tse-tung, scored the U.S. government but emphasized a Chinese desire for friendship with the American people. The article said "U.S. imperialism" had committed "aggression, intervention, subversion and sabotage everywhere" but that its "fascist rule over the American people" had provoked "violent revolutionary storms in the U.S.," where people were dealing imperialism "heavier and heavier blows from within . . . and have become an important vigorous force in the world peoples' struggle." The editorial dismissed U.S. government overtures toward the People's Republic of China made earlier in May as "humbug."

Chou wants U.S. exit from Taiwan. Communist Chinese Premier Chou En-lai said in Peking June 21 that a withdrawal of U.S. support for Taiwan (Nationalist China) would facilitate the solution of "all other problems" between the U.S. and the People's Republic of China.

Chou declared: "If the U.S. government withdraws all forces from Taiwan and the Taiwan Strait and no longer considers Chiang Kai-shek as the representative of China, then the logical result will be that Chiang Kai-shek and Taiwan would be matters internal to China. This would be recognition that the People's Republic of China is the only lawful government."

He said that in the event of U.S. withdrawal, Peking's assumption of control over Taiwan, which would "not be all that difficult," would not involve "exacting revenge" against Chiang's supporters. "If Taiwan returns to the motherland, then its people would be making a contribution to the motherland for which we should give them a reward," Chou remarked. Unemployed islanders coming to the mainland "could go back to their home provinces and they will not be discriminated against."

Chou's statements were made at a dinner given for William Attwood, publisher of Newsday; Robert I. Keatley, a reporter for the Wall Street Journal; and Seymour Topping, assistant managing editor of the New York Times.

Nixon Announces Plan to Visit Communist China

Trip arranged by Kissinger. President Nixon announced to an astonished American public July 15, 1971 that he would visit Peking before May 1972 to confer with Communist Chinese leaders "to seek the normalization of relations between the two countries and to exchange views on questions of concern to the two sides." A follow-up announcement by the Western White House in San Clemente, Calif. July 16 said the President's trip might be made as early as late 1971 and that he would confer with both Communist Party Chairman Mao Tse-tung and Premier Chou En-lai. No American President had ever been received by a Chinese government.

In his address, broadcast from Los Angeles, Nixon disclosed that arrangements for the projected meeting with Chinese leaders had been worked out in secret talks held in Peking July 9-11 by Henry A. Kissinger, his national security affairs adviser, and Chou En-lai. Kissinger, while on a fact-finding tour of Asia, had made the secret flight to Peking from Pakistan, one of his stopover points. During his visit to the Chinese capital, Kissinger had been publicly reported to be resting in Nattria Gali, a Pakistani mountain resort, temporarily incapacitated by a stomach ailment.

Nixon said the plan for the proposed trip was being announced simultaneously in the U.S. and Peking. Alluding to the Nationalist Chinese government on Taiwan, the President emphasized that "our action in seeking a new relationship with the People's Republic of China will not be at the expense of our old friends." Nixon called his forthcoming visit "a major development in our efforts to build a lasting peace in the world." He said it was in accord with his oft-stated belief that "there can be no stable and enduring peace without the participation of the People's Republic of China and its 750 million peoples."

Nixon said that Chou had extended the invitation to him to come to Peking in response to his [Nixon's] expression of interest in a visit to China. The Chinese premier was reported to have confirmed to a visiting French group July 17 that it was the President who had suggested the trip.

The President's announcement was totally unanticipated. In an announcement earlier July 15 that Nixon would address the nation on radio and television, the White House had said that the broadcast would be of the highest importance, but it had cautioned the news media against fruitless speculation on the subject of the speech.

In a dispatch from Peking July 17, visiting New York Times correspondent James Reston reported that the Chinese news media had devoted little attention to the announcement of Nixon's planned visit. The Communist party newspaper Jenmin Jih Pao carried only seven lines on the story on its front page July 16, Reston wrote. He said the journal made no further mention of the event in its July 17 issue and ignored further comments by Nixon and Henry A. Kissinger. Peking radio July 16 had limited its report to a reading of the official communique on the visit and ignored the topic in its July 17 news programs, broadcasting instead its usual denunciations of "American imperialism" and "Japanese militarism," according to Reston.

Kissinger mission described. Further comment on the President's plans to visit China and details of Henry A. Kissinger's mission to Peking were outlined in the Western White House's July 16 announcement. Kissinger had returned to the U.S. July 13 and reported to President Nixon at San Clemente.

In a press briefing, White House officials made these points:

■ There were "risks" in a meeting of Nixon and the Chinese leaders because of the enormous differences between the two countries, particularly over the issue of U.S. support of Nationalist China and Peking's demand that this backing be withdrawn.

Nixon's Statement on his Visit to Peking

Good evening:

I have requested this television time tonight to announce a major development in our efforts to build a lasting peace in the world.

As I have pointed out on a number of occasions over the past three years, there can be no stable peace and enduring peace without the participation of the People's Republic of China and its 750 million people. That is why I have undertaken initiatives in several areas to open the door for more normal relations between our two countries.

In pursuance of that goal, I sent Dr. Kissinger, my assistant for national security affairs, to Peking during his recent world tour for the purpose of having talks with Premier Chou En-lai.

The announcement I shall now read is being issued simultaneously in Peking and in the Unites States:

"Premier Chou En-lai and Dr. Henry Kissinger, President Nixon's assistant for national security affairs, held talks in Peking from July 9 to 11, 1971. Knowing of President Nixon's expressed desire to visit the People's Republic of China, Premier Chou En-lai on behalf of the government of the People's Republic of China has extended an invitation to President Nixon to visit China at an appropriate date before May, 1972.

"President Nixon has accepted the invitation with pleasure.

"The meeting between the leaders of China and the United States is to seek the normalization of relations between the two countries and also to exchange views on questions of concern to the two sides."

In anticipation of the inevitable speculation which will follow this announcement, I want to put our policy in the clearest possible context. Our action in seeking a new relationship with the People's Republic of China will not be at the expense of our old friends.

It is not directed against any other nation. We seek friendly relations with all nations. Any nation can be our friend without being any other nation's enemy.

I have taken this action because of my profound conviction that all nations will gain from a reduction of tensions and a better relationship between the United States and the People's Republic of China.

It is in this spirit that I will undertake what I deeply hope will become a journey for peace, peace not just for our generation but for future generations on this earth we share together.

Thank you and good night.

■ No specific date had been set for Nixon's visit because it required considerable "preparatory work, . . . but it will be well before May 1972. May was set as the date because the President directed that a step of such importance for world peace . . . should not get mixed up" in the 1972 Presidential election campaign.

■ The Peking journey was not directly connected with the war in Indochina. However, when "countries of the magnitude and world concerns of the United States and the People's Republic of China alter their relationship, it must affect other parts of the world."

■ Nixon would not extend his trip to include the Soviet Union: ". . . the occasion of a visit to Peking is not the best to also visit Moscow. The issues to be discussed between the two countries are too various. But in principle we are prepared to meet with the Soviet leaders whenever our negotiations have reached a point where something fruitful can be accomplished."

On the Kissinger mission, the White House officials disclosed that:

■ Preparations for it and the mission itself were shrouded in such secrecy that only Nixon, Kissinger, Secretary of State William P. Rogers and "a very few White House staff members" knew what was going on. The arrangements were drawn up between April and June. Nixon did not work out plans for the project in his office "for fear that papers would be left behind and people might walk in and see [the President and Kissinger] working on the papers. So they usually met in the Lincoln sitting room [of the White House]. . . ."

■ Kissinger flew to Peking from Islamabad, Pakistan aboard a U.S. Air Force plane. (He had conferred with President Mohammad Agha Yahya Khan in Rawalpindi during his visit July 8–9.) Kissinger was accompanied by three members of his staff—John Holdridge, Winston Lord and Richard Smyser. During their 49-hour stay, the officials conferred with Premier Chou and four unidentified senior Chinese officials in two places: a state guest house where the Americans were lodged and the Great Hall of the People, used by Chou for receptions and dinners.

■ The negotiations leading up to the Kissinger trip were accomplished in two stages. The first required the establishment of a framework for negotiations and success in convincing the Chinese leaders that Americans were flexible and were "not prisoners of history." "The second phase started in April when we moved from this general framework to a more specific exploration of where we might go from here. Then in April, May and June this meeting was set up through a series of exchanges."

Kissinger flew back to Washington from San Clemente with President Nixon July 18. Speaking to newsmen aboard the Presidential jet, Kissinger warned that a poorly prepared Peking summit conference would be a disaster. Both sides must be assured, Kissinger stressed, that something tangible can result from the talks and detailed preliminary work already was underway.

Congressional leaders briefed. President Nixon briefed Congressional leaders July 19 on his plans for the visit to China.

White House Press Secretary Ronald L. Ziegler said Nixon had told the eight senators and nine representatives present that he would not speculate on "the effect of these discussions [in Peking] on any other matters" including the war in Indochina, and that "general speculation on this matter would not be helpful."

The President's plans were discussed later at a Cabinet meeting attended by Nixon, Rogers and Kissinger.

Rogers held separate meetings July 19 with the envoys of nine countries to acquaint them with Nixon's plans for talks with the Chinese leaders. Rogers told them that despite Washington's move toward a rapprochement with Peking, the U.S. was still seeking ways of keeping Nationalist China in the U.N. Rogers met with the ambassadors of Nationalist China, Japan, Australia, Britain, New Zealand, Thailand, France and West Germany and the charge d'affaires of Italy.

Domestic political reaction. The announcement of Nixon's intention to visit China drew generally favorable comment, mainly within Congress, from U.S. political figures July 15–20.

Senate Majority Leader Mike Mansfield (D, Mont.) described himself July 15 as "flabbergasted, delighted and happy" that Nixon had accepted the Chinese invitation and said he was "looking forward to a new day" as a result of the decision. Sen. Hugh Scott, the Republican leader from Pennsylvania, called the planned visit "an extremely important step in producing world peace." Sen. Hubert H. Humphrey (D, Minn.) said the President's move was "a dramatic turn in American foreign policy and, in my mind, one that can lead to constructive developments." Sen. George S. McGovern (D, S.D.) said he hoped the trip would "mark the end of a long period of nonsense in our relations with China and the beginning of a new era of common sense."

A similar view was taken July 16 by Sen. John Sherman Cooper (R, Ky.), who said the planned trip was "a step that may help bring stability and peace to Southeast Asia."

Former Secretary of State Dean Rusk said July 17 he thought the visit might bring a period in which "things can be talked out a little more clearly," since "in a nuclear world, two big countries like mainland China and the U.S. ought to have regular channels of contact with each other, even though there may be some important points on which they disagree."

Sen. Jacob K. Javits (R, N.Y.) said July 19 that Nixon would not have planned the visit to China unless the two powers "were already on the way to agreement" on major issues. Approving Nixon's move, Sen. Edward M. Kennedy (D, Mass.) remarked: "Rarely, I think, has the action of any President so captured the imagination and support of the American people as President Nixon's magnificent gesture last week of the improvement in our relations with China."

Strong opposition to the move was voiced July 16 by Sen. James L. Buckley (R, N.Y.), who said he was "deeply concerned" over its possible results. Buckley added: "At home it will inevitably strengthen the hand of those seeking accommodation with the Communist world at almost any price" and in Asia "the grand scale of this overture to Peking will be anything but reassuring to those who have to live with the aggressive reality

of mainland China." Sen. John G. Tower (R, Tex.) said he was "disturbed by the scheduled visit, which he said might be a result of "our steadily diminishing capability to cope with Soviet expansionism and . . . military might." Rep. John Schmitz (R, Cal.), who represented the President's home Congressional district, charged that Nixon was "surrendering to international communism."

Addressing a meeting of the American Bar Association in London July 19, Former Undersecretary of State George W. Ball accused the President of "flamboyant diplomacy" and said that the likelihood of the trip's having an influence on the Indochina war was not great because "one cannot reasonably expect Peking to twist the arm of Hanoi on a basis less than Hanoi would like to see."

Gov. George C. Wallace (D, Ala.) said July 20 he had been "shocked" by the announcement but hoped that Nixon's visit "pays off in world peace" although he had "my doubts." Wallace added that he found it difficult to believe the Communist Chinese were truly interested in peace as long as they were "exporting heroin [and] subversion."

Taiwan scores U.S. move. Nationalist China expressed shock and dismay at the prospect of closer U.S.-Communist Chinese ties.

Ambassador James C. H. Shen delivered a strong protest to the State Department in Washington July 15. Shen said "I couldn't believe my ears" when he heard of President Nixon's announcement. He complained that his government was "getting a shabby deal."

U.S. Ambassador Walter P. McConaughy July 16 was called into Tapei's Foreign Ministry, where Vice Foreign Minister Yang Hsi-kun lodged a vehement protest.

Premier C. K. Yen expressed regret in Taipei July 16 that the U.S. had been "deceived by the Chinese Communists." He warned that "this could lead to a tragedy far more serious than that involved in the fall of the Chinese mainland" to the Communists in 1949. Despite the apparent improvement in Peking-Washington relations, Nationalist China had "the faith and determination to recover the Chinese mainland

and to resist any external adverse tide," Yen said. "Under no circumstances shall we relax or weaken our stand."

A senior official of Nationalist China's ruling Kuomintang party July 17 expressed his government's continued irreconcilable stand against an agreement with Peking. He said: "We want to liberate the mainland and they want to liberate Taiwan. I don't see any time when there is a possibility of negotiations between the Chinese Communists and us."

■ The White House reported July 20 that President Nixon had assured Chinese Nationalist leader Chiang Kai-shek that despite his friendly overtures to Peking, the U.S. would continue to provide Taiwan with military support. The Nationalist Foreign Ministry confirmed that Nixon had sent such a message to Chiang, adding that "the letter conveys assurances of the United States to honor its defense treaty commitments to the Republic of China and maintain the continuing friendship with her."

Chou sets terms. In a July 19 interview with members of the Committee of Concerned Asian Scholars, a group of visiting U.S. graduate students, Communist Chinese Premier Chou En-lai set terms for establishment of diplomatic relations between China and the U.S. and for Peking's membership in the U.N.

Chou declared that the U.S. would have to recognize Peking as the sole legitimate government of China and acknowledge Taiwan as an "internal affair" of China which "brooks no foreign intervention." He opposed the "Taiwan Independence Movement" because he said it was known for its "special manipulation from foreign forces" and because the native Taiwanese were Chinese people.

The U.S. would have to declare "illegal and null and void" its 1954 treaty of defense with Taiwan, he said.

Chou said his government was opposed to a "two-China" policy or a "one-China, one-Taiwan" policy "or any similar policy" and that "if such a situation continues in the United Nations, we will not go there."

Vietnamese, other foreign reaction. The response of other nations to President Nixon's announcement ranged from positive acclaim to sharp criticism in a few instances.

Mrs. Nguyen Thi Binh, chief Viet Cong delegate to the Paris peace talks, July 16 voiced confidence that China would not reach an Indochina agreement with President Nixon behind the backs of the Viet Cong leadership. She said "this would be inconceivable" in view of China's support of "our struggle for independence."

A Viet Cong broadcast July 20 warned Nixon against attempting to impose an Indochina solution on the Vietnamese people with the aid of other nations. The statement said "Nixon should remember that the source of all his problems and misfortunes was and is in Vietnam and Indochina" and that he should deal directly with the Vietnamese people.

South Vietnamese Vice President Nguyen Cao Ky predicted July 18 that Nixon's move would bring about an early settlement of the Indochina war. Ky said he believed China would pressure North Vietnam to agree to a peaceful solution and already may have done so. President Nguyen Van Thieu said "I just nourish the hope" that Nixon's decision would lead to peace.

Japanese Premier Eisaku Sato July 17 said he trusted that Nixon's meeting with Peking's leadership would help improve relations between Japan and China.

The Soviet government newspaper Izvestia published a terse report on the Peking invitation July 16 without comment. Western diplomats in Moscow said Soviet officials had reacted with stunned surprise to the news.

Elsewhere in Eastern Europe comment varied. The Bulgarian state radio July 16 condemned Washington's action, charging that Nixon "does not view relations with the Chinese People's Republic as an instrument of peace and understanding between nations but rather as a means to keep disunited the anti-imperialist forces and the national liberation movement."

The Polish press foresaw a radical change in international relations resulting from a U.S.-Chinese rapprochement. One newspaper, Express Wieczorny, said July 16 that "Peking's shocking turn-about is not surprising at all."

Belgrade radio said July 16 that Nixon's "arrival in Peking will cause more thinking among the Chinese than among the American public, since the latter is accustomed to various political and diplomatic turns."

The Hungarian newspaper Esti Hirlap July 16 characterized Nixon's decision to establish contacts with Communist China as "baseball diplomacy." The journal said "it is hardly an accident that the Nixon trip is scheduled to take place five to six months before the Presidential election."

■ Rumania July 21 lauded Nixon's decision to visit China. The Communist party newspaper Scienteia said "there can be no efficient settlement of any of the big problems facing mankind today without the participation of China."

All Western European governments, including those of France, Britain and West Germany, July 16 welcomed Nixon's decision to visit China.

Moscow reacts to Nixon's China trip. The Soviet Union July 21 endorsed the criticism of President Nixon's proposed trip to Communist China.

The weekly Literaturnaya Gazeta reprinted an article distributed by the Bulgarian Telegraph Agency, an official press agency, that was highly critical of the U.S.-China action. The agency article asserted that Peking's continued silence on the President's projected journey "put Nixon's assurances" that the visit is not directed against any country "in a different light."

Charging that the U.S. and China were "in secret collusion" against the Soviet Union, the Bulgarian statement said: "There are no signs that either the United States or the Chinese leaders have changed or are about to change any basic way the policy carried on up to now or to alter in a positive way their attitude toward preserving peace in the world."

The news agency Tass Aug. 10 distributed an article by Georgi A. Arbatov, a specialist in U.S. affairs, which expressed hope that President Nixon's forthcoming visit to Peking would not harm U.S.-Soviet relations or hinder the solution of major world problems.

Arbatov noted that the thaw in U.S.-Chinese relations had come at a time when "the hostility of the Chinese leaders toward the Soviet Union and their

splitting line in the revolutionary and liberation movement were revealed" but he said from this evidence "one cannot deduce that all Americans who favor an improvement in U.S.-Chinese relations are motivated by hostility toward other Socialist countries."

If the Nixon visit resulted in a "more constructive position" on such problems as "Vietnam, the Middle East, European security, limiting the arms race," Arbatov said, "then there would be grounds for taking the statements about Washington's peace-loving intentions and goodwill seriously."

Arbatov's article appeared to represent a softening of the first official Soviet reaction to the announcement of Nixon's planned visit, which took the form of a July 25 statement in the Communist party newspaper Pravda warning that "any designs to use the contacts between Peking and Washington for some pressure against the Soviet Union, or the states of the Socialist community, are nothing but the result of a loss of touch with reality." The statement had also repeated Soviet rejection of the "great-power chauvinistic policy of Peking and the slanderous fabrications of Chinese propaganda about the policy of our party and state."

Nixon stresses dialogue. President Nixon cautioned Aug. 4 against expectation that his forthcoming visit to Peking would produce "instant detente." At a news conference the President said, "We expect to make some progress, but to speculate about what progress will be made on any particular issue—to speculate, for example, as to what effect this might have on Vietnam—would not serve the interests of constructive talks."

What his visit "really" meant, he said, was "moving, as we have moved, I believe, in the situation with regard to the Soviet Union, from an era of confrontation without communication to an era of negotiations with discussion. It does not mean that we go into these meetings on either side with any illusions about the wide differences that we have. Our interests are very different, and both sides recognize this. . . . We do not expect that these talks will settle all of those differences. What is important is that we will have opened communication to see where our differences are irreconcilable, to see that they can be settled peacefully, and to find those areas where the United States, which today is the most powerful nation in the world, can find an agreement with the most populous nation in the world, which potentially in the future could become the most powerful nation in the world."

In response to a question, Nixon disclosed that he had discussed with Soviet Foreign Minister Andrei Gromyko when he was in Washington the possibility of a summit meeting and that Soviet leaders agreed with his position that "a meeting at the highest level should take place and would be useful only when there was something substantive to discuss that could not be handled in other channels." Nixon pointed out that progress was being made, as regards to the Soviet Union, on Berlin and disarmament and that discussions on the Mideast were continuing.

U.S. A-arms barred from near China. In view of President Nixon's efforts to improve relations with Peking, the nuclear weapons that were to be removed from Okinawa would not be placed closer to Communist China, U.S. government officials announced July 19. A proposal submitted to Nixon in June had called for shifting the atomic arms to Taiwan, South Korea and the Philippines, but the officials said the plan, which required Presidental approval, would be rejected by Nixon in the wake of his new policy on China.

The Joint Chiefs of Staff had proposed the atomic weapons shift before the President announced he would travel to China. Some Defense and State Department officials had opposed the plan on the ground that China would regard the action as nuclear encirclement.

A June 17 accord under which the U.S. agreed to return Okinawa to Japan alluded to the withdrawal of American nuclear weapons from the island. This was in accord with Japan's policy of banning such weapons from Japanese territory. The U.S. had never officially acknowledged the presence of nuclear weapons on Okinawa.

U.S. halts spy flights over China. The U.S. government announced July 28 a

suspension of American intelligence-gathering missions over Communist China by manned SR-71 reconnaissance planes and unmanned drones. The decision was aimed at preventing any incident that might mar President Nixon's scheduled trip to Peking. U.S. earth satellite missions were to continue over China, however. They were considered less provocative since they were well above China's airspace.

It was presumed that Nationalist China would continue to fly U-2 spy planes over China. A Washington informant was quoted as saying that "the mainland Chinese have good enough radar to distinguish between an overflight by the kind of aircraft we possess and the kind flown by the Chinese Nationalists."

The decision to stop the espionage flights over China was in accord with a July 16 White House statement commenting on the meeting between Chinese Premier Chou En-lai and Henry A. Kissinger. The statement said that neither the U.S. nor China would "knowingly do something that would undermine the prospects of something that it took so long to prepare and that it took such painful decisions to reach."

Chou's comments. In an interview Aug. 9 with New York Times columnist James Reston, Red Chinese Premier Chou En-lai discussed Nixon's forthcoming trip and other foreign policy matters.

Chou made it clear that while he was looking forward to Nixon's trip, he did not expect the visit to settle all the outstanding problems between the U.S. and China. Chou said:

"China is a country which was blockaded by the U.S. for more than 20 years. Now since there's a desire to come and look at China, it's all right. And since there is a desire to talk, we are also ready to talk. Of course, it goes without saying that the positions of our two sides are different. And there are a lot of differences between our points of view. To achieve relaxation, there must be a common desire for it, so various questions must be studied, and all these questions may be placed on the table for discussion. We do not expect a settlement of all questions at one stroke. That is not possible. That would not be practicable. But by contacting each other, we may be able to find out from where we should start in solving these questions."

The Chinese premier accused the U.S. of having "promoted the development of Japan toward militarism by the indefinite prolongation of the Japan-U.S. security treaty," which he said had not curbed Japan's ability to produce nuclear weapons. He said Japan had "ambitious designs with regard to Taiwan." Chou expressed fear that Japan might use its treaty with South Korea to occupy that country when all U.S. troops had been withdrawn.

Kissinger in Peking. Kissinger visited Peking again Oct. 20–25 to arrange the agenda and itinerary for Nixon's trip.

The White House announced on Kissinger's return to Washington Oct. 26 that he and his accompanying aides had made "good progress in their discussions" with Premier Chou En-lai and other Chinese officials in the six days of talks.

Kissinger briefed Nixon on his trip Oct. 27. The Presidential adviser later reported to newsmen that Nixon and the Chinese leaders hoped to restrict their substantive talks to issues involving only the two countries. Other matters, such as Soviet-Chinese relations and the Indochina war, would not be discussed, he said.

"We expect to settle the Vietnam war either by the unilateral policies we are pursuing or by negotiations with Hanoi," he said. "We are not going to settle it in Peking." He emphasized that the Sino-American talks that were to be held in Peking would not be aimed at exploiting China's relations with other nations and that they would not be "directed against third countries."

(Direct phone service between the U.S. and mainland China, terminated by Peking without explanation in 1968, had been restored Sept. 2.)

Trip to U.S.S.R. Set

Nixon's decision to visit Peking provoked comment that he would also have to visit Moscow, if only to keep the Soviets from *fearing that the U.S. was veering too far toward the U.S.S.R.'s chief Communist rival. Although Administration spokesmen denied that the President was swayed by any such motivation, Nixon soon arranged to make a trip to the Soviet Union.*

Nixon to visit Moscow. It was announced simultaneously in Washington and Moscow Oct. 12 that President Nixon would visit the Soviet Union "in the latter part of May 1972" for discussions with Soviet leaders on "all major issues, with a view toward further improving . . . bilateral relations and enhancing the prospects of world peace."

At a White House news conference in which he disclosed the plans for the trip, Nixon said his visit to Moscow had no connection with his visit to Peking.

"Neither trip is being taken for the purpose of exploiting what differences may exist between the two nations. Neither is being taken at the expense of any other nation," the President remarked.

It was time for a summit meeting, Nixon said, because in "significant areas" like biological weapons, agreements to prevent nuclear accidents and improve the Washington–Moscow "hot line" and in the preliminary Berlin settlement, there had been progress toward better relations between the two nations.

A two-hour meeting Sept. 29 with Soviet Foreign Minister Andrei A. Gromyko, Nixon said, made it clear that there were still "very great differences," although "the interest of neither country would be served by war. . . . It is because we have reached the point that the competition in terms of escalating arms race cannot gain an advantage, and both of us emphasized this in our meeting, it is for that reason that now the time has come to negotiate our differences . . . recognizing that they are still very deep, recognizing, however, that there is no alternative to negotiation at this point."

Nixon spoke Oct. 24 of his trips to Moscow and Peking in a brief radio address for Veterans Day (Oct. 25). He said "we go with no false hopes and we intend to leave behind us in America no unrealistic expectations." There were "great differences" between the government of the U.S. and those of the Soviet Union and the People's Republic of

China, he said, "but we have much in common with the Russian people and the Chinese people. We share this earth. We share a love for our children. And we share an understanding of the ultimate futility of war."

Kissinger added at a press conference Nov. 30 that the trip to China was not expected to result in establishment of formal diplomatic relations between the U.S. and China, nor a settlement of the differences between Peking and the Nationalist Chinese on Taiwan nor an end to the war in Southeast Asia.

"We're not sentimental about this," he said. "We recognize that the People's Republic is led by highly principled men whose principles are diametrically opposed to ours."

It was in the interest of both countries, Kissinger said, "that we understand what we are about and that on those matters that are in our common interest we know how to cooperate." The minimum objective of the trip, he said, would be to establish a system of communication on opposing views and thus avert "very dramatic, set-piece encounters."

Chou on Taiwan issue—Chinese Premier Chou En-lai implied in an interview with Australian author Neville Maxwell, published Dec. 5, that President Nixon would have to solve "the Taiwan question" during his forthcoming visit to China.

Chou said support of two Chinas amounted to "contradictions in U.S. foreign policy" and that it was "up to President Nixon to answer this question—otherwise, if he comes to China and yet the Taiwan question remains unsettled, how will he account for himself when he gets back?" Chou acknowledged that not all problems could be "solved at once" and that "we should not expect too much" to come from Nixon's visit. However, he added: "But if he solves nothing, will the American people agree to it?"

Lin Piao's fall, crisis in China. In the midst of preparations for Nixon's visits, Soviet and U.S. sources began to circulate reports of a crisis in mainland China and of Lin Piao's fall from power.

Tass and other Soviet newspapers, carrying a version of a report filed by the French news agency Agence France-Presse, said Nov. 13 that "in many diplomatic circles in Peking, even among persons closest to the Chinese government, there is growing doubt of Lin Piao remaining the 'Number 2 man' in China." The newspaper said it was becoming more difficult "to find in Peking's bookshops the Chinese edition of the party statutes adopted by the 9th Party Congress in 1969." These statutes, Tass noted, referred to Lin "as the successor" to Mao Tse-tung.

In a further comment on the alleged turmoil in China, Tass reported Nov. 19 that "although the Chinese leaders persist in keeping a veil of secrecy over the nature and causes of the events that took place in China recently, information reaches here from Peking and the press reports indicate the existence of a grave crisis in the Chinese leadership."

A Washington dispatch Nov. 16 said U.S. intelligence sources had been receiving reports that Communist party groups throughout China were being informed by top CP leaders that Lin "no longer holds power."

The U.S. intelligence sources were reported as saying that the crisis in Peking had come to a head about Sept. 11 when Lin and his followers were forced out by Mao and Premier Chou En-lai. Lin and some military leaders were said to have advocated economic priorities favorable to the armed forces while the Mao-Chou faction preferred to have the country's economic resources allocated largely for non-military use, according to the U.S. report. Lin also was said to have opposed Peking's new policy of detente with the West.

Chinese free two Americans. Two Americans released Dec. 12 from prisons in Communist China arrived in the U.S. Dec. 13.

A dispatch Dec. 13 from the official Communist Chinese press agency Hsinhua identified the former prisoners as Richard G. Fecteau and Mary Ann Harbert.

Hsinhua said Fecteau of Lynn, Mass., and John T. Downey of New Britain, Conn. had been shot down in a military aircraft over China in 1952 after dropping espionage agents trained in Japan into Manchuria. Downey's life sentence was being reduced to five more years because "both men had admitted their crimes during the trial and their behavior was not bad while serving their terms."

Miss Harbert had strayed into Chinese waters off southern Kwangtung Province in 1968 while sailing from Hong Kong in a yacht with Gerald R. McLaughlin, a family friend. Hsinhua declared that McLaughlin had "behaved badly" during detention, "resisted investigation and, taking the warders unawares, committed suicide on March 7, 1969."

White House Press Secretary Ronald L. Ziegler released a statement Dec. 13 saying that President Nixon "welcomes the act of clemency of the People's Republic of China" in commuting Downey's sentence and releasing Fecteau and Miss Harbert. Ziegler revealed that Nixon had been given "advance knowledge" that these actions were forthcoming. He also said that on two visits to China, Kissinger had discussed the prisoners with Chou En-lai.

Indo-Pakistan complication. U.S.-Soviet detente and the Nixon trip to Moscow seemed threatened during December 1971 by the fighting from which East Pakistan emerged as the independent state of Bangladesh. The war embroiled India on the side of the emerging Bangladesh against (West) Pakistan. The Soviet Union supported India in this dispute, and the U.S. aided Pakistan.

At one point, a White House official Dec. 14 warned that Nixon would reconsider his trip to Moscow unless the U.S.S.R. used its influence to get India to accept a cease-fire. The aide was identified by the Washington Post as Kissinger.

Kissinger told newsmen aboard a plane en route from the Azores that if the Soviets continued to spur Indian military action, the U.S. would have to reassess its entire relationship with Moscow. Kissinger was said to have taken particular issue with the Soviet Union's repeated vetoes of cease-fire resolutions in the Security Council, a position which also was said to have irked Nixon. Kissinger said Nixon believed that Soviet policy in South Asia was aimed at humiliating China by proving its inability to protect its Pakistani ally. Nixon's views were re-

ported to have been conveyed to Soviet Foreign Minister Andrei A. Gromyko by Ambassador Jacob Beam Dec. 13.

White House Press Secretary Ronald L. Ziegler amended Kissinger's reported remarks later Dec. 14. Without mentioning Kissinger by name, Ziegler said, "The United States is not considering canceling the U.S.-Soviet summit and no U.S. government official intended to suggest this." He called the accounts of Nixon's alleged attitude toward the Soviet Union on the Indian-Pakistani war as "highly speculative and taken out of context." He explained, "If the Soviets continued to support Indian military action and the Indians should move into West Pakistan, this could very well affect future relations with the Soviet Union. But we have no reason to suspect this will occur. We have every expectation the fighting will stop in South Asia."

Ziegler Dec. 15 reaffirmed the Administration's displeasure with the Soviet Union's strong support of India, but he said the possibility of canceling Nixon's trip to Moscow was not "a live issue."

The White House was displeased with the fact that Kissinger had been identified as the source of the comments on the controversy, in violation of long-standing procedures.

U.S.-Soviet naval curb asked. A U.S. State Department official revealed Feb. 2, 1972 that the U.S. had asked the Soviet Union to discuss reducing the naval forces of both countries but had not been given an answer.

Charles W. Bray 3rd, the spokesman, disclosed the U.S. overture in answer to questions raised by newsmen about a hearing conducted the previous day by the Senate Foreign Relations Committee, which had been interviewing Undersecretary of State U. Alexis Johnson about U.S. agreements for the use of naval facilities at Bahrain and the Azores.

In answer to a question whether the U.S. had ever approached the Soviet Union about limiting the size of both countries' naval forces in the Indian Ocean, Johnson was said to have replied without elaboration: "We have made such an approach. There have been discussions."

U.S.-Soviet medical pact. The formation of a Soviet-American Committee for Health Cooperation, to begin work in Moscow in March on pooling medical research efforts, was announced Feb. 11.

The accord, reportedly concluded in secret more than a year before, was revealed at a Washington news conference conducted by Soviet Ambassador Anatoly F. Dobrynin and Elliot L. Richardson, secretary of health, education and welfare. It provided for the committee to meet once a year, alternately in each country, to review the work of subcommittees that would be established to coordinate research in cancer, heart disease and environmental health problems.

In a related development, Porter International, a U.S. consulting firm, said Feb. 1 it had agreed to cooperate with the Soviet news agency Tass to issue a newsletter twice a month on Soviet economic developments.

Red China Wins U.N. Seat

The People's Republic of China was accepted as a member of the U.N. in October 1971, and Nationalist China was expelled. The change took place after the U.S. abandoned its fight to keep the Peking government out of the world body and agreed to "support" plans to seat it.

Membership move initiated. Albania and 17 co-sponsors submitted a resolution July 15 calling on the General Assembly to admit Communist China, seat it in the Security Council, and expel Nationalist China from all U.N. bodies.

A similar resolution had been supported by the Assembly in 1970 by a vote of 51-49, but Peking's admission was blocked because the General Assembly had decided the question required a two-thirds majority. The 1971 resolution was submitted well in advance of the assembly's Sept. 21 opening date, reportedly to emphasize Peking's insistence on the expulsion of Nationalist China as a condition for its own membership.

U.S. backs Red China's seating. The U.S. Aug. 2 ended 20 years of opposition to the Peking government's membership in the U.N. by announcing that it would "support action at the General Assembly this fall calling for seating the People's Republic of China." But the U.S. also emphasized its continued resistance to any move to expel Nationalist China "or otherwise deprive it of representation" in the U.N.

The announcement came at a State Department news briefing by Secretary of State William P. Rogers, who said the change in policy had occurred because "in Asia and elsewhere in the world we are seeking to accommodate our role to the realities of the world today."

During the news briefing, Rogers said he had received no indication from Peking or Taipei that either government would accept a place in the U.N. if the other government were also represented there. According to the New York Times Aug. 2, Rogers' statement mentioned support for the "seating" of Peking rather than for its "admission"—as would be the case with a new member—in order to convince Peking that the U.S. was not in favor of a two-China policy. The Times also noted that under the provisions of the U.N. Charter, new members were subject to approval of the Security Council, of which Nationalist China was a member.

On the question of whether Peking's seating in the U.N. would also bring seating on the Security Council, Rogers declared that "in the final analysis" the council itself would "make that decision."

Peking scores Rogers text—In a commentary on the Rogers statement Aug. 4, the official Communist Chinese news agency Hsinhua accused the U.S. of playing a "clumsy 'two Chinas' trick" that was "absolutely illegal and futile."

Hsinhua declared that in promoting a seat for Peking while asking that one be retained for Taipei, the U.S. was continuing "to obstruct the restoration to the People's Republic of China all of her legitimate rights in the U.N. and insists on being the enemy of the Chinese people."

Rogers was accused of practicing sophistry by asserting that President Nixon's policies were based both on the heritage of the past and the realities of the present. "Everybody knows clearly that the 'legacies of the past' Rogers talked about mean the Chiang Kai-shek clique, which has long been spurned by the Chinese people, and this was created single-handed by U.S. imperialism through occupying China's Taiwan Province and the Taiwan Strait by armed forces," the agency said. Rogers' "so-called realities of 'two Chinas' " were described as "his sheer fancy."

The article concluded: "We are deeply convinced that the justice-upholding countries and peoples of the world will also never allow anyone under the signboard of 'two Chinas' to continue to forcibly occupy China's territory Taiwan and obstruct the restoration to the People's Republic of China of her legitimate seats in the U.N."

Diplomatic observers noted that although the statement was critical of U.S. policy it did not imply that the Rogers text had fallen short of Peking's expectations or that it in any way influenced Nixon's proposed visit to China.

U.S. resolutions discussed—At the U.S. mission to the United Nations Aug. 3, Ambassador George Bush discussed two draft resolutions on Chinese seating with some of the 18 nations that supported the U.S. position in 1970.

The first resolution, according to the New York Times Aug. 5, affirmed Peking's right to take, and Nationalist China's right to maintain, a U.N. seat and recommended that the organization's "specialized agencies take into account the provisions of this resolution in deciding the question of Chinese representation in those agencies."

The other text asserted that "any proposal in the General Assembly which would result in depriving the Republic of China of representation in the U.N. is an important question under Article 18 of the Charter." Such a ruling

Text of Secretary of State Rogers' Statement on China

The world is approaching the midpoint between the end of World War II and the end of the 20th century. The United Nations, founded in the aftermath of the war, has passed its 25th anniversary.

President Nixon has been adapting American foreign policy with these facts in mind—forging policies directed to the future while taking fully into account the legacies of the past.

From its inception the United Nations was designed above all else to keep the peace shattered by two world wars within a single generation. The first words of the United Nations Charter, adopted at San Francisco in 1945, express a common determination to "save succeeding generations from the scourge of war."

In October 1969, President Nixon said with regard to Latin America that "we must deal realistically with governments . . . as they are." Both in Asia and elsewhere in the world we are seeking to accommodate our role to the realities of the world today. Our objective is to contribute, in practical terms, to the building of a framework for a stable peace.

No question of Asian policy has so perplexed the world in the last 20 years as the China question— and the related question of representation in the United Nations. Basic to that question is the fact that each of two governments claims to be the sole government of China and representative of all the people of China.

Representation in an international organization need not prejudice the claims or views of either government. Participation of both in the United Nations need not require that result.

Rather it would provide governments with increased opportunities for contact and communication. It would also help promote cooperation on common problems which affect all of the member nations regardless of political differences.

The United States accordingly will support action at the General Assembly this fall calling for seating the People's Republic of China. At the same time the United States will oppose any action to expel the Republic of China or otherwise deprive it representation in the United Nations.

Our consultations which began several months ago have indicated that the question of China's seat in the Security Council is a matter which many nations will wish to address. In the final analysis, of course, under the charter provision, the Security Council will make this decision. We, for our part, are prepared to have this question resolved on the basis of a decision of members of the United Nations.

Our consultations have also shown that any action to deprive the Republic of China of its representation would meet strong opposition in the General Assembly. Certainly, as I have said, the United States will oppose it.

The Republic of China has played a loyal and conscientious role in the U.N. since the organization was founded. It has lived up to all of its charter obligations. Having made remarkable progress in developing its own economy, it has cooperated internationally by providing valuable technical assistance to a number of less developed countries, particularly in Africa.

The position of the United States is that if the United Nations is to succeed in its peacekeeping role, it must deal with the realities of the world in which we live. Thus, the United States will cooperate with those who, whatever their view on the status of the relationship of the two governments, wish to continue to have the Republic of China represented in the United Nations.

The outcome, of course, will be decided by 127 members of the United Nations. For our part we believe that the decision we have taken is fully in accord with President Nixon's desire to normalize relations with the People's Republic of China in the interests of world peace and in accord with our conviction that the continued representation in the United Nations of the Republic of China will contribute to peace and stability in the world.

would make Nationalist China's ouster dependent on a two-thirds vote.

U.S. submits China resolution. George Bush, U.S. representative to the U.N., asked Secretary General U Thant Aug. 17 to place on the agenda of the forthcoming General Assembly session a resolution supporting a "two-China" policy.

The document, entitled "Representation of China in the U.N.," asked the assembly to recognize "the incontestable reality" that there were two Chinese governments and to avoid taking "a position on the respective conflicting claims of the People's Republic of [Communist] China or the Republic of [Nationalist] China." The resolution also requested that "provision should be made that the Republic of China is not deprived of its representation."

The New York Times said Aug. 23 that the Nationalist Chinese government had been informed of the impending announcement of U.S. support for Peking's admission to the U.N. when former Undersecretary of State Robert D. Murphy visited Taiwan in April as an emissary of President Nixon.

Detente debated at U.N. The General Assembly opened its general debate Sept. 27 with Brazilian Foreign Minister Mario Gibson Barbosa citing the admission of Communist China as one of the most important issues before the Assembly. Gibson Barbosa said the admittance to the U.N. of the "new partner" was taken for granted, "whether it was today or tomorrow."

Iranian Foreign Minister Abbas Sli Khalatbari told the Assembly Sept. 27 that his country recognized Peking as "the sole government of China" which should take its "rightful place at the U.N."

Speaking Sept. 28, Soviet Foreign Minister Andrei A. Gromyko made "detente" his key theme. Gromyko said the Soviet Union "in principle" regarded the improvement of relations between the U.S. and Communist China "as a natural development."

On the question of disarmament, Gromyko said "unless the deployment of antimissile defense is brought to a halt now, a chain reaction of competition between offensive and defensive weapons is bound to develop."

French Foreign Minister Maurice Schumann Sept. 27 had also emphasized the need for detente.

Rogers argues for Taiwan. In an address to the U.N. General Assembly Oct. 4, Secretary of State William P. Rogers argued for the U.S. resolution calling for the seating of Communist China on the Security Council and spoke against the Albanian resolution which called for expulsion of Nationalist China (Taiwan) from the General Assembly.

Rogers said the U.S. text, which would allow Peking to "assume, as a permanent member of the Security Council, the rights and responsibilities which go with that status," should "commend itself to member states of various policies." The proposal would, Rogers said, "assure that the long-prevailing de facto situation in China is reflected in U.N. representation" without requiring U.N. members "to alter their recognition policies or their bilateral relations." The move would "provide representation for the people concerned by those who actually govern them" without dividing "China into two separate states."

The Albanian resolution, on the other hand, Rogers described as "punitive in substance and in intent" and likely to "weaken, not strengthen, the moral and political fiber of this organization." He warned: "The path of expulsion is perilous. To open it for one would be to open it for many." Rogers said it would be "unrealistic" to expel a country which "governs a population on Taiwan greater than the populations of two-thirds of the 130 U.N. members" and which "has participated for over 25 years in the work of this organization with unfailing devotion to the principles set forth in the Charter."

Albania presents case—Nesti Nase, Albanian foreign minister, told the Assembly Oct. 5 that "nothing has changed" in the U.S.' "deep hostility against socialism and the great Chinese people," although Washington "has changed its tactics and now pretends to have adopted a new attitude."

Nase quoted from a statement, distributed Aug. 20 by the official Communist Chinese press agency Hsinhua, which said Peking "will have absolutely nothing to do with the U.N. if a two-China or a China-and-Taiwan situation should appear, a situation in which the status of Taiwan would remain to be determined, or any other such position."

In a speech devoted to numerous foreign policy issues, Nase condemned both the "U.S. imperialists and the Soviet social imperialists" for their tendency to "unite when it comes to carrying out their plans to establish their dominion in the world."

Nixon gets House petition on Taiwan. President Nixon Oct. 13 received a petition signed by 336 members of the U.S. House of Representatives opposing expulsion of Nationalist China from the U.N.

White House Press Secretary Ronald Zeigler reported that Nixon had thanked the group that had presented him with the petition for their "support of the Administration on this issue."

China debate opens. The historic debate on seating a delegation from the People's Republic of China opened Oct. 18 in the United Nations.

Albanian criticism—Opening the debate Oct. 18, Albanian Foreign Minister Nesti Nase criticized both "American imperialists" and "Soviet revisionists" for "serious crimes against the Chinese people."

Since 1950, he said, the U.S. had "continued to occupy a Chinese province, the island of Taiwan." The draft resolutions cosponsored by the U.S. and others were "contradictory and erroneous" because there was "no question of the admission of a new member nor the expulsion of any member that would be a subject governed by special procedure and would, therefore, require a majority of two-thirds." Countries supporting the U.S. texts did so "because they have not yet reached the point where they could throw off the political, economic and military chains that bind them to American imperialism."

U.S. position founded on 'reality'—U.S. delegate George Bush opened his address

by rejecting the "outrageous slanders of the delegate from Albania" which he termed an "old-fashioned tirade complete with the cliches of the cold war."

Bush argued that the substantive U.S. resolution, which would seat Peking on the Security Council and retain Taiwan in the General Assembly, "does not in any way purport to divide China into two separate states" and was "founded on the reality of the present situation as we all know it to be, but it does not seek to freeze this situation for the future." He added that the resolution "does not, to be sure, accept the claims of the parties; but neither does it deny or reject or prejudice those claims."

Bush warned that expulsion was "most ill-advised and dangerous" and "an unacceptable price to pay for the entry of the People's Republic of China." It was unfair, he said, to take this action, likely to be irreversible, against Taiwan "solely because certain other governments question its legitimacy." Delegates were advised that "this session of the U.N. cannot and should not try to write the last chapter in the complicated history of China's relations with itself or with the rest of the world."

Bush pointed out that the U.N. charter, which was "flexible enough to allow for the representation of Byelorussia, the Ukraine and the U.S.S.R.," might be able to "accommodate this situation."

Yvon Beaulne, the Canadian representative, noted that the question to be decided in the Assembly was not one of "membership or of expulsion of a member, it is the question of who represents China."

Taiwan takes exception—Nationalist Chinese Foreign Minister Chow Shu-kai warned that the seating of a delegation from Peking, which ruled by "torture and terror," would damage the U.N. "This being so, the deceptive change of attitude on the part of Peking toward the U.S. and the rest of the world cannot be taken as anything more than tactical maneuvers. There can be no question that the new posture is designed to exploit the prevailing pacificist-isolationist mood of the American people, to force the complete withdrawal of American influence from Asia."

Japan backs U.S. position—Speaking Oct. 19 in favor of the U.S. resolutions, which his country was cosponsoring, Japanese delegate Kiichi Aichi advocated adoption of the proposals as a "transitional step for solving the Chinese representation issue within the context of one China." Aichi spoke against the Albanian resolution, which he described as "an unreasonable and peremptory demand" which was "punitive in substance and intent" and likely to "entail an abrupt change in the delicate international situation prevailing in the past."

U.S.S.R. scores U.S. plan—On the third day of the debate Oct. 20, the Soviet delegate to the U.N., Yakov A. Malik, said the U.S. argument against the expulsion of Nationalist China as a member state was an effort "to frighten the members of the United Nations" and amounted to "absurd inventions and ridiculous fairy tales composed for children of preschool age." He insisted that Taiwan was not a state but "a province of China" and that the Albanian resolution would simply "expel a group of private persons who seized a seat and restore this seat to its lawful occupants."

He denounced the U.S. proposal for dual representation as "a retreat concealed by rear-guard battles" now that the U.S. was forced by the reality of world politics to find accommodation with the Peking regime.

Yugoslav delegate Lazar Mojsov also backed the Albanian resolution and argued against the U.S. contention that the departure of Nationalist China would be the expulsion of a member state. He said it was a matter "of having the government truly representing the Chinese people take its seat in the United Nations."

France supports Albanian resolution— Jacques Kosciusko-Morizet of France declared there was only one member state, China, and therefore there should be only one representative nation: the People's Republic of China. He said France would vote for the Albanian resolution and would oppose any resolution that would support dual representation or that would create "new obstacles" to Peking's membership in the U.N.

The Swedish delegate, Olof Rydbeck, also insisted that the "sole legitimate

Chinese government" was the People's Republic of China.

U.N. seats Peking delegation and ousts Nationalist regime. The U.N. General Assembly voted overwhelmingly Oct. 25 to admit Communist China and expel the Chinese Nationalist government of Taiwan. The vote, taken at an unexpected evening session, assured that the Peking government would take China's seats in the Assembly and the Security Council. The resolution, sponsored by Albania and 20 other nations, was approved by 76–35 vote, with 17 abstentions.

The Assembly earlier had defeated the U.S. resolution to declare the expulsion of Taiwan an important question requiring a two-thirds majority. That vote was 59–55 with 15 abstentions.

The rapid resolution of the U.N.'s "China question" followed the Assembly's defeat of a motion introduced as part of a complex maneuver by Saudi Arabian Ambassador Jamil Baroody to delay voting on the key resolutions until Oct. 26. The cosponsors of the American resolution supported the motion, but the cosponsors of the Albanian resolution voiced opposition, claiming it amounted to a U.S. delaying tactic to gather support for its resolution. The U.S. side lost, 56–53, with 19 abstentions.

Moments before the vote on the Albanian resolution and after the "important question" issue had been defeated, Liu Chieh, the Chinese Nationalist representative, announced from the podium that his government would no longer take part in the proceedings. After a brief speech in which he reviewed his country's 26 years as a U.N. member and the "crimes against the Chinese people" he said the Peking regime had committed, he led the Nationalist delegation out of the Assembly.

After the vote on the Albanian resolution, Ambassador Bush told reporters he hoped the U.N. would "not relive this moment of infamy." He said that the "U.N. crossed a very dangerous bridge tonight" in expelling a member nation. He added that he had believed "we would win and it would be very, very close."

U.S. officials said Oct. 26 that the fight to keep Taiwan in the U.N. was lost because seven countries had reneged on

Resolution on Admitting Peking

The General Assembly,

Recalling the principles of the Charter of the United Nations,

Considering that the restoration of the lawful rights of the People's Republic of China is essential both for the protection of the Charter of the United Nations and for the cause that the United Nations must serve under the Charter.

Recognizing that the representatives of the Government of the People's Republic of China are the only lawful representatives of China to the United Nations and that the People's Republic of China is one of the five permanent members of the Security Council,

Decides to restore all its rights to the People's Republic of China and to recognize the representatives of its Government as the only legitimate representatives of China to the United Nations, and to expell forthwith the representatives of Chiang Kai-shek from the place which they unlawfully occupy at the United Nations and in all the organizations affiliated to it.

Sponsored by Albania, Algeria, Ceylon, Congo [Brazzaville] Cuba, Equatorial Guinea, Guinea, Iraq, Mali, Mauritania, Nepal, Pakistan, Rumania, Somalia, Southern Yemen, Syria, Sudan, Tanzania, Yemen, Yugoslavia and Zambia.

their commitments. While the officials refused to name the seven, the Washington Post reported Oct. 27 that they were Belgium, Cyprus, Morocco, Oman, Qatar, Tunisia and Trinidad-Tobago. In Washington, Secretary of State William P. Rogers said: "We'll make it clear to the nations that told us one thing and did another—that we don't particularly like that."

Official U.S. reaction—In a statement approved by President Nixon and read to newsmen by Rogers Oct. 26, the Administration welcomed Communist China's admission to the U.N. as "consistent with the policy of the U.S." but said that "at the same time, the U.S. deeply regrets the action taken by the U.N. to deprive the Republic of China of representation in that organization."

The statement added: "Although we believe that a mistake of major proportions has been made in expelling the Republic of China from the United Nations, the U.S. recognizes that the will of a majority of the members has been expressed. We, of course, accept that decision."

After reading the statement, Rogers, answering questions, said that Nixon's plans to travel to Communist China would not be altered by the setback in the U.N.

Nixon on 1971 & Future

1971 a 'breakthrough' year. President Nixon's third annual report on foreign affairs, sent to Congress Feb. 9, 1972, viewed 1971 as a "breakthrough" year in which U.S. initiatives constituted "a profound change in America's world role." "The heart of our new conception of that role," he said, "is a more balanced alliance with our friends—and a more creative connection with our adversaries."

The major focus of the report was on U.S. relations with its "two principal adversaries," the Soviet Union and China.

Although the prevailing tone of the report was optimistic—that the U.S. was "once again acting with assurance and purpose on the world stage"—the President listed numerous "disappointments" in the foreign policy area in 1971. The greatest, he said, was the failure to negotiate a Vietnam settlement.

The President also listed among "unfinished business" of the U.S. in foreign affairs:

■ "We need to prove, through additional concrete accomplishments, the benefit to both the Soviet Union and ourselves of mutual self-restraint and willingness to accommodate rather than merely assert our respective national interests."

■ "We need to continue the hopeful but delicate process of creating a better relationship between ourselves and the People's Republic of China."

■ "We need to bring the arms race under control."

■ "We need to continue with both our friends and our adversaries to build an international system which all will work to preserve because all recognize their stake in its preservation."

But, in essence, the President viewed 1971 as a "watershed year" in which "we stopped reacting" to events and began to deal "with the realities of today and the opportunities of tomorrow."

Among other highlights of the report:

Soviet Union—The President cautioned that for a long time competition would likely be "the hallmark of our relationship with the Soviet Union." He said the U.S. would be confronted with "ambiguous and contradictory trends in Soviet policy."

Despite progress toward arms control, the continuing buildup of Soviet military power was an "obvious source of deep concern," he said. And Soviet "attitudes" during the Indo-Pakistani crisis—when it seemed the U.S.S.R. preferred to let "events boil toward crisis in the hope of political gain"—held "dangerous implications for other regional conflicts, even though in the end the U.S.S.R. played a restraining role." Similarly, he said, "the U.S.S.R.'s position in the Middle East reflects a mixture of Soviet interest in expansionist policies and Soviet recognition of the dangers of confrontation."

In 1971, however, the President continued, "we have also had evidence that there can be mutual accommodation of conflicting interests, and that competition need not be translated into hostility or crisis. We have evidence that on both sides there is an increasing willingness to break with the traditional patterns of Soviet-American relations. A readiness to capitalize on this momentum is the real test of the summit" meeting planned later in the year in Moscow.

"On balance," Nixon summarized, the Soviet willingness "to take positive steps toward peace in the past year makes a meeting at the highest level timely, particularly in arms limitation and economic cooperation."

Again, there were reservations. It was unclear, the President said, whether "we. are now witnessing a permanent change in Soviet policy or only a passing phase concerned more with tactics than with a fundamental commitment to a stable international system."

As for the "tasks ahead," the President presented a list:

■ An accord on an initial strategic arms limitation agreement or on the issues to be addressed in the second stage of the SALT negotiations.

■ A discussion of the problem of the Middle East and the reasons for the failure to reach a peaceful settlement there.

■ A discussion of the problem of European security in all its aspects and the identification of mutually shared objectives which will provide a basis for further normalization of intercourse between Eastern and Western Europe.

■ An exploration of our policies in other areas of the world and the extent to which we share an interest in ●stability.

■ An examination of the possibility of additional bilateral cooperation, such as in economic relations.

The report disclosed the latest strategic arms status and continuing Russian buildup—an increase during 1971 for the U.S.S.R. in land-based intercontinental-ballistic missiles from 1,440 to 1,520, and in submarine-launched nuclear rockets from 350 to 500, while the U.S. deterrent remained constant at 1,054 ICBMs and 656 submarine-launched missiles.

This posed the question, the President said, "whether the Soviet Union seeks the numbers and types of forces needed to attack and destroy vital elements of our own strategic forces."

"Under no circumstances," Nixon pledged, "will I permit the further erosion of the strategic balance with the U.S.S.R." He said he was confident that "Congress shares these sentiments."

Nevertheless, the President expected a strategic-arms-limitation agreement to be reached soon. He suggested (a) that antiballistic-missile (ABM) systems have "comprehensive limitations" placed on them by a "long-term commitment formalized in a treaty," and (b) that offensive weapons, such as ICBMs and missile-firing submarines be frozen at current strength levels by "an interim agreement." The separate agreements, he said, would preserve "an essential linkage" between limitation of offensive and defensive forces.

China—Nixon said he looked forward to his trip to Peking, cautioning anew that it would open a political dialogue but would "certainly not bring a quick resolution of the deep differences" between the two nations. But the "hope of genuine communication" with China, he said, should promote Asian stability and world peace.

He emphasized that this new initiative in U.S. policy toward China was "not aimed against Moscow" and should not "be read as shifting our priorities from Tokyo to Peking."

Nixon in China

President Richard M. Nixon's visit to the People's Republic of China took place Feb. 21–28, 1972. It produced a joint statement that recognized differences in views and goals of the U.S. and Peking but emphasized the need for improved contacts between the two countries.

Pre-departure activity. Three days before his Feb. 17 departure for China, Nixon further relaxed barriers to trade with China and conferred with Andre Malraux, the French writer and specialist in Chinese affairs.

Ronald L. Ziegler, White House press secretary, said Feb. 14 that the effect of Nixon's directive on trade with China was to place that country under the same liberalized trade restrictions as those applying to the Soviet Union and to remove China from an export control group which included North Korea, North Vietnam and Cuba. China would now be able to buy under general licenses from U.S. firms such items as locomotives, construction equipment, industrial chemicals, internal combustion engines and rolling mills. Special licenses would still be needed for the purchase of items considered strategic.

Nixon met for nearly an hour and a half with Malraux in a session attended by Kissinger and by a State Department interpreter. Malraux said at a news conference before returning to Paris Feb. 15 that he had discussed with Nixon the prospect of the U.S. aiding the Chinese economy by "a Marshall Plan, with all the dangers it entails." He said he thought the President would "envisage" and "consider" the proposal if it were advanced by China's leaders.

In a farewell statement made during ceremonies at the White House, Nixon described himself as being "under no illusions that 20 years of hostility between the People's Republic of China and the U.S. are going to be swept away by one week of talks that we will have there." Referring to the words of a toast given by Chinese Premier Chou En-lai to Kissinger at the time of Kissinger's visit to Peking in October 1971, the President said that both the Americans and the Chinese were "a great people" and that their separation by "a vast ocean and great differences in philosophy should not prevent them from finding common ground." He noted "that if there was a postscript that I hope might be written with regard to this trip, it would be the words on the plaque which was left on the moon by our first astronauts when they landed there. We came in peace for all mankind."

Members of President Nixon's official party had been announced by the White House Feb. 12. They were: Secretary of State William P. Rogers; Kissinger; H.R. Haldeman, assistant to the President; Ziegler; Brig. Gen. Brent Scowcroft, military assistant to the President; Marshall Green, assistant secretary of state for East Asian and Pacific affairs; Dwight L. Chapin, deputy assistant to the President; John A. Scali, special consultant to the President; Patrick J. Buchanan, special assistant to the President; Rose Mary Woods, personal secretary to the President; Alfred L. Jenkins, State Department director for Asian Communist affairs; John Holdridge, staff member of the National Security Council, and Winston Lord, special assistant to Kissinger.

Ziegler also said that an "unofficial" party of "approximately 21" would include Gerald L. Warren, deputy White House press secretary; Brig. Gen. Walter R. Tkach, the President's physician; Ronald Walker, staff assistant to the President; Timothy Elbourne, a press aide, and a number of "secretarial assistants." The total press contingent was to number 168, including 87 newsmen, 13 satellite ground station technicians and 68 other communications personnel.

A party of 61 U.S. radio and television technicians flew into Peking Feb. 1 and were joined by 18 others Feb. 14, the

New York Times reported.

A new communications satellite, Intelstat 4, which would broadcast reports of Nixon's visit to China, went into operation Feb. 14 and a temporary receiving station in Peking, built by the Hughes Tool Company, was reported to have been leased to the Chinese government. RCA Global Communications, Inc. announced Feb. 15 that it was installing a permanent station in Shanghai, which would be purchased by China for $2.9 million.

Visit begins. Nixon arrived in China Feb. 21. Although the airport reception was restrained, Nixon later in the day met with Chairman Mao Tse-tung, an event which had not been announced beforehand.

With Mrs. Nixon and other members of the traveling party, the President had stopped Feb. 17 and 18 at the Kaneohe Marine Corps Air Station in Hawaii. The party then flew to Guam, crossing the international dateline, for another overnight stay Feb. 20. After landing at Shanghai to pick up a Chinese navigator for the last leg of the 11,500-mile journey, the Presidential jet touched down at Hung Chiao Airport in Peking.

On hand to greet the U.S. visitors were Premier Chou En-lai, several other Chinese dignitaries and a 500-man military honor guard. There were no crowds, no apparent efforts to decorate the city and no speeches.

President Nixon's visit with Chairman Mao, which took place at Mao's residence somewhere in the old Forbidden City, lasted one hour and was described afterwards as "frank and serious." Spokesmen for both sides declined to say what had been discussed. Nixon was accompanied by Kissinger. Mao was aided by Premier Chou and by Wang Hai-jung, deputy director of protocol, and Tang Wen-sheng, an interpreter.

The Chinese were hosts at a banquet the evening of Feb. 21 at the Great Hall of the People. Chou offered a toast to the Nixon party in which he said that Nixon's visit "provides the leaders of the two countries with an opportunity of meeting in person to seek the normalization of relations between the two countries and also to exchange views on questions of concern." Calling the trip a "positive move," he said that Sino-U.S. "contacts" had been suspended "owing to reasons known to all." The social systems of the two countries were "fundamentally different and there exist great differences between the Chinese government and the U.S. government."

Nonetheless, Chou said, "normal state relations" could still be established "on the basis of the five principles of mutual respect for sovereignty and territorial integrity; mutual nonaggression; noninterference in each other's internal affairs; equality and mutual benefits, and peaceful coexistence."

President Nixon responded by noting that "more people are seeing and hearing what we say than on any other occasion in the whole history of the world." He said that if the two countries could "find common ground to work together, the chance for world peace is immeasurably increased." The U.S. and China had "at times in the past been enemies. We have great differences today. What brings us together is that we have common interests which transcend those differences." There was "no reason for us to be enemies. Neither of us seeks the territory of the other. Neither of us seeks domination over the other. Neither of us seeks to stretch out our hands and rule the world."

In the central portion of his toast, Nixon referred to the legendary Long March of 1934-35, in which Mao's army broke through an encirclement by the forces of Chiang Kai-shek and traveled some 6,000 miles from their base in Kiangsi Province to the caves of Yenan, in Shensi Province, where they lived for more than a decade.

Nixon declared: "And so let us, in these next five days, start a long march together. Not in lockstep, but on different roads leading to the same goal: the goal of building a world structure of peace and justice in which all may stand together with equal dignity and in which each nation, large or small, has a right to determine its own form of government free of outside interference of domination."

4-hour meeting with Chou—Nixon and Chou met Feb. 22 for four hours of policy discussions. Accompanying the President were Kissinger and John H. Holdridge and Winston Lord of the National Security Council.

Those attending with Chou were: Yeh Chien-ying, deputy chairman of the Communist party Central Committee's military commission; Li Hsien-nien, a deputy premier; Wang Hai-jung; Chiao Kuan-hua, a deputy foreign minister; and Chang Wen-chin, head of the European, American and Australian section at the Foreign Ministry.

Secretary of State William P. Rogers and Foreign Minister Chi Peng-fei held a separate conference.

In the evening, after a private dinner, the Nixons attended a special performance of "Red Detachment of Women," a revolutionary opera fashioned by Chiang Ching, Mao's wife and a member of the Politburo. Chou and his wife, Teng Ying-chiao, also attended the performance.

Chinese told of visit—The Communist party newspaper Jenmin Jih Pao, after publishing only a formal announcement of Nixon's visit the previous day, devoted two of its six pages Feb. 22 to the President's arrival, featuring photos of Nixon and Mao shaking hands. Chinese television, which had ignored the event in its evening news bulletin Feb. 21, carried a 10-minute film of Nixon's activities Feb. 22.

(Mrs. Nixon disclosed Feb. 22 that at the previous evening's banquet Premier Chou had offered as a gift to the U.S. two giant pandas, apparently being given in recognition for two musk oxen President Nixon had ordered sent to China.)

Nixon and Chou met Feb. 23 for four more hours of talks. They were followed in the evening by exhibitions of gymnastics and table tennis. Mrs. Nixon visited the Evergreen People's Commune, an agricultural cooperative near the capital, and the Peking Glassware Factory. Jenmin Jih Pao, in an article at the bottom of the front page, printed four more photographs showing aspects of the Nixon trip.

Sino-American exchanges hinted—President Nixon Feb. 24 made excursions to the Great Wall of China, a fortification built in pre-Christian times to keep out barbarian invaders, and to the Ming Tombs, which had been constructed by members of a dynasty that ruled China from the 14th to the 17th centuries. Some of Nixon's comments to newsmen were taken as an indication that his talks with Premier Chou had explored the prospect of Sino-U.S. tourist exchanges.

Speaking informally to reporters for the first time during his visit, Nixon said: "I think that you would have to conclude that this is a great wall and it had to be built by a great people. Many lives, of course, were lost in building it. There was no machinery or equipment at the time. It had to all be done by hand. But under the circumstances it is a certain symbol of what China in the past has been and what China in the future can become.... As we look at this wall, we do not want walls of any kind between peoples."

He hoped one result of the journey to Peking might be that "peoples, regardless of their differences and backgrounds and philosophies, will have an opportunity to communicate with each other, and to share with each other those particular endeavors that will mean peaceful progress in the years ahead."

According to the Washington Post Feb. 25, Nixon remarked on his way to the Ming Tombs that one outcome of his talks with Chou might be "apart from relations between governments, that people will be able to come here and that, of course, Chinese people would be able to come to the U.S."

President Nixon held talks for three hours again Feb. 24 with Chou En-lai. The session was followed by a private dinner, which was also attended by Secretary Rogers and Foreign Minister Chi, whose meetings were reported to be continuing.

Visit to Forbidden City—In their last full day in Peking, Nixon and his party Feb. 25 visited the Forbidden City, where the Nixons viewed the palaces and courtyards of ancient Chinese emperors. Later in the afternoon Nixon and Chou met for about an hour of private talks. That night at the Great Hall of the People, Nixon gave a banquet for Chou at which their mutual toasts suggested the substance of a joint communique released in Shanghai Feb. 27.

The President remarked that the U.S. and China had "begun the long process of removing that wall between us" and he ended his toast with a quotation from George Washington's farewell address: "Observe good faith and justice toward all nations, cultivate peace and harmony with all."

Chou said the two sides had exchanged views on "the normalization of relations" although there existed "great differences of principle" between them. He added: "The times are advancing and the world changes. We are deeply convinced that the strength of the people is powerful and that whatever zigzags and reverses there will be in the development of history, the general trend of the world is definitely toward light and not darkness."

The Nixons Feb. 26 journeyed to Hangchow, a resort city 100 miles southwest of Shanghai, where they were the guests of Nan Ping, chairman of the Revolutionary Committee of Chekiang Province, of which Hangchow was the capital.

The following day, in the company of Chou En-lai, the Nixons flew to Shanghai.

Shanghai communique favors contacts. Nixon and Premier Chou En-lai released a joint communique Feb. 27 indicating that their talks had resulted in agreement on the need for increased Sino-U.S. contacts and for eventual withdrawal of U.S. troops from Taiwan, held by the Nationalist Chinese. The communique was issued in Shanghai.

Nixon and his party then left China Feb. 28 to return to the U.S.

The 1,800-word communique, showing the results of talks by the two sides, had been reached after several nights of intensive negotiation and was divided into five sections. The first was a general account of the President's stay in China.

In the second part of the statement, each nation recorded separately its views on Asian policy issues.

The U.S. emphasized its support for an eight-point plan proposed by the U.S. and South Vietnam in January as a basis for bringing the Indochina war to an end. It added: "In the absence of a negotiated settlement the U.S. envisages the ultimate withdrawal of all U.S. forces from the region consistent with the aim of self-determination for each country of Indochina." The U.S. would "maintain its close ties with and support for the Republic of [South] Korea." Washington "places the highest value on its friendly relations with Japan; it will continue to develop the existing close bonds." Regarding the India-Pakistan dispute, the U.S. favored a continuation of the cease-fire and "the withdrawal of all military forces to within their own territories and to their own sides of the cease-fire line in Jammu and Kashmir."

In its statement, China announced its support for Viet Cong and North Vietnamese proposals, favored North Korean proposals for the "peaceful unification" of Korea and opposed the "revival and outward expansion of Japanese militarism."

The third section of the communique pointed out that although there were "essential differences" in the "social systems and foreign policies" of the U.S. and China, "the two sides agreed" on general rules of international relations.

These were that countries "should conduct their relations on the principles of respect for the sovereignty and territorial integrity of all states, nonaggression against other states, noninterference in the internal affairs of other states, equality and mutual benefit, and peaceful coexistence."

(These principles had been enunciated by Chou En-lai as early as 1955 at the Bandung Conference of Asian and African Peoples.)

The two sides further agreed that progress toward "the normalization of relations" between them was "in the interests of all countries"; both wished "to reduce the danger of international military conflict"; neither "should seek hegemony in the Asia-Pacific region and each is opposed to the efforts by any other country or group of countries to establish such hegemony"; neither "is prepared to negotiate on behalf of any third party or to enter into agreements or understandings with the other directed at other states."

The fourth part of the text was given over to separate statements on Taiwan. The Chinese declared that the "Taiwan question is the crucial question obstructing the normalization of relations" between Washington and Peking. In the remainder of the passage, China reaffirmed its traditional claims to the island, emphasizing that the "liberation of Taiwan is China's internal affair."

The communique said: "The Chinese government firmly opposes any activities which aim at the creation of 'one China, one Taiwan,' 'one China, two governments,' 'two Chinas' and 'independent Taiwan,' or advocate that 'the status of Taiwan remains to be determined.'"

The U.S. said: "The U.S. acknowledges that all Chinese on either side of the Taiwan Strait maintain there is but one China and that Taiwan is a part of China. The U.S. government does not challenge that position. It reaffirms its interest in a peaceful settlement of the Taiwan question by the Chinese themselves. With this prospect in mind, it affirms the ultimate objective of the withdrawal of all U.S. forces and military installations from Taiwan. In the meantime, it will progressively reduce its forces and military installations on Taiwan as the tension in the area diminishes."

In the communique's final section, both sides said they had discussed joint contacts "in such fields as science, technology, culture, sports and journalism" and that they planned to "facilitate the further development of such contacts and exchanges." The desirability of increasing "bilateral trade" was stressed. It was agreed to send "a senior U.S. representative to Peking from time to time for concrete consultations to further the normalization of relations between the two countries and continue to exchange views on issues of common interest."

At a banquet given after the release of the communique, Nixon declared that "our two peoples tonight hold the future of the world in our hands." He said the talks with Mao and Chou had been "characterized by frankness, by honesty, by determination and above all by mutual respect."

The President noted that both the Chinese and the American people were dedicated to the principle "that never again shall foreign domination, foreign occupation, be visited upon this city or any part of China or any independent country in this world."

Kissinger briefing on communique—
Henry A. Kissinger briefed the press in Shanghai Feb. 27 on aspects of the Sino-U.S. communique. Kissinger was accompanied by Marshall Green, assistant secretary of state for East Asian and Pacific Affairs, who had been with Secretary of State William P. Rogers in his talks with Chinese Foreign Minister Chi Peng-fei.

In explaining how the communique was produced, Kissinger said both sides had tried to insure that the document "would not pretend to an agreement that did not exist and which would have to be interpreted away in the subsequent implementation." To assemble materials for the text of the communique, he said, "issues of general principle" were first discussed in meetings between President Nixon and Premier Chou. Then the discussions were transferred "to the meetings chaired by" Secretary Rogers and Foreign Minister Chi. If "any additional issues arose," they were sent back to Nixon and Chou.

Kissinger said that for the previous "few nights" this process had gone on until "the early hours of the morning." He remarked that the document "ought to be seen in two aspects: first, in terms of the specific principles and conclusions it states, and secondly, in terms of the direction to which it seeks to point."

Green explained that the meetings he attended had been notable for their "candor, friendliness and courtesy" but that participants had been "outspoken" with "no effort to cover up or paper over differences."

Responding to questions from newsmen, Kissinger declared that the portion of the text promising a gradual reduction of the U.S.' armed forces on Taiwan was "a general statement of our policy which we have enunciated on innumerable occasions in innumerable forms." He said the communique was "a fair characterization of the basic positions" of both sides regarding the issue of U.S. prisoners of war in Vietnam.

Asked what features of the communique indicated significant steps by China since its 1971 invitation brought a U.S. table-tennis team to mainland China, Kissinger replied: "The formalization of exchanges encouraged by the two governments, the opening of trade encouraged by the two governments, the establishment of a diplomatic mechanism for continued contact, the joint statement of some general principles of international relations, the joint statement of some basic approaches to the view of the world with respect to, for instance, the section which includes the reference to hegemony—these, I believe, are matters that most of us would have considered unthinkable at the time of the invitation to the ping-pong team."

President's return home. President and Mrs. Nixon were greeted by crowds and a military band Feb. 28 at Andrews Air Force Base in Maryland following a nine-hour stopover near Anchorage, Alaska to allow a period of rest after the flight from Shanghai.

In a nationally televised address to the crowd, the President said his trip had shown "that nations with very deep and fundamental differences can learn to discuss those differences calmly, rationally and frankly without compromising principles" and that this amounted to "the basis of a structure for peace."

Nixon said he and his Chinese hosts had "agreed on some rules of international conduct which will reduce the risk of confrontation and war in Asia and the Pacific," and had "set up a procedure whereby we can continue to have discussions in the future." They had also decided, he said, "that we will not negotiate the fate of other nations behind their back and we did not do so in Peking. There were no secret deals of any kind."

The President described the Shanghai communique as "unique in honestly setting forth differences rather than trying to cover them up with diplomatic double-talk." He explained "We did not bring back any written or unwritten agreements that will guarantee peace in our time. We did not bring home any magic formula which will make unnecessary the efforts of the American people to continue to maintain the strength so that we can continue to be free."

Chinese premier visited Hanoi. Former Cambodian Chief of State Prince Noro-

dom Sihanouk disclosed March 9 that Chinese Premier Chou En-lai had briefed North Vietnamese leaders on his talks with President Nixon and assured them of Peking's support in the Indochina struggle. The U.S. government was said to have received authoritative reports confirming that the discussions had been held in Hanoi March 3-4 and that Chou had returned to China March 5.

Speaking in Shanghai, Sihanouk said March 9 that Chou had informed him in a three-hour conversation that Nixon had been told in the Peking summit talks that China would not mediate the Indochina war by acting as an intermediary between Washington and the "Indochinese resistance." Chou "told me it was China's duty to support these resistance movements until total victory," Sihanouk said.

According to the exiled Cambodian leader, Peking had informed Nixon that "if the U.S. desires sincerely to improve and normalize relations with China it should end the aggressive war against Indochina." Chou had told Nixon that if the U.S. continued to stay in Indochina, "tensions will be lasting and perhaps will increase if you continue your air escalation," Sihanouk said. The prince said Chou had told the President that the U.S. must solve the Indochina problem before the Taiwan dispute.

White House Press Secretary Ronald L. Ziegler refused March 9 to make a direct comment on Sihanouk's statement that Nixon had sought to have China serve as intermediary in Indochina. Ziegler only referred to that section of the Feb. 27 joint U.S.-Chinese communique that stated neither country was "prepared to negotiate on behalf of any third party or to enter into agreements or understandings with the other directed at other states."

China Trip's Aftermath

Conservatives critical of communique. The President's trip and final communique drew criticism from conservative Republicans, who objected to the U.S. withdrawal from Taiwan and the absence in the communique of any mention of the mutual defense pact with the Nationalist Chinese.

According to Sen. James L. Buckley (Conservative-Republican, N.Y.) Feb. 28, the communique was "being widely interpreted both at home and abroad as signaling the ultimate abandonment of Taiwan" by the U.S. "If we permit doubts about our intentions to persist with respect to our security agreement with Taiwan," he said, "we will undercut the credibility of our arrangements with Japan, South Korea and our other Asian allies as well."

The senator's brother, William F. Buckley Jr., publisher of the National Review, joined in the criticism. Buckley, a member of the press party accompanying the President to China, objected Feb. 29 to the President's acknowledgment that the Peking-Taiwan dispute was an internal matter and to the U.S. making it clear it was "pulling out of that area and yielding to Red China's dominance in that area."

"His desire for the spotlight in China," Buckley said, "transformed, subtly, his analysis of what was going on into a desire for maximum political publicity." By so doing, he said, concessions had been made that undermined the "whole moral basis" of U.S. treaty commitments in Asia.

Buckley made the comments in Manchester, N.H., where he endorsed Rep. John M. Ashbrook (R, Ohio) in his campaign against Nixon in the presidential primary. Ashbrook, with Buckley in agreement, deplored the Taiwan aspect of the communique as a "sellout of principle."

Ashbrook had said Feb. 27 that he was "shocked and dismayed at President Nixon's decision to accept Communist China's central demand of the past 22 years—unilateral withdrawal of all U.S. forces from the Republic of China on Taiwan."

Some conservatives satisfied—Reassuring statements that the President had not undermined basic conservative positions concerning Taiwan were issued March 1 by GOP Sens. Barry M. Goldwater (Ariz.) and Gordon Allott (Colo.), chairman of the Senate Republican Policy Committee. Goldwater expressed satisfaction "we have not given away one single thing to the Red Chinese."

Allott said there was "no basic change in policy regarding Taiwan involved in the joint communique."

Humphrey, Jackson criticism. Only a few of the many Democratic presidential contenders criticized the Nixon trip to China. Sen. Henry M. Jackson (Wash.) observed Feb. 28 "it appears that we are doing the withdrawing and they are doing the staying." He said "that does not strike me as a good horse trade."

Sen. Hubert Humphrey (Minn.) said Feb. 28 on first interpretation it appeared that Nixon had made concessions but the Chinese had not.

Many of the Democratic candidates, however, considered the Nixon trip and communique a step forward diplomatically. Sen. Edward M. Kennedy (Mass.), a major critic of the Administration, Feb. 28 called the communique "one of the most progressive documents" in the history of American diplomacy and hailed "the bridge that has now been built to Peking."

International reaction. The Assembly of Nationalist China Feb. 21 adopted unanimously a resolution declaring that Nixon's visit "deeply and greatly hurts the interests of the Republic of China."

It said that since Nixon "is going to negotiate with an illegal entity, the government and people of the Republic of China will consider null and void any agreement that may emerge from his talks with the Peking leadership." Taiwan would "never change its national policy of regaining the Chinese mainland and will under no circumstances negotiate or reach a compromise with the Chinese Communists at any time."

A Viet Cong radio broadcast Feb. 24 accused Nixon of trying to "capitalize on the internal disagreements of the Socialist camp in order to further his interests."

Indian Prime Minister Indira Gandhi told an election rally Feb. 21 in New Delhi: "If the meetings between the American and Chinese leaders are meant to forge friendship, it is welcome to us. But apprehensions are being expressed that the talks are meant to form some sort of a new power group. If so, India—

though a small nation—will not be bound by any such decision which seeks to dictate terms to Asian countries."

The Soviet government newspaper Izvestia Feb. 21 said China was keeping silent about the U.S. bombing of North Vietnam during Nixon's visit. The paper declared: "At present it is no secret for anyone that Nixon's trip to Peking, advertised in every way by Washington propaganda as 'a visit in the name of peace,' is taking place against a background of severe enlargement of the U.S. military clique's piratical actions in Indochina."

While acknowledging that the journey might be valuable if it did not run directly counter to Soviet interests, Yuri Zhukov had said Feb. 17 in the Communist party newspaper Pravda that there was "evidence of a desire both in the Peking leadership and in certain quarters in Washington to use the process of development of American-Chinese contacts to the detriment of a relaxation of international tension."

In Rumania, the party newspaper Scinteia Feb. 23 said the trip was proof of "a realistic stand" and "an important positive act with broad impacts on international life as a whole."

South Vietnam's first official comment on the trip was in remarks March 1 by Foreign Minister Tran Van Lam, who said he was not upset by the Sino-U.S. communique's reference to the ultimate withdrawal of U.S. forces from Indochina.

Lam declared: "It has already been agreed between our two governments that when Vietnamese troops are fully trained and equipped the American troops will go home." He also said: "We fully approve of Mr. Nixon's trip. No one can deny that it helped create an atmosphere of eased tensions. . . . The U.S. has been very correct and faithful in its commitments to Vietnam, and we especially appreciate the mention of our eight-point peace proposal."

U.N. Secretry General Kurt Waldheim commented Feb. 28 that Nixon's visit had been "about what I had expected" and said he hoped it would help bring about "further contacts and possibly further actions."

Taiwan scorns communique. The Nationalist Chinese Foreign Ministry issued a statement Feb. 28 denouncing the Sino-U.S. communique. Taiwan newspapers joined in condemning the document.

The Foreign Ministry dispatch repeated the government's earlier warning that it would consider "null and void" any agreement "which has been and which may not have been published, involving the rights and interests of the government and people of the Republic of China, reached between the U.S. and the Chinese Communist regime."

The "so-called 'question ot Taiwan' " would be "solved only when the government of the Republic of China, the sole legitimate government elected by all people of China, has succeeded in its task of the recovery of the mainland, the unification of China and the deliverance of our compatriots. There is definitely no other alternative." These efforts "have as their objectives not only the salvation of China but also that of Asia and the world."

The daily newspaper Chung-kuo Shih Pao said President Nixon had "gained nothing in return for his statement about the withdrawal. Not even a specific commitment that the Chinese Communists will not resort to the use of force in the Taiwan area." Lien Ho Pao, the largest paper on the island, said the Nixon journey had been a "complete failure."

Rogers assures Taiwan—James C. H. Shen, Nationalist Chinese ambassador to the U.S., said in Washington March 2 that Secretary of State William P. Rogers had assured him that day of the U.S. commitment to the 1954 Taiwan defense treaty.

Nationalist Foreign Minister Chow Shu-kai said in an interview March 2 that there was now less prospect than ever of a negotiated settlement between Peking and Taipei because in the Shanghai communique, Peking had noted its plan to "liberate" Taiwan. This seemed to Chow to rule out any "sensible" discussion of the matter. (Andre Malraux, the French writer, said in an interview with Agence France-Presse March 2 that he believed there was a secret Peking-Taipei accord under terms of which Taiwan would be controlled by the mainland government after Chiang Kai-shek's death. Malraux asserted: "I don't think

Nixon gave up anything over Formosa because there has been for at least five years an agreement between Peking and Taipei, linked with the death of Chiang Kai-shek.")

Taiwan March 7 announced its intention to seek diplomatic contacts with Communist nations "if they are not the puppets of" the Peking government. The policy was enunciated at a meeting of the Kuomintang party by Foreign Minister Chow, who added: "Since the confrontation between Soviet Russia and Communist China, the relationship between Communist countries has become more complicated.... Whether to establish diplomatic relations with any other country should be decided on the basis of whether it would be good for us."

Soviet Union equivocal. The official Soviet news agency Tass Feb. 28 gave a long account of the Sino-U.S. communique, noting with approval Peking's support for the Viet Cong peace proposal and mentioning that the communique had stressed "essential differences between China and the U.S."

The trade union newspaper Trud declared Feb. 29, however, that the Chinese leaders had "broken all records to curry favor" with the U.S. It added: "The entire progressive world, along with the condemnation of the activities of American imperialism against the peace and freedom of peoples, also condemns the Maoists for having entered a dangerous plot with the ruling circles of the U.S." Trud cited favorably what it claimed were evaluations of the Nixon trip made by U.S. newsmen, who "jokingly called it the show of the century because it was well-rehearsed, combed and sleek."

A Feb. 25 statement by the Soviet Defense Ministry, appearing in the armed forces newspaper Krasnaya Zvezda, had said China was annually setting aside approximately one-third of its budget ($8 billion to $8.5 billion) for military expenditures.

It asserted that Peking was intensifying "purely military measures to prepare for war, such as the development and stockpiling of modern weapons, widespread military construction in border districts, and military training of the population through the system of people's volunteers functioning even in

peacetime." The paper said of China's trade with capitalist countries that "a greater and greater proportion consists of goods of a strategic character: nonferrous and rare metals, equipment and materials necessary for the production of nuclear weapons and the means of their delivery, and even military equipment."

U.S. assures Japan. Marshall Green, assistant secretary of state for East Asian Affairs, and John H. Holdridge, an Asian specialist for the National Security Council staff, arrived in Tokyo from Shanghai Feb. 28 to discuss President Nixon's visit to China with officials of the Japanese government.

Green and Holdridge met Feb. 28 with Foreign Minister Takeo Fukuda, who had told newsmen the previous day he thought the President's visit had been fruitful.

Green in Seoul—Green told South Korean Foreign Minister Kim Yong Shik March 1 that President Nixon had made no secret deals during his China visit. Green repeated his message the following day in interviews with Premier Kim Chong Pil and President Chung Hee Park.

Foreign Minister Kim had told newsmen Feb. 28: "We welcome the American support for our position on the Korean problem, opposing Communist China's stand." Kim said his people regarded the Shanghai communique as "reaffirmation of the U.S. pledge to stand with us for the defense of our nation."

Green reassures South Vietnamese— Green met South Vietnamese President Nguyen Van Thieu March 6 in Saigon. A March 7 dispatch from the Vietnamese Foreign Ministry said Green had "strongly affirmed that there had been no secret arrangements between the U.S. and Communist China concerning the Vietnam issue" and that "there had been no secret contacts between the U.S. and North Vietnam under any form and by any persons during the China visit."

Green left that morning for Thailand and made stops on the way in Laos and Cambodia. He had a meeting with Laotian Premier Souvanna Phouma in Vientiane and later saw Cambodian Deputy Premier Sisowath Sirik Matak and Foreign Minister Koun Wick. He reportedly told them that the U.S. was looking for a settlement in which "the armed forces of all Indochinese states will remain within their national frontiers." Sirik Matak remarked March 8 that he had been assured by Green that the Nixon trip to China had not affected the Cambodian situation. "We will continue to receive U.S. aid and all guarantees that we would desire to have," he said. In Bangkok March 8, Green met with Thai Premier Thanom Kittikachorn.

Review of alliances rejected. U.S. Secretary of State William P. Rogers March 8 rejected a suggestion by a Democratic senator that the U.S. review its military alliances in the Pacific in light of Washington's new relations with China.

The suggestion was made by Sen. Frank Church (D, Idaho) during Rogers' appearance before a Senate Foreign Relations Committee hearing.

In response to Church's suggestion, Rogers said it would be "very unfortunate to leave the impression that, now that the visit to the People's Republic of China has taken place, we are thinking of treaty revisions with countries who have based their foreign policy on such treaties."

One of the treaties Church said should be subject to review was the Southeast Asia Treaty Organization (SEATO), originally set up in the 1950s to counter possible Chinese expansion in the Pacific area.

Church called the SEATO pact "a corpse," which had been abandoned by at least three U.S. allies. He said it deserved a "decent burial" to avoid use in foreign entanglements.

Rogers expressed concern at the timing of Church's remarks. He pointed out that the Administration had gone to considerable lengths to reassure its Asian allies that Nixon's trip to China would not undermine the various alliances with the U.S.

Congress leaders in China. As a result of the Nixon trip, visits to China were made

by Senate Democratic leader Mike Mansfield (Mont.) and Republican leader Hugh Scott (Pa.) and by House Democratic leader Hale Boggs (La.) and Republican leader Gerald R. Ford (Mich.). The Senators went to China on Chinese Premier Chou En-lai's invitation, and the Representatives received an invitation later after House leaders protested their exclusion from the original invitation.

White House Press Secretary Ronald L. Ziegler said the invitation, which had originated with Chou, had been extended to the leaders by President Nixon when he met with Congressional leaders Feb. 29 to brief them on his recent China trip. Other members of Congress also were briefed Feb. 29 by Henry A. Kissinger, the President's chief foreign policy adviser. The President also briefed his cabinet Feb. 29.

Mansfield commented after the briefing that the group meeting with the President had been "unanimously in favor of the President's trip and what he accomplished."

Scott said he had "no doubt whatever . . . that we have in no way by this visit altered our treaty commitments to Korea, Taiwan or Japan."

Scott also said Nixon had stressed that the promise to withdraw U.S. troops from Taiwan, as mentioned in the final communique, was not to be considered a separate item and was not unrelated to a decrease in tensions in Asia, particularly in Vietnam. Scott indicated that the current U.S. force of 8,000 men on Taiwan would be reduced to 2,000 with total withdrawal contingent upon a peaceful settlement of differences between Taiwan and Peking.

Mansfield and Scott arrived in China April 18 and met with Chou April 20. They returned May 7 and filed separate reports with the Senate May 11.

Mansfield said he thought it "illusory" to hope that, out of a desire to improve relations with the U.S., China would influence North Vietnam to end the war or release American prisoners. He also declared that "the new sorties into North Vietnam have tarnished the significance of the President's visit to China and, of course, the visit of the Senate's joint leadership. They have thrown into at least temporary eclipse the possibilities of Chinese-U.S. rapprochement."

Scott said the U.S. and China should "normalize relations to the greatest extent possible. At the same time we must remain alert to the fact that there are basic philosophical differences in our views of man and society."

The two Representatives filed their reports July 8 after a 10-day visit. They informed the House that Chinese officials had expressed concern to them about the possible combination of a Soviet arms buildup and U.S. disarmament and withdrawal from the Pacific and other regions.

Boggs asserted that the concern had been expressed in conversations with Premier Chou En-lai and other Chinese officials. "As they put it," he reported, "there are two superpowers—the United States and Russia—and if Russia becomes the greater superpower then much of the world is in difficulty."

Ford said the Chinese officials had shown "a great deal of interest" in "the sufficiency of our military capability and what our direction might be in the future with respect to the Defense Department funding and its programs." "They don't want the United States to withdraw from the Pacific or the world at any point," Ford said.

The Soviet Communist party newspaper Pravda published an attack July 16 on the Chinese leadership on the basis of the Boggs and Ford remarks, which were categorically denied by Chinese sources July 17. The sources denied that China desired a continued U.S. presence in the Far East and said Chou had protested to the visiting congressmen about the apparent strengthening of U.S. forces in other areas, particularly in Thailand and off the coast of Vietnam, while the U.S. withdrew its troops from Vietnam.

Sino-U.S. talks in Paris. The U.S. and Chinese ambassadors to France met March 13 in Paris for the first in what was described as a projected series of private discussions on matters of interest to the two countries.

The talks, conducted for the U.S. by

Arthur K. Watson and for China by Huang Chen, took place in the Chinese embassy and lasted nearly an hour. Afterwards they were described as "warm and cordial" by Watson, who added: "Today's was just the beginning of several meetings and we hope we will be continuing the dialogue."

In announcing the talks March 10, White House Press Secretary Ronald L. Ziegler had said Paris was chosen "primarily because it was felt that it would be a mutually convenient location." He emphasized, however, that the choice "does not close other channels." He said that in the following meetings, the problems discussed would be "far broader than anything ever taken up in Geneva and Warsaw."

U.S. represented at Canton fair. The New York Times reported April 8 that several U.S. companies had been invited to send representatives to the Canton Trade Fair, a month-long event beginning April 15 at which more than half of China's $2 billion in yearly exports were sold.

The firms were R. H. Macy & Co., Inc., the May Lee Import-Export Corp., the Sino-American Council and the Industrial Chemical and Dye Co., Inc., all of New York and a San Francisco group representing the U.S. Committee for a New China Policy, the Greater San Francisco Chamber of Commerce and the California Council on International Trade.

Chinese team tours in U.S. A table-tennis team from the People's Republic of China ended a tour of the U.S. April 30 after arriving in the country April 12 from Canada and playing exhibition matches in major cities.

The visitors traveled to Detroit, Ann Arbor, Mich., and Washington, where they met President Nixon April 18. Following a tour of Williamsburg, Va., the Chinese played a match at the United Nations in New York April 19. They then went to Memphis, Los Angeles and San Francisco before leaving for a two-week stay in Mexico.

Detente Advances: 1972-74

U.S.-Soviet Cordiality

In May 1972 Richard M. Nixon became the first U.S. President to visit Moscow. Despite major and minor disagreements between the U.S. and Soviet Union before and after Nixon's visit, the President's trip appeared to symbolize an overwhelming net improvement in U.S.-Soviet cooperation and cordiality. ·

Brezhnev welcomes Nixon visit. Soviet Communist Party General Secretary Leonid I. Brezhnev said March 20, 1972 in a talk at a trade union convention in Moscow that he hoped President Nixon's planned visit to the Soviet Union would lead to a better understanding between the two countries.

In a speech covering a range of domestic and foreign policy issues, Brezhnev declared:

"We approach the forthcoming Soviet-American talks from business-like, realistic positions. We are fully aware of the importance of the state of Soviet-American relations for the life of the people of both countries, as well as for the entire international situation, for its further development in the direction of lasting peace or in the direction of growing military danger. That is why we consider it our duty to find such areas in relations between the U.S.S.R.

and the U.S. that would make it possible, without retreating from the principles of our policy, to establish a certain degree of mutually advantageous cooperation in the interests of the peoples of both countries and the strengthening of universal peace." Such cooperation was "desirable, but, of course not at the expense of third parties."

On Nixon's recent visit to China, Brezhnev said that it was "quite natural" for Washington and Peking to want to establish normal relations. It would be up to "future actions of the U.S. and China" to reflect "the significance of the Peking talks."

Brezhnev remarked that there was cause to wonder whether the talks might have gone "beyond the framework of the bilateral relations" between the two states. "How else can one assess the statement made at a banquet in Shanghai that 'our two peoples tonight hold the future of the world in our hands'?"

Referring to Chinese insistence that relations with the Soviet Union be conducted on the basis of peaceful coexistence, the Soviet leader commented: "Well, if the people in Peking are not prepared for more in relations with a Socialist state, we are ready to develop Soviet-Chinese relations on that basis, too."

The Soviet Union attached "serious importance to the Soviet-American strategic arms limitation talks," Brezhnev said. "The key to their success is recognition by both parties of the principle of equal security of the sides and readiness to genuinely adhere to this principle." He added, however, that in "our foreign and defense policies we cannot ignore the fact that a buildup of arms is being continued in a number of imperialist states. The new budget that is now being discussed in Washington provides for a considerable growth in military spending, especially on long-term programs of strategic armaments. The U.S. is demanding of its NATO allies an increase in military allocations."

Licenses & debts. The Nixon Administration Feb. 16 approved licenses for export of another $367 million worth of machine tools to the Soviet Union's Kama River truck plant.

Washington announced Feb. 17, 1972 that the Soviet Union had agreed to reopen talks with the U.S. on debts it owed Washington from lend-lease assistance received during World War II. The U.S. had originally asked for $2.6 billion in compensation, but when the talks were broken off in 1960 the Soviet Union was offering some $300 million.

Jewish emigration curbs. A major barrier to U.S.-Soviet detente was a campaign in the U.S. for a relaxation of Soviet oppression of its Jewish citizens and of restrictions against the emigration of Jews and other residents of the U.S.S.R.

The Soviet restrictions had been protested in the U.S. by rallies and by several extremist attacks on Soviet diplomats and on organizations dealing with the U.S.S.R. George Bush, U.S. representative at the U.N., asked Congress March 16 for legislation making it a crime to harass foreign diplomats. Bush, testifying before a House judiciary committee, enumerated "senseless acts of violence" that had taken place in New York. He declared: "Bricks have been thrown through windows, paint has been thrown against walls of buildings, motor oil has been

placed in car radiators, burning rags in gas tanks and Molotov cocktails have been thrown at mission vehicles. . . . As a result, there is a general, and, I am sad to say, justified consensus among the representatives of members of the U.N. that their physical security is threatened."

William B. Macomber Jr., deputy undersecretary of state for management, told the committee of an incident which had occurred March 15 at a reception at American University in Washington in which a girl who said she was a member of the Jewish Defense League (JDL) had poured blood on the head of Gennadi F. Domakhin, a Soviet third secretary. A spokesman for the JDL had said afterwards that the blood symbolized "our determination to continue our fight until amnesty is given to all prisoners of conscience [in Russia] and until exodus instead of deceptive token emigration is granted to all Soviet Jews."

U.S.-Soviet cultural pact. The U.S. and the Soviet Union reached agreement April 11 on a 1972–73 cultural exchange accord, the latest in a series dating from 1958.

The document was signed by U.S. Ambassador Jacob D. Beam and Andrei A. Smirnov, a Soviet deputy foreign minister. It provided for the first time for the exchange of up to eight full-time university instructors who would teach courses lasting from a semester to a full year. In the performing arts, six major groups would be exchanged, instead of the five stipulated in the 1970–71 pact.

In a related development, the first meeting of the Soviet-American Committee for Health Cooperation ended in Moscow April 1 after a week of talks.

Butz sets grain deal. U.S. Secretary of Agriculture Earl L. Butz visited the U.S.S.R. April 8–12 and ended his visit with the prediction of a big U.S.-Soviet grain sale and the announcement that he was carrying a message for President Nixon from Communist Party General Secretary Leonid I. Brezhnev.

Butz, who began talks during his stay on a proposed $200 million grain transaction, was returning the visit of his Soviet counterpart Vladimir V. Matskevich, who traveled to the U.S. in 1971. Butz asserted that Brezhnev had indicated that the Soviet government was "looking forward to the visit of the American President." Butz reported that Brezhnev had said "he would like to have a minimum of ceremony and a maximum of substantive discussion during the Nixon visit."

U.S.-Soviet shipping pact. The U.S. and the Soviet Union announced April 21 that they had reached agreement after five days of talks on procedures governing access to each other's seaports.

According to the U.S. Embassy in Moscow, "The understanding includes provisions relating to port access, entry and treatment of the ships of one country in the ports of the other country, cargo carriage and other maritime matters."

Kissinger visits Moscow secretly. The White House announced April 25 that Henry A. Kissinger had secretly visited the U.S.S.R. April 20–24 and had conferred with Brezhnev on a variety of problems.

In a briefing given to newsmen April 26, Kissinger said that his journey had grown out of correspondence between Nixon and Brezhnev initiated early in 1971 and that "in the course of these exchanges, it was felt in the last few weeks that a more direct exchange might be desirable."

Kissinger remarked that as a result of his conversations with Brezhnev all negotiations with the Soviet Union were "on course" and "they may have received an additional impetus." He was accompanied by four members of the National Security Council Staff: Helmut Sonnenfeldt, Winston Lord, Peter Rodman and John Negroponte.

U.S. mines North Vietnam's ports. A fresh problem threatening detente appeared May 8, 1972 when Nixon announced that he had ordered the mining of Haiphong harbor and six other North Vietnamese ports plus an intensified air offensive on North Vietnam's rail and other supply lines. The announcement

followed a National Security Council meeting for which State Secretary William Rogers had been called back from Europe and for which Henry Kissinger had postponed a trip to Japan.

At a White House news conference May 9, Kissinger called these decisions "very painful and difficult" but necessary because "no honorable alternative was available." While the closing of North Vietnam supply routes "involves some risks" and "short-term difficulties" for Soviet leaders, he said, the Administration concluded that it "did not involve an unacceptable risk" to the U.S.

Kissinger spoke of the "massive difficulties" for the U.S. arising from a situation the Soviet Union "permitted to evolve," the "real choices" facing both sides and of his opinion that "if one wants a genuine improvement in relations, as we do, one cannot also at the same time maximize the pressures all around the periphery."

The Administration still believed, he said, that "a new era in East-West relations" was possible and would "pursue it with the same intensity as before." The Administration was proceeding with preparations for Nixon's Moscow visit, he said, and saw no reason at the moment to postpone it.

Kissinger said the Vietnam situation had been discussed during his recent (April 21-24) secret trip to Moscow and he did not believe "that there could be any doubt in the minds of the Soviet leaders of the gravity with which we would view an unchecked continuation of a major North Vietnamese offensive and of an attempt by the North Vietnamese to put everything on the military scales." He noted that the enemy had launched three "major onslaughts" after his return from Moscow and the renewal, at Soviet urging, of secret and public peace talks in Paris.

While he did not think the Soviet Union had "a deliberate plan to inflict a humiliation" on the U.S. in Vietnam, Kissinger stressed, "we are saying that any thoughtful national leader, looking at the masses of offensive equipment, might have considered the consequences and, prior to a meeting that had, and still has such high prospects, should ask himself whether it can be in the interest of either party to impose a major setback on the other."

Kissinger disclosed details of a secret meeting he had held May 2 in Paris with Le Duc Tho, a member of North Vietnam's Politburo. The meeting (rumored at the time and thereafter confirmed by the White House May 5) had been six months in the making, Kissinger said, and the result of "innumerable exchanges." Then, he said, Tho had refused to negotiate and presented previously published demands. "What we heard could have been clipped from a newspaper and sent to us in the mail," Kissinger said. The unproductive meeting, and its nature, and the Soviet role in getting the U.S. to attend, were said to have been part of the planning background influencing Nixon's decision to cut off North Vietnam's war supply routes.

In a statement distributed May 11 by the press agency Tass, the Soviet Union called on the U.S. to end its "blockade" of North Vietnam, declaring that the mining of ports in the area and the bombing of rail lines were "fraught with serious consequences for international peace and security."

The dispatch characterized the mining of North Vietnam's harbors as an "inadmissable" threat to "the safety of Soviet and other ships" and urged that the "blockade" be "canceled without delay" and that the U.S. cease its "acts of aggression" against North Vietnam. (The New York Times May 12 reported the belief in journalistic circles that two Soviet freighters had been hit in the previous three days during raids on Haiphong.) "All responsibility for the possible consequences of these illegal actions will be borne by the government of the U.S.," the message said.

It described the U.S. measures as a "gross violation of the generally recognized principle of freedom of navigation —ignoring the fact that the Geneva conventions of 1958 on maritime law affirming that principle bear, alongside other signatures, the one of the U.S." The U.S. had thereby "demonstrated its contempt for one of the basic requirements of international law: the observance by states of commitments assumed under international treaties."

Moscow asserted that the "real purpose of these actions is clear. It is not to 'save the U.S. from humiliation,' but to save the notorious policy of 'Vietnamization,' which has obviously failed. It is not to enable the Vietnamese to settle their affairs through negotiation, but to extend American military support to the antipopular puppet regime in Saigon." The Soviet Union "has rendered and will continue to render the necessary support" to the "heroic Vietnamese people."

A Tass dispatch from Washington May 9, viewed as a preliminary Kremlin reaction to the Nixon announcement, had called the bombing and mining "overt acts of aggression" which violated "norms of international law."

Soviet aides visit Nixon—At the time of the Russian announcement criticizing the latest U.S. moves against North Vietnam, two Soviet officials were in Washington visiting President Nixon. One of them indicated after the meeting that the President's trip to the Soviet Union was likely to take place as scheduled.

The Soviet officials were Ambassador Anatoly F. Dobrynin and Foreign Trade Minister Nikolai S. Patolichev. They met Nixon; Kissinger; Secretary of Commerce Peter G. Peterson; and Peter Flanigan, assistant to the President for international economic affairs.

After the meeting, which lasted about an hour, Patolichev reportedly answered a newsman's question about Nixon's proposed Soviet visit by remarking: "We never had any doubts about it. I don't know why you asked this question. Have you any doubts?"

Chinese ships hit by U.S. jets—Two Chinese freighters anchored off Hon Ngu island in North Vietnam were shelled by U.S. warships May 6 and bombed and strafed by U.S. planes May 7 and 8, the Peking Foreign Ministry charged May 9. The statement said the vessels were badly damaged and Chinese crew members and Vietnamese civilians were injured. The ministry called the attack "a grave provocation against the Chinese people" and said the government had "lodged a strong protest with the U.S."

Peking sees U.S. 'provocation'—An article appearing May 11 in the Chinese Communist party newspaper Jenmin Jih Pao and distributed by the official news agency Hsinhua called Nixon's action a "dangerous move" and a "flagrant provocation against the people of Vietnam and the world over."

The statement declared: "The Chinese people express the gravest indignation at and the strongest condemnation of this grave act of war escalation of U.S. imperialism."

As long as the war "against Vietnam and Indochina continues in any form," the article said, "we shall firmly support the Vietnamese and other Indochinese peoples . . . to the end and final victory."

The Chinese Foreign Ministry May 12 released an official statement calling the U.S. actions against North Vietnam a "grave new step" that "grossly violates the freedom of international navigation and trade and wantonly tramples upon the charter of the United Nations and international public law."

Nixon's Trip to Moscow

President Richard M. Nixon's trip to the Soviet Union took place May 22-29, 1972. The first American President to visit the U.S.S.R., Nixon signed several U.S.-Soviet agreements, the most important being the SALT accord limiting U.S. and Soviet offensive and defensive missiles.

Nixon arrives in Moscow. President and Mrs. Nixon arrived in Moscow May 22 after a two-day visit to Austria and were met at the airport by Soviet Premier Aleksei N. Kosygin and President Nikolai V. Podgorny. Approximately 100,000 persons gathered to watch the Nixon motorcade pass down Lenin Prospekt, a thoroughfare leading to the visitors' guest quarters in the Great Kremlin Palace.

Nixon met Leonid I. Brezhnev, the Communist party general secretary, for two hours May 22 and held further discussions with him in the following days. At a dinner given in Nixon's honor

May 22, President Podgorny declared in a toast that the visit of the American leader was "a momentous event" which would "have an effect on the further development of the international situation either toward a lasting peace and stronger universal security or toward greater tension."

Podgorny said that although his government did "not underestimate" the "serious complications" affecting relations between the two countries, the Soviet Union wanted to establish "not merely good but friendly relations between the U.S.S.R. and the U.S." Such cooperation, he emphasized, would not take place "at the expense of any third countries or peoples."

Podgorny added: "Experience confirms that whenever our two countries succeeded in insuring by joint efforts the sane balance of interests [of] both of our two countries and other states concerned, opportunities opened for solving acute conflicts and situations and concluding important international agreements and treaties."

In his response, Nixon said the "courage of the Russian people," who "generation after generation have heroically defended this city from invaders," made clear that the "only way to enter Moscow is to enter it in peace." He noted that the U.S. and the Soviet Union had "never fought each other in war" and he expressed the hope that during his visit leaders of the two countries could "make decisions now which will help insure that we shall never do so in the future."

President Nixon cautioned that "great nuclear powers have a solemn responsibility to exercise restraint in any crisis, and to take positive action to avert direct confrontation." Such powers were also obliged "to influence other nations in conflict or crisis to moderate their behavior."

He specified "the exploration of space, the conquest of disease, the improvement of our environment" and "an initial limitation of strategic arms" as areas in which U.S.-Soviet agreements could be expected, even though there would be "hard negotiating ahead, and statesmen with real differences will have their share of obstacles." Nixon concluded: "Let us be worthy of the hopes of the Soviet people, the American people and all the people on this earth as we work together toward the goal of a peaceful world."

General Secretary Brezhnev and President Nixon held five hours of talks May 23. In the morning session Nixon was joined by Secretary of State William P. Rogers; Henry A. Kissinger, the President's national security adviser; Martin J. Hillenbrand, assistant secretary of state for European affairs, and Jacob D. Beam, ambassador to the Soviet Union. Brezhnev was accompanied by President Podgorny, Premier Kosygin, Foreign Minister Andrei A. Gromyko and by Brezhnev's personal aide, Andrei M. Aleksandrov. Afternoon and evening sessions of the talks featured only Brezhnev, Nixon, Kissinger, Aleksandrov and a Soviet interpreter, Viktor M. Sukhodrev.

Secretary Rogers held discussions in the afternoon with Soviet Foreign Trade Minister Nikolai S. Patolichev, who had concluded talks in Washington May 16 with U.S. Commerce Secretary Peter G. Peterson described as having "covered all basic aspects of present and potential commercial relationships."

President Nixon began May 24 by laying a wreath at the Tomb of the Unknown Soldier in the Alexander Gardens near the Kremlin. Mrs. Nixon toured Moscow University, made several purchases in the GUM department store in Red Square and, in the evening, attended the circus.

Later May 24 Nixon returned to St. Catherine's Room of the Great Kremlin Palace, accompanied by Kissinger and Hillenbrand, and had a two-hour meeting with Brezhnev, Podgorny, Kosygin, Gromyko, Aleksandrov and Anatoly F. Dobrynin, Soviet ambassador to the U.S. In the evening Nixon retired to Brezhnev's country residence for five hours of discussions. The talks were understood to have dealt with plans to convene a European security conference and to achieve mutual and balanced reduction of military forces in Europe.

Health, environment pacts—The health agreement was signed May 23 by Secretary Rogers and Boris V. Petrovsky,

Soviet minister of public health. It was understood to be a formalization of a Feb. 11 exchange of letters between officials of the two governments.

Elliot L. Richardson, U.S. secretary of health, education and welfare, said in Washington May 23 that the accord would put previous contacts on an institutional basis and would provide for the exchange of equipment and pharmaceuticals for research purposes.

President Nixon and President Podgorny signed the environmental research agreement, described as an expansion of a U.S.-Soviet cultural pact reached in April. Under the accord, a joint panel would meet semi-annually to deal with such problems as pollution and urban sprawl.

Space, technical accords—Officials of the two governments signed agreements May 24 on space exploration and technological cooperation based on the April U.S.-Soviet cultural exchange accord. Each pact was to take effect immediately and remain in force for five years.

The space agreement, signed by President Nixon and Premier Kosygin, pledged each nation to "develop cooperation in the fields of space meteorology, study of the natural environment, exploration of near earth space, the moon and the planets, and space biology and medicine." This was to take place partly "by means of mutual exchanges of scientific information and delegations, through meetings of scientists and specialists of both countries."

The main feature of the space accord was a project to develop "compatible rendezvous and docking systems of U.S. and Soviet manned spacecraft and stations to enhance the safety of manned flights in space and to provide the opportunity for conducting joint scientific experiments in the future."

An agreement on technological cooperation was signed by Secretary Rogers and Vladimir A. Kirillin, chairman of the State Committee on Science and Technology. It provided for a joint commission to meet once a year in Washington and Moscow alternatively for the purpose of "establishing contacts and arrangements between U.S. firms and

Soviet enterprises where a mutual interest develops." The exchange of scientists and of "technical information and documentation" as well as the promotion of joint research were given as further objectives.

Naval accidents accord—U.S. and Soviet officials May 25 signed an agreement designed to avoid possible accidents between each other's ships at sea. The pact, concluded before President Nixon's Moscow visit, was described as the first military agreement between the two states since World War II.

The document was signed by U.S. Navy Secretary John W. Warner and Adm. Sergei G. Gorshkov, commander in chief of the Soviet navy. It recognized that operations in open waters were subject to regulation by the 1958 Geneva Convention on the High Seas and it forbade both ships and aircraft to engage in "simulated attacks by the simulated use of weapons against aircraft and ships, or performance of various aerobatics over ships, or dropping various objects near them in such a manner as to be hazardous to ships or to constitute a hazard to navigation." The risk of collision was to be decreased by avoiding "maneuvering in a manner which would hinder the evolutions of formation."

Trade commission created—U.S. and Soviet officials announced May 26 the formation of a joint trade commission to resolve outstanding differences on economic issues and supervise the beginning of large-scale economic interchange between the countries. Negotiations failed to yield a hoped-for trade pact, however, and remained snagged on questions of shipping and settlement of the Soviet World War II lend lease debt.

The commission, which was to meet first in Moscow in July, and alternate between that city and Washington thereafter, would attempt to negotiate a trade accord including most-favored-nation tariff treatment for each side. The commission would also arrange credit procedures, set up trade offices in both countries and establish arbitration machinery for any future dis-

putes. U.S. Secretary of Commerce Peter G. Peterson would be chief American negotiator at commission meetings.

The agreement had been worked out in talks attended by Secretary of State William P. Rogers, Henry A. Kissinger, Peter Flanigan, Nixon's assistant for international economic affairs, Soviet President Nikolai V. Podgorny, Premier Aleksei N. Kosygin and Soviet Ambassador to the U.S. Anatoly F. Dobrinin.

According to the New York Times May 29, the Soviet Union had objected to paying high U.S. shipping rates for the 50% of mutual trade that would be carried in American ships, according to a 50-50 split already agreed upon. American negotiators, on the other hand, were under pressure from U.S. maritime unions not to yield on the issue. The disagreement had reportedly helped block an expected short term $130 million grain sale to the U.S.S.R.

Money differences over settlement of the lend lease debt had reportedly narrowed from the $800 million asked by the U.S. and $300 million offered by the U.S.S.R. at the start of the talks, but disagreement remained over the length of time to be allowed for repayment. The U.S. Administration was reported to feel that a lend lease accord would help assure Congressional approval of most-favored-nation treatment for the Soviet Union.

A Soviet planning official, Mikhail I. Misnik, told American newsmen May 29 that the U.S.S.R. hoped to go beyond "classic trade" with U.S. businessmen into "large scale arrangements in which the United States would provide plant and equipment and we would pay with raw materials and the end products of such plants." He cited the natural gas, automotive and aviation industries as possible areas for such cooperation.

Arms agreements signed. President Nixon and General Secretary Brezhnev signed agreements in the Great Hall of the Kremlin May 26 limiting offensive and defensive strategic weapons. Although the accords, which had been worked out in months of negotiations between U.S. and Soviet officials in Helsinki, required approval by the U.S.

Senate, both leaders promised to abide by them immediately.

There were two agreements—one limiting ABM (antiballistic missile) systems and the other limiting offensive missile launchers. The offensive pact, known as an interim agreement, was accompanied by a protocol specifying the number of missile launchers each side could possess.

The ABM accord allowed each nation two antiballistic missile systems. One of these would be "centered on the party's national capital," the other would be located elsewhere in the country to guard a portion of the nation's offensive missile force. No site could employ more than 100 ABM interceptor missiles and the same number of launchers. Radar complexes at each site were limited. The "modernization and replacement of ABM systems and their components" was to be permitted.

Violations were to be monitored by spy satellites, referred to in the treaty as "national technical means of verification," and each side agreed not to interfere with the other's satellites or to "use deliberate concealment measures which impede verification." A "standing consultative commission" was to be established to deal with such questions as "unintended interference" with satellites, "possible changes in the strategic situation which have a bearing on this treaty" and "procedures and dates for destruction and dismantling of ABM systems" in excess of what the agreement allowed. The treaty was to be "of unlimited duration."

In the interim agreement on offensive weapons, the parties agreed "not to start construction of additional fixed land-based intercontinental ballistic missile (ICBM) launchers after July 1, 1972." Submarine-launched ballistic missile (SLBM) launchers and "modern ballistic missile submarines" were to be limited "to the numbers operational and under construction on the date of signature of this interim agreement." Modernization and replacement of existing missiles and launchers could be undertaken. The accord was to last five years and, as with the ABM treaty, there was to be no interference with satellites. Both parties agreed "to continue active

negotiations for limitations on strategic offensive weapons."

The protocol attached to the interim agreement limited the U.S. to no more than 710 SLBMs and no more than 44 missile-launching submarines. The Soviet Union was limited to 950 SLBMs and 62 modern submarines. Some replacements were to be permitted for "launchers of older types deployed prior to 1964."

Texts of the arms agreements:

Treaty on ABMs

The United States of America and the Union of Soviet Socialist Republics, hereinafter referred to as the parties,

PROCEEDING from the premise that nuclear war would have devastating consequences for all mankind,

CONSIDERING that effective measures to limit antiballistic missile systems would be a substantial factor in curbing the race in strategic offensive arms and would lead to a decrease in the risk of outbreak of war involving nuclear weapons,

PROCEEDING from the premise that limitation of antiballistic missile systems, as well as certain agreed measures with respect to limitation of strategic offensive arms, would contribute to the creation of more favorable conditions for further negotiations on limiting strategic arms,

MINDFUL of their obligations under Article VI of the treaty on the nonproliferation of nuclear weapons,

DECLARING their intention to achieve at the earliest possible date the cessation of the nuclear arms race and to take effective measures toward reductions in strategic arms, nuclear disarmament, and general and complete disarmament,

DESIRING to contribute to the relaxation of international tension and the strengthening of trust between states,

HAVE AGREED as follows:

ARTICLE I

(1) Each party undertakes to limit antiballistic missile (ABM) systems and to adopt other measures in accordance with the provisions of this treaty.

(2) Each party undertakes not to deploy AMB systems for a defense of the territory of its country and not to provide a base for such a defense, and not to deploy ABM systems for defense of an individual region except as provided for in Article III of this treaty.

ARTICLE II

(1) For the purpose of this treaty an ABM system is a system to counter strategic ballistic missiles or their elements in flight trajectory, currently consisting of:

(A) ABM interceptor missiles, which are interceptor missiles constructed and deployed for an ABM role, or of a type tested in an ABM mode:

(B) ABM launchers, which are launchers constructed and deployed for launching ABM interceptor missiles, and

(C) ABM radars, which are radars constructed and deployed for an ABM role, or of a type tested in an ABM mode.

(2) The ABM system components listed in Paragraph 1 of this article include those which are:
(A) operational,
(B) under construction,
(C) undergoing testing,
(D) undergoing overhaul, repair or conversion or
(E) mothballed.

ARTICLE III

Each party undertakes not to deploy ABM systems or their components except that:
(A) Within one ABM system deployment area having a radius of 150 kilometers and centered on the party's national capital, a party may deploy: (1) No more than 100 ABM launchers and no more than 100 ABM interceptor missiles at launch sites, and (2) ABM radars within no more than six ABM radar complexes, the area of each complex being circular and having a diameter of no more than three kilometers, and
(B) Within one ABM system deployment area having a radius of 150 kilometers and containing ICBM silo launchers, a party may deploy: (1) No more than 100 ABM launchers and no more than 100 ABM interceptor missiles at launch sites, (2) Two large phased-array ABM radars comparable in potential to corresponding ABM radars operational or under construction on the date of signature of the treaty in an ABM system deployment area containing ICBM silo launchers, and (3) No more than 18 ABM radars each having a potential less than the potential of the smaller of the above-mentioned two large phased-array ABM radars.

ARTICLE IV

The limitations provided for in Article III shall not apply to ABM systems or their components used for development or testing, and located within current or additionally agreed test ranges. Each party may have no more than a total of 15 ABM launchers at test ranges.

ARTICLE V

(1) Each party undertakes not to develop, test or deploy ABM systems or components which are sea-based, air-based or mobile land-based.
(2) Each party undertakes not to develop, test or deploy ABM launchers for launching more than one ABM interceptor missile at a time from each launcher, nor to modify deployed launchers to provide them with such a capability, nor to develop, test or deploy automatic or semiautomatic or other similar systems for rapid reload of ABM launchers.

ARTICLE VI

To enhance assurance of the effectiveness of the limitations on ABM systems and their components provided by this treaty, each party undertakes:
(A) Not to give missiles, launchers or radars, other than ABM interceptor missiles, ABM launchers, or ABM radars, capabilities to counter strategic ballistic missiles or their elements in flight trajectory and not to test them in an ABM mode, and
(B) Not to deploy in the future radars for early warning of strategic ballistic missile attack except at locations along the periphery of its national territory and oriented outward.

ARTICLE VII

Subject to the provisions of this treaty, modernization and replacement of ABM systems or their components may be carried out.

ARTICLE VIII

ABM systems of their components in excess of the numbers or outside the areas specified in this treaty shall be destroyed or dismantled under agreed procedures within the shortest possible agreed period of time.

ARTICLE IX

To assure the viability and effectiveness of this treaty, each party undertakes not to transfer to other states, and not to deploy outside its national territory, ABM systems or their components limited by this treaty.

ARTICLE X

Each party undertakes not to assume any international obligations which would conflict with this treaty.

ARTICLE XI

The parties undertake to continue active negotiations for limitations on strategic offensive arms.

ARTICLE XII

(1) For the purpose of providing assurance of compliance with the provisions of this treaty, each party shall use national technical means of verification at its disposal in a manner consistent with generally recognized principles of international law.
(2) Each party undertakes not to interfere with national technical means of verification of the other party operating in accordance with Paragraph 1 of this article.
(3) Each party undertakes not to use deliberate concealment measures which impede verification by national technical means of compliance with the provisions of this treaty. This obligation shall not require changes in current construction, assembly, conversion or overhaul practices.

ARTICLE XIII

(1) To promote the objectives and implementation of the provisions of this treaty, the parties shall establish promptly a standing consultative commission, within the framework of which they will:
(A) Consider questions concerning compliance with the obligations assumed and related situations which may be considered ambiguous;
(B) Provide on a voluntary basis such information as either party considers necessary to assure confidence in compliance with the obligations assumed;
(C) Consider questions involving unintended interference with a national technical means of verification;
(D) Consider possible changes in the strategic situation which have a bearing on the provisions of this treaty;
(E) Agree upon procedures and dates for destruction or dismantling of ABM systems or their components in cases provided for by the provisions of this treaty;
(F) Consider, as appropriate, possible proposals for further increasing the viability of this treaty, including proposals for amendments in accordance with the provisions of this treaty;
(G) Consider, as appropriate, proposals for further measures aimed at limiting strategic arms.
(2) The Parties through consultation shall establish, and may amend as appropriate regulations for the standing consultative commission governing procedures, composition and other relevant matters.

ARTICLE XIV

(1) Each party may propose amendments to this treaty. Agreed amendments shall enter into force in accordance with the procedures governing the entry into force of this treaty.
(2) Five years after entry into force of this treaty, and at five-year intervals thereafter, the parties shall together conduct a review of this treaty.

ARTICLE XV

(1) This treaty shall be of unlimited duration.
(2) Each party shall, in exercising its national sovereignty, have the right to withdraw from this treaty if

it decides that extraordinary events related to the subject matter of this treaty have jeopardized its supreme interests. It shall give notice of its decision to the other party six months prior to withdrawal from the treaty. Such notice shall include a statement of the extraordinary events the notifying party regards as having jeopardized its supreme interests.

ARTICLE XVI

(1) This treaty shall be subject to ratification in accordance with the constitutional procedures of each party. The treaty shall enter into force on the day of the exchange of instruments of ratification.

(2) This treaty shall be registered pursuant to Article 102 of the Charter of the United Nations.

Done at Moscow on May 26, 1972, in two copies, each in the English and Russian languages, both texts being equally authentic.

For the United States of America
President of the United States of America
For the Union of Soviet Socialist Republics
General Secretary of the Central Committee of the C.P.S.U.

The Interim Agreement

The Union of Soviet Socialist Republics and the United States of America, hereinafter referred to as the parties,

CONVINCED that the treaty on the limitation of antiballistic missile systems and this interim agreement on certain measures with respect to the limitations of strategic offensive arms will contribute to the creation of more favorable conditions for active negotiations on limiting strategic arms as well as to the relaxation of international tension and the strengthening of trust between states.

TAKING into account the relationship between strategic offensive and defensive arms,

MINDFUL of their obligations under Article VI of the treaty on the nonproliferation of nuclear weapons,

HAVE AGREED as follows:

ARTICLE I

The parties undertake not to start construction of additional fixed land-based intercontinental ballistic missile (ICBM) launchers after July 1, 1972.

ARTICLE II

The parties undertake not to convert land-based launchers for light ICBM's, or for ICBM of older types deployed prior to 1964, into land-based launchers for heavy ICBMs of types deployed after that time.

ARTICLE III

The parties undertake to limit submarine-launched ballistic missile (SLBM) launchers and modern ballistic missile submarines to the numbers operational and under construction on the date of signature of this interim agreement, and in addition launchers and submarines constructed under procedures established by the parties as replacements for an equal number of ICBM launchers of older type deployed prior to 1964 or for launchers on older submarines.

ARTICLE IV

Subject to the provisions of this interim agreement, modernization and replacement of strategic offensive ballistic missiles and launchers covered by this interim agreement may be undertaken.

ARTICLE V

(1) For the purpose of providing assurance of compliance with the provisions of this interim agreement, each party shall use national technical means of verification at its disposal in a manner consistent with generally recognized principles of international law.

(2) Each party undertakes not to interfere with the national technical means of verification of the other party operation in accordance with Paragraph I of this article.

(3) Each party undertakes not to use deliberate concealment measures which impede verification by national technical means of compliance with the provisions of this interim agreement. This obligation shall not require changes in current construction, assembly, conversion, or overhaul practices.

ARTICLE VI

To promote the objectives and implementation of the provisions of this interim agreement, the parties shall use the standing consultative commission established under Article XIII of the treaty on the limitation of antiballistic missile systems in accordance with the provisions of that article.

ARTICLE VII

The parties undertake to continue active negotiations for limitations on strategic offensive arms. The obligations provided for in this interim agreement shall not prejudice the scope or terms of the limitations on strategic offensive arms which may be worked out in the course of further negotiations.

ARTICLE VIII

(1) This interim agreement shall enter into force upon exchange of written notices of acceptance by each party, which exchange shall take place simultaneously with the exchange of instruments of ratification of the treaty on the limitation of antiballistic missile systems.

(2) This interim agreement shall remain in force for a period of five years unless replaced earlier by an agreement on more complete measures limiting strategic offensive arms. It is the objective of the parties to conduct active follow-on negotiations with the aim of concluding such an agreement as soon as possible.

(3) Each party shall, in exercising its national sovereignty, have the right to withdraw from this interim agreement if it decides that extraordinary events related to the subject matter of this interim agreement have jeopardized its supreme interests. It shall give notice of its decision to the other party six months prior to withdrawal from this interim agreement. Such notice shall include a statement of the extraordinary events the notifying party regards as having jeopardized its supreme interests.

Done at Moscow on May 26, 1972, in two copies each in the Russian and English languages, both texts being equally authentic.

For the Union of Soviet Socialist Republics
General Secretary of the Central Committee of the C.P.S.U.
For the United States of America
The President of the U.S.A.

The Protocol

The United States of America and the Union of Soviet Socialist Republics, hereinafter referred to as the parties,

Having agreed on certain limitations relating to submarine-launched ballistic missile launchers, and modern ballistic missile submarines, and to replacement procedures, in the interim agreement,

Have agreed as follows:

The parties understand that, under Article III of

the interim agreement, for the period during which that agreement remains in force:

The U.S. may have no more than 710 ballistic missile launchers on submarines (SLBMs) and no more than 44 modern ballistic missile submarines. The Soviet Union may have no more than 950 ballistic missile launchers on submarines and no more than 62 modern ballistic missile submarines.

Additional ballistic missile launchers on submarines up to the above-mentioned levels, in the U.S.—over 656 ballistic missile launchers on nuclear powered submarines, and in the U.S.S.R.—over 740 ballistic missile launchers on nuclear-powered submarines, operational and under construction, may become operational as replacements for equal numbers of ballistic missile launchers of older types deployed prior to 1964 or of ballistic missile launchers on older submarines.

The deployment of modern SLBMs on any submarine, regardless of type, will be counted against the total level of SLBMs permitted for the U.S. and the U.S.S.R.

This protocol shall be considered an integral part of the interim agreement.

For the United States of America
The President of the United States of America
For the Union of Soviet Socialist Republics
The General Secretary of the Central Committee of the C.P.S.U.

Kissinger, Smith briefing—After the arms documents were signed, a briefing for newsmen was given by Kissinger and Gerard C. Smith, chief U.S. negotiator at the SALT talks in Helsinki.

Kissinger said the two signatory parties had agreed that the existing total of offensive missiles for the Soviet Union was 2,328 (1,618 ICBMs and 710 SLBMs) and for the U.S. was 1,710 (1054 ICBMs and 656 SLBMs). He added: "If you compare megatonnage, the Soviets have about three times as much. If you count warheads, we have about three times as much."

In emphasizing the curbs on defensive weapons, Ambassador Smith remarked: "This is an admission of tremendous psychological importance, a recognition that the deterrence force of either side is not going to be challenged."

Toasts at state dinner—Several hours before the signing of the arms agreements May 26, President Nixon gave a state dinner at the American embassy in Moscow for the Soviet leaders.

In a toast, Nixon said he was "greatly honored by the presence of our Soviet guests" and that he looked forward "to a time when we shall be able to welcome you in our country and in some way respond in an effective manner to the way

in which you have received us so generously in your country."

Of the strategic arms pact, he declared: "It is an enormously important agreement; but again, it is only an indication of what can happen in the future as we work toward peace in the world. But I have great hopes on that score."

Premier Aleksei N. Kosygin responded by calling the treaty "a great victory for the Soviet and American peoples in the matter of easing international tension" and noting that it was also "a victory for all peace-loving peoples, because security and peace is their common goal." He cautioned, however, that any "agreement, any treaty only then leaves a trace in history when its proclaimed principles and intentions become the content of the practical activities of states."

U.S. halts ABM project—One day after the treaty was signed, Defense Secretary Melvin R. Laird ordered the Army to halt construction work on the Safeguard antimissile base in Montana and to drop construction plans for projected sites not already under way.

Laird said in a statement accompanying the order May 27 that "we want to move with prudent speed to abide by the obligations of the historic arms limitations agreements."

Under his order, work would be stopped on the Safeguard missile site at the Malmstrom Air Force Base, which was in its early stages. Laird's order, however, would not affect the nearly-completed Safeguard site at the Grand Forks (N.D.) Air Force Base. The Grand Forks site was the first Safeguard battery to be constructed.

Laird said the Administration recognized that the halt on ABM work would cause "some temporary economic hardships," but that the Defense Department would do everything it could to help those affected.

Laird's directive included orders to appropriate U.S. personnel to suspend all antimissile research and development programs prohibited by the U.S.-Soviet treaty.

TV address to Soviet people. President Nixon made a televised speech to the

Soviet people May 28 from Moscow in which he discussed relations between the U.S. and the Soviet Union.

Nixon said the most important aspect of relations between the two countries was that they had "never fought one another in war." He said that as "great powers" they would "sometimes be competitors, but we need never be enemies."

Referring to U.S.-Soviet agreements concluded during the summit talks, Nixon declared: "If we continue in the spirit of serious purpose that has marked our discussions this week, these agreements can start us on a new road of cooperation for the benefit of our people, for the benefit of all peoples."

Much of the address concerned the role of "great nations," which had "often been dragged into war without intending it by conflicts between smaller nations." He observed: "Together with other advanced industrial countries, the U.S. and the Soviet Union share a twofold responsibility in this regard. On the one hand, to practice restraint in those activities such as the supply of arms that might endanger the peace of developing nations. And, second, to assist them in their orderly economic and social development without political interference."

The President concluded his speech by citing a visit he had made the previous day to the Piskarevska Cemetery in Leningrad, where he had read the diary of Tanya Savicheva, a young girl whose family had died during the siege of the city in World War II. (At a luncheon in his honor in Leningrad May 27, Nixon had remarked: "I only hope that the visit that we had at the highest level with the Soviet leaders will have contributed to that kind of world in which the little Tanyas and their brothers and sisters will be able to grow in a world of peace and friendship.")

President Nixon traveled from Moscow to Kiev, the Ukrainian capital, May 29 and attended a dinner given in his honor that evening by the Supreme Soviet Presidium and the Ukrainian government. In his toast, Nixon said that "we should drink tonight to the heroes who fought in war and the heroes who have rebuilt this city in peace." He expressed the hope that

"the tragedy of war will never again be visited upon this city or any city like it in the world."

Declaration of principles. The summit talks were concluded May 29 with the signing of a U.S.-Soviet declaration of principles and the release of a joint communique. The documents appeared to signal an improvement in relations between the two countries.

The declaration of principles bound the U.S. and the Soviet Union to work for "peaceful coexistence" on the basis of respect for "sovereignty, equality, noninterference in internal affairs and mutual advantage." They attached "major importance" to preventing "exacerbation of their relations." Both sides would "do their utmost to avoid military confrontations" and to practice the "renunciation of the use or threat of force."

The parties agreed to "continue their efforts to limit armaments on a bilateral as well as on a multilateral basis." They made "no claim for themselves and would not recognize the claims of anyone else to any special rights or advantages in world affairs."

In their May 29 communique, the U.S. and the Soviet Union promised to conduct their bilateral affairs on the basis of the declaration of principles and to work for the implementation of agreements concluded between them during the previous week.

The remainder of the text was devoted to international issues. Both sides "took note of favorable developments in the relaxation of tensions in Europe," particularly the 1971 Berlin accord and West Germany's nonaggression treaty with the U.S.S.R. "Multilateral consultations" for a European security conference could take place after the Berlin accord had been signed. The conference itself, which was to be held "without undue delay," was to be "carefully prepared" so that it would be able to "concretely consider specific problems." Talks on "reciprocal reduction of armed forces and armaments" in Europe should be held "in a special forum."

The communique set forth the standard positions of both countries on Vietnam. The U.S. insisted that the "political future of South Vietnam should be left for the South Vietnamese people to decide for themselves, free from outside interference." The Soviet Union called for "a cessation of bombings" of North Vietnam and "a complete and unequivocal withdrawal of the troops of the U.S. and its allies from South Vietnam."

Regarding disarmament, both sides approved the recent treaty against the use of biological weapons in warfare and promised to invest their efforts for a similar ban on chemical weapons, with the "ultimate purpose" being "general and complete disarmament."

The communique ended with the announcement that President Nixon had invited General Secretary Brezhnev, President Podgorny and Premier Kosygin to visit the U.S. and that the invitation had been accepted.

In explaining the communique for newsmen May 29, Henry A. Kissinger elaborated thus: "We are not naive. It is perfectly possible that in six months we could be in a period of extreme hostility. That would mean a great opportunity lost." He said there had been "long, sometimes difficult, and very detailed discussions on Vietnam" but no efforts to correlate possible U.S.-Soviet trade agreements with a Vietnam settlement. Kissinger said: "I am denying that we ever said to the Soviet leaders, if you do this for us in Vietnam, we will do that for you on trade. . . . You have to recognize that these are serious people and that we didn't come here to buy them."

Text of the declaration of principles:

The United States of America and the Union of Soviet Socialist Republics,

GUIDED by their obligations under the Charter of the United Nations and by a desire to strengthen peaceful relations with each other and to place these relations on the firmest possible basis,

AWARE of the need to make every effort to remove the threat of war and to create conditions which promote the reduction of tensions in the world and the strengthening of universal security and international cooperation,

BELIEVING that the improvement of U.S.-Soviet relations and their mutually advantageous development in such areas as economics, science and culture will meet these objectives and contribute to better mutual understanding and businesslike cooperation, without in any way prejudicing the interests of third countries,

CONSCIOUS that these objectives reflect the interests of the peoples of both countries,

HAVE AGREED as follows:

First. They will proceed from the common determination that in the nuclear age there is no alternative to conducting their mutual relations on the basis of peaceful coexistence. Differences in ideology and in the social systems of the U.S.A. and the U.S.S.R. are not obstacles to the bilateral development of normal relations based on the principles of sovereignty, equality, noninterference in internal affairs and mutual advantage.

Second. The U.S.A. and the U.S.S.R. attach major importance to preventing the development of situations capable of causing a dangerous exacerbation of their relations. Therefore, they will do their utmost to avoid military confrontations and to prevent the outbreak of nuclear war. They will always exercise restraint in their mutual relations, and will be prepared to negotiate and settle differences by peaceful means. Discussions and negotiations on outstanding issues will be conducted in a spirit of reciprocity, mutual accommodation and mutual benefit.

Both sides recognize that efforts to obtain unilateral advantage at the expense of the other, directly or indirectly, are inconsistent with these objectives.

The prerequisites for maintaining and strengthening peaceful relations between the U.S.A. and the U.S.S.R. are the recognition of the security interests of the parties based on the principle of equality and the renunication of the use or threat of force.

Third. The U.S.A. and the U.S.S.R. have a special responsibility, as do other countries which are permanent members of the United Nations Security Council, to do everything in their power so that conflicts or situations will not arise which would serve to increase international tensions. Accordingly they will seek to promote conditions in which all countries will live in peace and security and will not be subject to outside interference in their internal affairs.

Fourth. The U.S.A. and the U.S.S.R. intend to widen the juridical basis of their mutual relations and to exert the necessary efforts so' that bilateral agreements which they have concluded and multilateral treaties and agreements to which they are jointly parties are faithfully implemented.

Fifth. The U.S.A. and the U.S.S.R. reaffirm their readiness to continue the practice of exchanging views on problems of mutual interest and, when necessary, to conduct such exchanges at the highest level, including meetings between leaders of the two countries.

The two governments welcome and will facilitate an increase in productive contacts between representatives of the legislative bodies of the two countries.

Sixth. The parties will continue their efforts to limit armaments on a bilateral as well as on a multilateral basis. They will continue to make special efforts to limit strategic armaments. Whenever possible, they will conclude concrete agreements aimed at achieving these purposes.

The U.S.A. and the U.S.S.R. regard as the ultimate objective of their efforts the achievement of general and complete disarmament and the establishment of an effective system of international security in accordance with the purposes and principles of the United Nations.

Seventh. The U.S.A. and the U.S.S.R. regard commercial and economic ties as an important and necessary element in the strengthening of their bilateral relations and thus will actively promote the growth of such ties. They will facilitate cooperation between the relevant organizations and enterprises of the two countries and the conclusion of appropriate agreements and contracts, including long-term ones.

The two countries will contribute to the improvement of maritime and air communications between them.

Eighth. The two sides consider it timely and useful to develop mutual contacts and cooperation in the fields of science and technology. Where suitable, the U.S.A. and the U.S.S.R. will conclude appropriate agreements dealing with concrete cooperation in these fields.

Ninth. The two sides reaffirm their intention to deepen cultural ties with one another and to encourage fuller familiarization with each other's cultural values. They will promote improved conditions for cultural exchanges and tourism.

Tenth. The U.S.A. and the U.S.S.R. will seek to insure that their ties and cooperation in all the above-mentioned fields and in any others in their mutual interest are built on a firm and long-term basis. To give a permanent character to these efforts, they will establish in all fields where this is feasible joint commissions or other joint bodies.

Eleventh. The U.S.A. and the U.S.S.R. make no claim for themselves and would not recognize the claims of anyone else to any special rights or advantages in the world affairs. They recognize the sovereign equality of all states.

The development of U.S.-Soviet relations is not directed against third countries and their interests.

Twelfth. The basic principles set forth in this document do not affect any obligations with respect to other countries earlier assumed by the U.S.A. and the U.S.S.R.

Moscow, May 29, 1972

For the United States of America

Richard Nixon
*President of the United States
of America*

*For the Union of Soviet
Socialist Republics*

Leonid I. Brezhnev
*General Secretary of the
Central Committee, C.P.S.U.*

Soviet ratifies summit results. The Soviet news agency Tass reported June 1 that the results of talks with U.S. leaders that week had been "entirely approved" by the Communist party Politburo and by the two highest organs of government—the Council of Ministers and the Presidium of the Supreme Soviet.

The dispatch said Soviet leaders regarded the Nixon-Brezhnev joint statement of principles as a statement which "creates the prerequisites under international law for building ties and cooperation in all field of mutual interest, on a firm and long-term basis, by no means to the detriment of third countries."

The arms agreement, featuring U.S. acceptance of "the principle of parity and equal security," was hailed as "the most important measure."

Tass added: "The Soviet Union comes out for developing trade and broad economic relations with the U.S., believing that reciprocally advantageous solutions can be found in this sphere too."

■ The Washington Post said June 2 that Jewish sources the previous day had disclosed the release from jail of two Soviet Jews held during the Nixon visit. They were Vladimir Slepak and his son Alexander, members of a group of seven others who were presumably still being detained.

Nixon reports to Congress. President Nixon reported to Congress on his Moscow visit within a half-hour of his return to the U.S. June 1. He told Congress, assembled in joint session that evening in the House chamber, that the foundation had been laid "for a new relationship" between the U.S. and the Soviet Union.

He described his visit as "a working summit" with "a solid record" of progress on solving difficult issues, and he urged Congress to inspect and approve the agreements reached there, especially the ones for arms limitations. "We can undertake agreements as important as these," he said, "only on a basis of full partnership between the executive and legislative branches of our government."

The President, in his nationally televised address, cautioned that the Soviet Union remained a dedicated ideological adversary and said America must maintain adequate defenses, keep its economy vigorous and its spirit confident. The American commitment to its way of life, he said, must be just as wholehearted as the Communist commitment to its system.

The President spoke of his trips to Peking and Moscow in 1972 as "part of a great national journey for peace" and he urged Congress and the nation to "see it through" so the world could be free of the "fears" and "hatreds" that had been mankind's lot for centuries.

■ Nixon referred to his China and

Russia trips as a move away from "perpetual confrontation" and toward "better understanding, mutual respect, point-by-point settlement of differences." While the threat of war had not been eliminated, he said, "it has been reduced" and progress was being made toward "a world in which leaders of nations will settle their differences by negotiation, not by force, and in which they learn to live with their differences so that their sons will not have to die for those differences."

On the arms limitation agreements, Nixon urged that "the fullest scrutiny" be made of the accords and expressed confidence that they were "in the interest of both nations" and would "forestall a major spiraling of the arms race." He added that such a race "would have worked to our disadvantage since we have no current building programs for the categories of weapons which have been frozen and since no new building program could have produced any new weapons in those categories during the period of the freeze."

He assured Congress and the American people that the present and planned strategic forces of the U.S. were "without question sufficient for the maintenance of our security and the protection of our vital interests." "No power on earth is stronger than the United States of America today," he asserted. "And none will be stronger than the United States of America in the future. This is the only national posture which can ever be acceptable to the United States and ... which with the responsible cooperation of the Congress I will take all necessary steps to maintain in our future defense programs."

In cautioning that the U.S. must maintain "our defenses at an adequate level until there is mutual agreement to limit forces," the President said, "the time-tested policies of vigilance and firmness which have brought us to this summit are the ones that can safely carry us forward to further progress in reaching agreements to reduce the danger of war."

The successes in the strategic arms talks and in the Berlin negotiations, he said, "which opened the road to Moscow, came about because over the past three years we have consistently refused

proposals for unilaterally abandoning the ABM, unilaterally pulling back our forces from Europe and drastically cutting the defense budget." Congress deserved "the appreciation of the American people for having the courage to vote such proposals down," he said, "and to maintain the strength America needs to protect its interests."

By the same token, he continued, "we must stand steadfastly with our NATO partners if negotiations leading to a new detente and a mutual reduction of forces in Europe are to be productive. Maintaining the strength, integrity and steadfastness of our free world alliances is the foundation on which all of our other initiatives for peace and security in the world must rest. As we seek better relations with those who have been our adversaries, we will not let down our friends and allies around the world."

Nixon said he had "full, very frank and extensive discussions" with Soviet leaders about Europe, the Vietnam war and the Middle East. Regarding Europe, he mentioned the agreement to engage in multilateral consultations for a conference on security and to move forward with negotiations on mutual force reductions in central Europe.

The President said he had reiterated in the Soviet discussions "the American people's commitment to the survival of the state of Israel and of a settlement just to all the countries in the area."

Nixon said the problem of ending the Vietnam war "was one of the most extensively discussed subjects on our agenda" of the Moscow talks. But "it would only jeopardize the search for peace if I were to review here all that was said on that subject," he declared. "I will simply say this: each side obviously has its own point of view and its own approach to this very difficult issue. But at the same time, both the United States and the Soviet Union share an overriding desire to achieve a more stable peace in the world."

The U.S.S.R.'s Grain Purchases

The Soviet Union bought more than 700 million bushels of grain from the U.S. in the summer of 1972 after the U.S.S.R.'s own crops failed. The biggest grain sale in

U.S. history, the deal included nearly 440 million bushels of wheat, 25% of the U.S.' total crop.

Nixon Administration officials hailed the sale as providing markets for U.S. farmers, reducing U.S.-Soviet tensions and improving the U.S.' balance of international payments. Critics charged that the sale depleted U.S. grain reserves, caused higher prices for food in the U.S. and abroad, cheated U.S. farmers of the higher prices they would have charged had they been informed of the U.S.S.R.'s situation, cost the U.S. heavily in subsidy payments and unduly enriched international grain traders.

The U.S. sale of 18 million tons of grain to the U.S.S.R. in 1972 was preceded and accompanied by Soviet purchases of 10 million tons of grain from other producers the same year.

Soviets to buy U.S. grain. President Nixon announced July 8 that the U.S. had concluded a three-year agreement for the sale of at least $750 million of American wheat, corn and other grains to the Soviet Union.

(The agriculture attache at the U.S. embassy in Moscow had informed the U.S. State Department in reports filed Feb. 9 and 18 that the Soviet winter grain crop had been heavily damaged and that the U.S.S.R. would probably try to buy large quantities of feed grain later in 1972. The U.S. embassy reported to Washington March 31 that the Soviet Union's winter wheat loss totaled 25 million acres and that low soil moisture made conditions unfavorable for the spring planting.)

Under the agreement, the Soviet Union would purchase grain on the commercial market from private grain dealers in the U.S.

Also included in the agreement was a U.S. pledge that it would provide long-term credits to the Soviet Union from the Agriculture Department's Commodity Credit Corporation.

In cash terms, the Soviet Union would purchase $200 million worth of American wheat for delivery during the first year of the agreement—Aug. 1 through July 31, 1973. Loans from the Commodity Credit Corp., which the Soviet Union would use to finance the purchases, had to be repaid within three years of delivery.

In a related development, U.S. Agriculture Department officials said Aug. 9 that Cook Grains had formalized the sale of $100 million worth of soybeans to the Soviet Union for use as cattle feed.

More Soviet grain purchases expected. An Agriculture Department analysis released Oct. 2 predicted that the Soviet Union would continue to be "a major importer of grain" for the next three to five years.

The forecast came in an appraisal of current Soviet crop conditions. The report said poor harvests had jeopardized plans to increase meat and dairy stocks by 1975.

Crop difficulties had also depleted grain stores for the population, and rather than divert that grain to livestock feeding requirements, the report said the Soviet Union would be forced to import.

"With Soviet living standards at a new high, people have been led to expect a more dependable supply of better foods, and it also appears that the Soviet government is determined that the Russian people aren't to be disappointed," the study said.

USDA ends wheat subsidy. The Agriculture Department (USDA) announced Sept. 22 that it was eliminating the export subsidy by setting the payment rate at zero because of the "strong demand for wheat and supplies."

The subsidy had been used to pay the difference between the relatively high domestic price of wheat and a lower world price to keep U.S. grain competitive on the world market.

The USDA had been criticized for using the subsidy to permit sales to the Soviet Union at prices of $1.63–$1.65 a bushel (while the U.S. price was climbing to $2.10 a bushel) when the U.S. was the Soviet's only supplier of grain and could have demanded a higher price.

U.S.-Soviet maritime accord. The U.S. and the Soviet Union signed a three-year maritime agreement in Washington Oct. 14 establishing premium rates for U.S. vessels carrying Soviet grain purchases and substantially increasing the number of ports in each country open to ships of the other nation.

The Soviet Union was to pay U.S. shippers either $8.05 a ton from Gulf Coast to Black Sea ports or 110% of the prevailing world rate, whichever was higher. American shipowners were to receive from the Maritime Administration a subsidy covering the difference between the Soviet rate and the cost of shipping.

The first U.S. ship carrying wheat to the U.S.S.R. docked in Odessa Dec. 20 after negotiations deadlocked over shipping rates were settled Nov. 22 in Washington.

A complex agreement covering only the period until Jan. 25, 1973 was arranged by Assistant Secretary of Commerce Robert J. Blackwell on the basis of a sliding scale of $10.34–$9.90 per ton of grain.

Another pact was signed Dec. 20 setting the carrier rate at $10.34 per ton until July 1, 1973.

Renewed shipping talks had become necessary after world charter rates climbed.

Total grain sale loss estimated. The Washington Star News Nov. 1 estimated the net loss to U.S. taxpayers as a result of the Soviet purchase of grain at $27 million.

Taxpayer Gains (In Millions)

Rise in value of surplus wheat	$183.5
Cut in 1972 farm subsidy	$120.
Cut in 1973 farm subsidy	$189.
Storage and interest savings	$ 73.
Total Gains	$565.5

Taxpayer Costs

Rise in bread price	$178.5
Rise in flour price	$ 20.
Wheat export subsidy	$300.
Shipping subsidy	$ 40.
Subsidy cost to farmers who sold early	$ 54.
Total Costs	$592.5

USDA corn subsidy attacked. The Agribusiness Accountability Project released a report Oct. 7 which was critical of the USDA subsidies given to Continental Grain Co. and Cargill Corp. for the 1971 sale of corn to the Soviet Union.

The nonprofit research group, which was funded by the Field Foundation Inc., entitled the report, 'The Great Grain Robbery and Other Stories.'

The study contended that the controversial government subsidy to U.S. wheat exporters during 1972 was part of standard USDA policy. That policy of favoring exporters began with the Nixon Administration "gutting the International Grains Agreement," the study stated.

In late 1971, according to the report, the USDA bought barley "at inflated prices" of $1.18 or more per bushel, and sold it to Cargil and Continental for 83¢ to 91¢ per bushel. The export companies then sold the barley to the Soviet Union.

The USDA defended the barley sale, the report said, as a necessary inducement to encourage Soviet purchases of corn (also surplus). The report, however, noted that another grain exporter, Louis Dreyfus Co., subsequently sold corn to the Soviet Union without special conditions and that the USDA permitted exporters to fulfill contracts with corn, half of which was taken from U.S. stocks.

GAO criticizes deal. In 1973 a Government Accounting Office (GAO) report held that the Agriculture Department had subsidized the 1972 U.S. grain sale to the U.S.S.R. "much beyond what appeared necessary or desirable" and had provided the Soviets with wheat at "bargain prices."

Comptroller General Elmer B. Staats presented the GAO report to the House Agriculture Committee March 8. Although there was "no indication of law violations," Staats noted that "farmers were not generally provided timely information with appropriate interpretive comments. Agriculture reports presented a distorted picture of market conditions."

Shultz: U.S. 'burned' on grain deal. Treasury Secretary George P. Shultz conceded at a White House press conference Sept. 7, 1973 that the U.S. had been "burned" in the Soviet grain deal.

"I think it is a fair statement that they [Soviet traders] were very skillful in their buying practices, and I think that we should follow the adage [that] if we are burned the first time, why, maybe they did it, but if we get burned twice, that is our fault and we shouldn't have that happen," Shultz said.

Sen. Walter D. Huddleston (D, Ky.) had charged earlier Sept. 7 that the Soviet

Union had profited doubly from the U.S. grain deal. In addition to obtaining U.S. supplies at very low prices, Huddleston said, the Soviet Union had resold some of its U.S. wheat to Italian dealers at inflated prices.

Assistant Agriculture Secretary Carroll G. Brunthaver, a defender of the U.S.-Soviet grain deal, told the New York Times Sept. 7 that the disputed purchases had been made by Swiss exporters and that the Soviet Union had not been involved. Italian officials also denied the charges Sept. 8.

China Also Buys Grain

China has been suffering drought since 1963. After a series of optimistic reports and predictions, the Chinese government conceded that the 1972 grain crop was about 10 million metric tons below the 1971 crop. Although good yields in other crops were reported, China had to go back to the world market to buy enough grain in 1972, and it made similarly large purchases in 1973.

China buys Canadian wheat. Canadian Justice Minister Otto Lang, who also had responsibility for the Canadian Wheat Board, announced June 2, 1972 the sale of 58.8 million bushels of wheat to China for $100 million.

Lang said nearly half the amount would be shipped in 1972, raising to 117.6 million bushels the total volume of wheat shipped to China by the end of the year, with the rest being sent between January and March 1973.

(Argentina and China had signed an agreement under which China would buy 100,000 tons of Argentine corn, according to the Argentine Foreign Ministry June 16.)

China buys U.S. wheat. U.S. Agriculture Secretary Early L. Butz said Sept. 14 that China had placed an order for wheat with the U.S. subsidiary of a French-based company.

Later Sept. 14, an official of the Louis Dreyfus Corp., the New York branch of the French firm Societe Anonyme Louis-Dreyfus et Cie., said the Chinese had agreed to purchase 18 million bushels of soft red wheat. The U.S. firm would "de-Americanize" the grain by selling it first to the parent firm in France for "business reasons."

During a political radio broadcast Oct. 27, President Nixon announced that China had purchased on the U.S. market in the past few days some 12 million bushels of corn at a cost of $18 million.

Nixon said the sale, reportedly made through the Louis Dreyfus Corp., pointed to an "immense trade potential between our two countries."

The Department of Agriculture announced Nov. 1 that China had purchased 970,000 bushels of U.S. wheat valued at about $2.5 million. The department said the sale had been made through the Louis Dreyfus Corp.

Trade, Scientific & Other Arrangements

Kissinger in Peking. Henry Kissinger conferred with Chinese officials in Peking again June 19-22, 1972.

Kissinger held four hours of talks June 19 with Premier Chou En-lai and afterwards attended a banquet given by Chou. Another four hours of discussions took place June 20 between Kissinger and Chou, with Foreign Minister Chi Peng-fei and other officials in attendance.

After reporting to President Nixon June 23, Kissinger told a White House news conference the following day that he had discussed the Indochina war at length with Chinese leaders, but detected no break in the political impasse.

Kissinger also said the Peking meetings had left him confident that the U.S. and China would make "steady progress" in bilateral talks on expanding trade and on arranging cultural, scientific and educational exchanges.

An official joint statement issued simultaneously in Washington and Peking June 24 said the Kissinger-Chou meetings "consisted of concrete consultations to promote the normalization between the two countries." The statement expressed the "desirability of continuing" these discussions in the future.

U.S. approves China plane sale. The U.S. Commerce Department announced July 5 it had granted an export license to the Boeing Co. for the sale of $150 million worth of aircraft, spare parts and ground equipment to China.

The contract, providing for China's purchase of ten 707s and related equipment, was signed Sept. 9.

RCA expands China station. The Wall Street Journal Aug. 18 reported the announcement by the RCA Corp. that RCA Global Communications, Inc., a subsidiary, had signed a $5.7 million contract with the China National Machinery Import & Export Corp. to install a new satellite communications earth station in Peking and to expand the one already in operation in Shanghai.

U.S.-Soviet pact on cancer drugs. The Soviet Union June 30 concluded an agreement on cancer drugs with U.S. scientists who had arrived in Moscow earlier in the month to exchange medical information.

The accord was reached after six days of talks and provided for an exchange of experimental drugs, known as antineoplastic agents, which would then be tested in each other's laboratories to determine their effectiveness in retarding the growth of malignant tumors.

In a related development, U.S. and Soviet medical officials Nov. 18 exchanged viruses and laboratory mice as part of mutual efforts to find a cure for cancer. The ceremony took place in Moscow between Dr. Nikolai N. Blokhin, an official of the Soviet Academy of Medical Sciences, and Dr. John B. Moloney of the National Cancer Institute.

U.S., U.S.S.R. sign research pact. Dr. Edward E. David Jr., President Nixon's science adviser, signed for the U.S. July 7 an agreement with the Soviet Union detailing the first areas of study in science and technology in which American and Soviet scientists would cooperate.

David, who signed the agreement in Moscow, expressed confidence that the envisoned projects to be undertaken by U.S. and Soviet scientists "show the promise of great benefits not only to our own nation but to the rest of the world as well."

U.S.-Soviet trade talks set. A delegation of U.S. negotiators, headed by Commerce Secretary Peter G. Peterson, were being sent to Moscow to begin discussions July 20 with Soviet officials on an overall trade agreement between the two countries, the White House announced July 10.

According to Administration officials, the main obstacle blocking such an agreement was the unresolved issue of the Soviet Union's World War II lend-lease debt to the U.S. The U.S. had said that extension of long-term credits and more favorable tariff policies for the Soviet Union would not be possible without a settlement of the lend-lease debt.

U.S.-Soviet tractor deal. International Harvester Co. would supply the Soviet Union with $40 million worth of tractors and equipment by the end of 1973, it was announced Aug. 16, 1972 by the firm's executive vice president, Omer G. Voss, and by Vladimir Sushkov, head of the Soviet delegation to the International Trade Fair in Seattle.

The large tractors, the International TD-25C, were to be used to construct natural gas pipelines.

The U.S.S.R. Oct. 20 signed a $68 million contract to buy tractors and pipelaying equipment from the Caterpillar Tractor Co. of Peoria, Ill. The machinery was intended for use in building pipelines for natural gas.

The contract was signed in New York by Albert V. Engibarov, chairman of V/O Tractoroexport, the Soviet agency importing agricultural and construction equipment, and by J. W. Busch, managing director of Caterpillar Overseas, a subsidiary of the parent firm with offices in Geneva.

Agreement on technological processes. U.S. and Soviet officials disclosed Aug. 24 a series of agreements between the two countries to exchange technological processes. The accords were revealed at a joint news conference at the National Press Club in Washington by

Boris E. Kurakin, a spokesman for Licensintorg, the official Soviet buyer and seller of technology, and Henry Shur, president of Patent Management, a U.S. patent and transfer firm that had signed six agreements with Licensintorg.

The two officials said the Kaiser Aluminum and Chemical Corp. had signed an agreement with the Soviet Union to buy technological information and licenses to manufacture aluminum at reduced costs by using a Soviet method of casting the metal in such a way as to avoid ingot "skin." Other agreements announced:

Andco of Buffalo had bought licenses for the manufacture of an evaporative cooling system to be used in the production of blast furnaces in Canada.

The American Magnesium Co. of Tulsa had contracted to use an advanced Soviet system for the extraction of magnesium at its plant in Snyder, Tex.

Licensintorg had bought the rights to make cash registers in the Soviet Union based on a model used by a West German subsidiary of the National Cash Register Co.

Cooper-Bessemer of Mount Vernon, Ohio had sold licenses and data to Licensintorg for making gas compressors for the Soviet Union's natural gas transmission network.

Boeing Associated Products of Seattle, a subsidiary of the Boeing Corp., had sold the Russians data for the manufacture of airplane doors similar to those on the Boeing 727.

Kurakin declared that Licensintorg was "moving more aggressively to adapt its operations to American-style transfer of know-how and patent rights" in order to "operate under the U.S. patent system and according to accepted rules and procedures familiar to American businessmen."

Shur noted that the Soviet Union "constitutes the world's largest single concentrated source of high technology with proven industrial results which eliminate the risk of costly R&D [research and development] efforts for U.S. industry."

Robert M. Boudeman, president of the Upjohn Co., announced Sept. 20 that his firm had reached agreement to provide the Soviet Union with technology for the construction of a plant that would produce urethane foam, to be used for auto crash pads and transportation equipment insulation.

'Progress' on trade pact. Kissinger conferred with Soviet officials in Moscow Sept. 11–13, 1972, and a joint communique released Sept. 14 announced that the talks had produced "significant progress" toward a comprehensive U.S.-Soviet trade agreement.

The statement said that during his visit Kissinger had held "frank and constructive" discussions with Leonid I. Brezhnev, the Soviet Communist party leader, and with Foreign Minister Andrei A. Gromyko. Described as a "general review of the course of Soviet-American relations since the summit meeting and of international problems of interest," the talks had included such matters as European security and early resumption of the SALT talks.

"Special attention was given to the status of commercial relations," the dispatch said, and progress "was made on several issues of principle."

The officials also "agreed to conclude promptly" a maritime agreement that would allow U.S. and Soviet ships to carry cargoes to each other's ports. (Victor Louis, Soviet correspondent for the London Evening News who was reported to have connections with Soviet intelligence, had reported Sept. 13 that the U.S. and the Soviet Union were "on the verge of signing a mammoth trade deal" which would be worth several billion dollars a year by 1977. Louis said the lend-lease problem "had been cleared.")

Soviet exit tax debated—Sen. Jacob K. Javits (R, N.Y.) said in an interview Sept. 14 that "a determined group of legislators can block" trade relations with the Soviet Union for several years unless "justice" was granted to Soviet Jews over an exit tax imposed by the U.S.S.R. Aug. 3 on all emigrants.

Sen. Henry M. Jackson (D, Wash.), with 72 other Senators as cosponsors, introduced Oct. 4 an amendment to the Trade Reform Act that would block the U.S.' extension of credits or most-favored-nation status to non-market economies that restricted or taxed the emigration of their citizens. (With 73 cosponsors, Jackson reintroduced the amendment March 15, 1973.)

U.S.-Soviet trade pact signed. After months of intensive negotiations, the U.S. and the Soviet Union reached agreement Oct. 18 on a three-year trade pact which included settlement of the U.S.S.R.'s World War II lend-lease debt and a U.S. promise to ask Congress for most-favored-nation treatment for Soviet imports.

The lend-lease agreement, which the U.S. had insisted upon before going ahead with favored tariff treatment, required that the Soviet Union should pay by July 1, 2001 a total of $722 million in principal and interest. The amount could go as high as $759 million if the U.S.S.R. took advantage of four postponements it was allowed if it paid interest at an additional 3% a year. The Soviet Union made its first payment of $12 million Oct. 18. Secretary of State William P. Rogers and Nikolai S. Patolichev, Soviet foreign trade minister, signed the accord.

The principal element of the trade agreement, signed by Patolichev and Commerce Secretary Peter G. Peterson, was the U.S. promise to secure Congressional authorization for a reduction of duties on Soviet imports "generally applicable to like products of most other countries."

(In what appeared to be an effort to soften Congressional opposition to the trade package, the Soviet Union Oct. 18 announced that 19 Jewish families would be allowed to leave the country without paying exit fees provided they departed before Oct. 28. Six of the families had been told only two days earlier to pay about $195,000 for their exit visas. None of those whose fees were waived were known activists.)

Among other items in the agreement:

President Nixon signed an official determination Oct. 18 stating it was "in the national interest" for the U.S. Export-Import Bank to extend credits and guarantees for sales to the Soviet Union.

Both parties stated that total U.S.-Soviet trade in the three years covered by the pact would reach about $1.5 billion, triple the rate of the 1969-71 period. Each country could request that the other not ship goods that "cause, threaten or contribute to a disruption of its domestic market," through unfair low pricing. Commercial disputes were to be settled under arbitration rules of a United Nations agency in a third country.

The U.S. was to set up a government-sponsored office in Moscow to help U.S. businessmen arrange commercial deals. The Soviet Union was to have a similar office in Washington and to expand the number of American firms (presently four) allowed to have offices in Moscow. For the use of U.S. and other foreign businessmen in Moscow, the Soviet Union would construct an office-hotel-apartment-trade center complex.

U.S.-Soviet environment projects. The U.S. and the Soviet Union ended three days of talks in Moscow Sept. 21 by agreeing to set up about 30 projects as a means of protecting the environment of both countries.

The agreement, an extension of one signed by President Nixon in Moscow in May, was reached by the Joint Committee on Cooperation in the Field of Environmental Protection. The U.S. delegation had been led by Russell E. Train, chairman of the White House Council on Environmental Quality, the Soviet team was led by Yevgeny K. Fedorov, chairman of his government's Hydrometeorological Service.

The joint studies were to deal with such problems as air and water pollution, urban environment, pest management, atmospheric pollution, problems found in permafrost regions and earthquake prediction methods. They would involve transfer of Soviet and U.S. specialists to research sites in each other's countries for periods of several months.

After three more days of meetings in March 1973, the committee signed an agreement to conduct joint water-pollution studies that would keep lakes and rivers fit "for the enjoyment of future generations." The studies would focus on river basins with high industrial concentration as well as on relatively unpolluted lakes such as Baikal in Siberia and Tahoe and Superior in the U.S.

Chase gets Moscow office. The Chase Manhattan Bank, third largest in the U.S., announced Nov. 14 that the U.S.S.R. had approved Chase's plans to open a representative office in Moscow.

First National City Bank, the second largest American bank, had applied to the Soviets for permission to open a full banking branch in Moscow, but said

Nov. 14 it had not received a reply. A predecessor bank of First National City maintained a Moscow office from 1917-1922, when all U.S. banks closed operations in the Soviet Union.

It took another half-year before it was reported (June 13, 1973) that First National City had received Soviet permission to open a Moscow branch.

U.S.S.R. to get U.S. soft drink. Pepsico Inc., producer of Pepsi-Cola, announced Nov. 16 that it had obtained agreement with authorities in Moscow to manufacture and sell its product in the Soviet Union in 1973.

Donald M. Kendall, Pepsico chairman, said that under terms of the agreement a Pepsico subsidiary, Monsieur Henri Wines, Ltd., would become the exclusive distributor of Soviet champagne, wine and brandy in the U.S. Kendall said the deal had been worked out during a series of meetings between Vladimir Alkhimov, vice minister of trade, and Grigory Nikolaev, president of V/O Sojuzplodoimport, a government trade organization.

In a related development, the Alliance Tool and Die Corp., Rochester, N.Y., announced Nov. 21 it had signed a $7 million contract with the Soviet Union to build a consumer tableware factory in Kiev. The deal, by which the U.S. firm would construct the plant and outfit it for production, had been reached Nov. 14 with officials of Stankoimport, a division of the Soviet Foreign Trade Ministry.

U.S.-Soviet accord on embassies. Representatives of the U.S. and the Soviet Union ended 10 years of negotiation Dec. 4 by signing an agreement authorizing each nation to construct a new embassy complex in the other's capital.

Under terms of the accord, local builders would construct the shell of both embassies but each country would be allowed to use workers of its own choice for surveillance-proof interior finishing. Both the U.S. and the Soviet Union would have "unrestricted access" to their respective job sites and would have an option to do exterior facing and final roofing.

Space planning. U.S. and Soviet space planners met at the U.S. Manned Spacecraft Center in Houston, Tex. July 6-17, 1972, at the Soviet Academy of Sciences in Moscow Oct. 6-18 and again in Moscow Dec. 7-15. During the meetings, scientists, astronauts and engineers exchanged data on each other's space achievements and findings and worked on coordinating plans for U.S.-Soviet cooperation in space. Major attention was directed to the joint U.S.-Soviet manned flight scheduled for mid-1975.

At the conclusion of the July meeting, leaders of the two delegations announced July 17 that these tentative agreements had been made: (a) The target month for the 1975 flight would be July. (b) The U.S.S.R.'s Soyuz spaceship would be launched first with two cosmonauts aboard. (c) The U.S. Apollo with three astronauts aboard would go up from Cape Kennedy, Fla. about $7\frac{1}{2}$ hours later. (d) The Apollo would carry a cylindrical docking module, about 10 feet long and 5 feet in diameter, which North American Rockwell Corp. was designing. (e) The two spaceships would dock during the Apollo's 14th revolution around the earth. (f) During the 48-hour period of docked flight, two astronauts would go through the docking module to join the two cosmonauts; they would then return to the Apollo for the night; two astronauts would visit the Soyuz again the next day, and one would return to the Apollo with a cosmonaut; the astronaut and cosmonaut would then return to their own spacecraft, and the two spacecraft would separate.

Details of the docking device were discussed at a press conference July 17 by the respective test directors of the joint flight, Konstantin D. Bushuyev of the U.S.S.R. and Glynn S. Lunney of the U.S. A problem they explained was the fact that the cabin atmosphere in the Soyuz, which roughly duplicated that on the earth, was nitrogen and oxygen at a pressure of 14.7 pounds a square inch whereas the Apollo atmosphere was almost pure oxygen at five pounds a square inch. Cosmonauts going from one spaceship to the other, therefore, would have to spend about two hours in the air lock allowing their bodies to adjust, and this consumed too much time to allow all personnel to visit back and forth. Lunney said that "all future flights of Soviet and American spacecraft will carry these compatible [docking] mechanisms." Boris N. Petrov, chairman of the Soviet Intercosmos Council and leader of the 22-member Soviet delegation, added that this arrangement "insures that one spacecraft could come to the aid of another [regardless of nationality] in case of need."

During the October meeting, the target date was narrowed to July 15 for the Soyuz launching, and the Soviet scientists agreed to lower the pressure of the Soyuz' atmosphere. Should the Apollo miss its first launching chance $7\frac{1}{2}$ hours after the Soyuz launching, two additional launching opportunities would be available during the next five days. It was also agreed that joint training of Soviet and U.S. crews would start in the summer of 1973 and that the first training session would take place at the Manned Spacecraft Center in Houston.

During the December meeting, space technicians successfully tested scale models of the docking mechanism.

U.S. eases China travel. An injunction against travel to China by U.S. ships and planes, established during the Korean War, was ended by President Nixon Nov. 22, 1972.

In announcing the move, White House Press Secretary Ronald L. Ziegler emphasized that such travel would continue to be subject to Chinese authorization in each instance and that there were no plans at present to establish regular commercial service to China. Commerce Department officials were reported as saying, however, that World Airways and Trans International Airlines, both charter firms, had been given permission by the department to fly to China.

Ziegler said the easing of restrictions was designed to "facilitate development of trade and contacts between the American and Chinese people in the spirit of the joint communique" issued after President Nixon's visit to China in February.

U.S.-Chinese visits. Eleven Chinese doctors toured medical facilities in the U.S. Oct. 12–Nov. 1, 1972.

They had arrived in New York Oct. 12 and met President Nixon in Washington Oct. 14. Later that day the Chinese specialists flew to Bethesda, Md. to visit the headquarters of the National Institutes of Health. Other stops on their tour included Kansas City and Palo Alto, Calif.

An unofficial delegation of 14 U.S. scholars paid a three-week visit to China December 1972–January 1973.

The group's leader, Alexander Eckstein of the University of Michigan, said that as a result of talks with Chinese officials the chances of increased exchanges between the two countries "look very promising." The organization, known as the National Committee on U.S.-China Relations, was a nonpartisan group based in New York and had sponsored the 1972 visit to the U.S. of a Chinese table tennis team.

In a related development, U.S. and Soviet cardiologists agreed Feb. 9 in Washington on a pilot project to collect information about deaths caused by sudden heart attacks.

U.S. & China set up liaison offices. In a joint communique released Feb. 22, 1973, after a five-day visit by Kissinger to Peking, the U.S. and China announced that each would establish a liaison office "in the capital of the other." Kissinger discussed his trip later Feb. 22 at a press conference in Washington.

The joint communique said Kissinger's meetings with Chinese officials had been "conducted in an unconstrained atmosphere and were earnest, frank and constructive." Both sides had "reaffirmed" the principles of the 1972 Shanghai declaration, made at the conclusion of President Nixon's visit to China, and had "agreed on a complete program of expanding trade as well as scientific, cultural and other exchanges."

In the press briefing, Kissinger said the "major point" of his Asian trip was that U.S. "contacts with the People's Republic of China have moved from hostility toward normalization." In addition to the liaison offices, which would be "established in the nearest future" and would "cover the whole gamut of relationships," the two states agreed to negotiate "on a global basis" U.S. private financial claims against the Chinese government and the question of blocked Chinese assets in the U.S.

Kissinger said the Chinese had also agreed to review the sentence against John T. Downey, a CIA agent shot down over China in 1952, and to release "within the same time period as our withdrawal from Vietnam" Navy Lt. Cmdr. Robert J. Flynn and Air Force Maj. Philip E. Smith, both shot down over Chinese territory while flying missions against North Vietnam.

The exchange program, Kissinger revealed, was to include visits to China by U.S. congressmen and the Philadelphia Orchestra and trips to the U.S. by Chinese athletes and nuclear physicists.

A statement issued Feb. 22 by the Foreign Ministry of the Nationalist Chinese government on Taiwan said the Washington-Peking communique "contravenes the wishes of the Chinese people." It added that Taiwan would "consider null and void" any future agreement between the U.S. and the "rebel group" now "occupying the Chinese mainland."

Liaison chiefs named—Nixon announced at his March 15 news conference that he had chosen Ambassador David K. E. Bruce to head the U.S. liaison office in Peking.

In an opening statement at his news conference, Nixon said he had chosen Bruce "because I thought it was very important to appoint a man of great stature to this position. The Chinese accepted that view themselves and we expect soon to hear from them as to the appointment of the man they will have as his opposite number here in Washington."

Nixon emphasized that Bruce was a Democrat who had "not engaged in partisan politics" and expressed hope that bipartisan appointments to the Peking office would "continue in the future, whether the Presidency is occupied by a Democrat or a Republican."

Peking announced the appointment of the head of its liaison office in Washington March 30.

Gen. Huang Chen, 66, the Chinese envoy, had recently ended an eight-year tour as his country's ambassador to France, where he participated in discussions with the former U.S. ambassador to Paris aimed at improving mutual relations.

Kennedy urges full diplomatic tie— Sen. Edward M. Kennedy (D, Mass.) had introduced in the U.S. Senate Feb. 21 a resolution calling for "prompt establishment of full diplomatic relations" with China. He said the U.S. should end its diplomatic recognition of the Nationalist government on Taiwan and announce a unilateral guarantee for Taiwan's security.

Other calls for U.S. diplomatic recognition of China had been made by Sens. Edward Brooke (R, Mass.) Feb. 1 and Henry M. Jackson (D, Wash.) Feb. 4.

China frees U.S. fliers—John T. Downey, a CIA agent shot down over China in 1952, arrived in New Britain, Conn. March 12 after he had been released by Chinese authorities that day. Two U.S. airmen were released by China three days later. They were Lt. Cmdr. Robert J. Flynn, 35, of Colorado Springs, Colo., shot down Aug. 21, 1967 aboard an A-6 in southern China and Maj. Philip E. Smith, 38, of Roodhouse, Ill., shot down Sept. 20, 1965 over Hainan Island near the Gulf of Tonkin when his F-104 veered off course.

In related developments, a West German believed to be the last foreigner detained in China crossed into Hong Kong April 11. Trutz von Xylander had been imprisoned in 1969 on charges of spying for the CIA.

U.S.-Soviet fishing pact. U.S. and Soviet negotiators Feb. 21, 1973 signed agreements regulating fishing off the U.S. Pacific coast and establishing fisheries review boards in each other's capitals.

The accords, resulting from talks begun Jan. 29 in Moscow, were signed for the U.S. by Donald L. McKernan, a State Department special assistant for fisheries, and for the Soviet Union by Vladimir M. Kamentsev, deputy fisheries minister.

One agreement limited the Soviet catch of king crab and tanner crab in the eastern Bering Sea and obliged the Russians to use traps, instead of nets, which had often become tangled with U.S. floating gear. The second accord restricted Soviet catch of Pacific hake and flatfish, including yellow-tail flounder. Under terms of this agreement Russian fishermen were forbidden to go for rockfish, flounder and sole off the coasts of Washington, Oregon and California but were to be given port access at Seattle, Portland and Honolulu equivalent to that extended the Soviet merchant marine fleet. The third pact, affecting crab fishing off Kodiak Island, increased the area closed to Soviet vessels during the U.S. fishing season.

Shultz in Moscow. U.S. Treasury Secretary George P. Shultz visited Moscow March 12–14, 1973 to discuss economic matters with Soviet leaders.

Shultz, whose appointment as chief U.S. representative on the U.S.-Soviet Joint Commercial Commission and head of the East-West Trade Policy Committee had been announced by the White House March 6, held talks with Finance Minister Vasily F. Garbuzov. He also met with Nikolai K. Baibakov of the State Planning Committee and Vladimir N. Novikov, a deputy premier with foreign economic responsibility.

After a three-hour discussion March 14 with Leonid I. Brezhnev, the Communist party general secretary, Shultz declared at a news conference he had not come to the Soviet Union "to negotiate anything in particular," although his meetings with officials had been "serious, professional and constructive."

Regarding efforts in the U.S. Congress to block favored tariff treatment for the Soviet Union until Moscow abandoned its exit tax on Jews and other emigrants, Shultz said: "I tried to explain the nature of the problem as we see it and to be sure that people were generally informed about that aspect. I also tried to explain the character of the American political process involving interaction between the President and Congress."

A group of 309 Soviet Jews appealed in an open letter March 8 to two U.S. Congressmen for help in obtaining permission to emigrate to Israel. In their letter to Sen. Henry M. Jackson (D, Wash.) and Rep. Wilbur D. Mills (D. Ark.), both of whom had sponsored bills aimed at getting the Soviet Union to modify its high exit tax, the signers claimed they were denied permission to leave because their work on government projects gave them access to secret information.

The White House announced April 18 that Nixon had received assurances from the U.S.S.R. that it was suspending the exit tax.

U.S. opens Moscow trade office. As provided for in the 1972 Soviet trade agreement, the U.S. opened a commercial office in Moscow March 28, located in its embassy chancery. A Soviet trade office had already been opened in Washington.

In a related development, the Soviet government agreed April 13 to provide U.S. businessmen living in Moscow with multiple visas and to abandon a procedure by which they had to fill out special applications every time they wanted to leave or re-enter the country.

U.S.-Soviet fertilizer deal. Officials of the Soviet government and the Occidental Petroleum Corp. signed a multibillion dollar barter arrangement in Moscow April 12.

Although the Soviet news agency Tass put the value of the deal at $8 billion, Dr. Armand Hammer, chairman of Occidential, said the figure was lower.

Under terms of the deal, Occidental would ship to the Soviet Union large quantities of superphosporic acid to be used in production of phosphate fertilizers. With the Bechtel Corp. of San Francisco, Occidental would help with construction of a fertilizer complex at Kuibyshev, 500 miles southeast of Moscow. It would receive as repayment liquid ammonia and urea from the Kuibyshev plant and potash from other parts of the country.

Kissinger in U.S.S.R. Kissinger had four days of intensive talks with Soviet leaders at Leonid I. Brezhnev's estate near Moscow May 6–9, 1973.

A joint communique expressed "satisfaction at the comprehensiveness and constructiveness of the exchange of views."

Brezhnev was joined at the talks by Foreign Minister Andrei A. Gromyko and Soviet Ambassador to the U.S. Anatoly F. Dobrynin. Kissinger was accompanied by Helmut Sonnenfeldt, Treasury undersecretary for East-West trade.

Major topics of discussion reportedly included U.S. concern over North Vietnamese troop and supply movements, continued fighting in South Vietnam and Cambodia and the Soviet desire for increased trade.

Brezhnev meets U.S. newsmen. In his first meeting with U.S. newsmen, Soviet Communist Party General Secretary Leonid I. Brezhnev said June 14 he had "great respect" for President Nixon, and hoped the upcoming summit talks would help lead to "further improvement of relations" between their two countries, "not based on momentary considerations."

The Soviet leader praised Nixon for his "realistic, constructive approach" to bilateral relations, and for living up to his appeal in his first inaugural address for an era of negotiation.

Brezhnev emphasized economic relations, calling for "large-scale trade, worthy of the scale of our two big countries." He said the Soviet Union was "prepared to give up part of its natural wealth to the United States," but said he expected tough negotiations on terms.

In response to a question about the Jewish issue, Brezhnev said there was no Soviet law forbidding an individual to emigrate "if that departure is justified." The exceptions, he said, were "certain categories of people connected with what is called national security." He said "countless documentary materials" would be given to Nixon showing that Jews were free to emigrate. Brezhnev said he had "a very warm-hearted feeling toward the Jews living in the Soviet Union," citing their disproportionately large role in science and the arts.

U.S. Soviet gas deal set. The Soviet Union and two U.S. companies signed a preliminary agreement in Moscow June 8 on a $10 billion, 25-year project to bring Siberian natural gas to the U.S. West Coast.

The agreement, which would require $4 billion in Western financing, was signed by the Occidental Petroleum Corp. and the El Paso Natural Gas Co. Under the plan, the Soviet Union would first conduct exploratory operations to determine whether 25 trillion cubic feet of gas reserves existed in the Yakutsk area in eastern Siberia. Howard T. Boyd, chairman of El Paso, who joined Occidental chairman Armand Hammer in a Moscow news conference, said about half that total had already been proven.

The Soviet Union, possibly with Japanese help, would borrow $2 billion to build a 2,000 mile pipeline to a new liquefaction plant in the Vladivostok area. The U.S. firms would borrow a further $2 billion for a fleet of 20 tankers, to begin deliveries in 1980 at the earliest.

The entire plan depended on favorable action by the U.S. administration, which was currently considering a decision on reliance on foreign energy sources, and by Congress, which was considering tariff and credit concessions for the Soviet Union. In addition, gas prices and volume remained to be negotiated.

Though the deal was still highly tentative, it was believed that Soviet Communist Party General Secretary Leonid Brezhnev wanted a signed accord before his trip to the U.S. to encourage additional support from American businessmen for Soviet development projects.

NBC exchange accord with U.S.S.R. The National Broadcasting Co. (NBC) of the U.S. and Soviet officials signed an agreement May 31 providing for exchanges of news and entertainment shows, and of technical and management personnel.

Soviet trade benefits cited. A staff study prepared for a U.S. House foreign affairs subcommittee and released June 9 said that expanded U.S.-Soviet trade would have only "relatively modest economic returns," but could produce important political benefits.

If expanded trade caused the U.S.S.R. to "reorder its priorities" and allow Western businessmen to influence its decision making, it might lead to a reduction in the Soviet threat to U.S. security, and to acceptance by the Soviet Union of the Western international system, the report said.

Total bilateral trade could rise to $5 billion yearly by 1980, the report said, if all contemplated natural gas projects materialized.

Arms Control Problems

Soviet warns U.S. on arms pact. A leading Soviet official warned the U.S. Aug.

23, 1972 against trying to put new interpretations on arms pacts signed by President Nixon in Moscow in May. The warning was understood to apply to an effort by Sen. Henry M. Jackson (D, Wash.) to amend the interim agreement on offensive weapons.

Mikhail A. Suslov, a member of the Communist party Politburo, in an address to a joint meeting of the foreign affairs committees of the two houses of the Supreme Soviet, declared: "Everyone must understand that the Soviet Union, proceeding from its own security interests, will attentively watch attempts of certain forces in the U.S. to distort the spirit and letter of the treaty and interim agreement, and will take into consideration in its policy all changes that may appear in the position of the American side."

He added: "The fulfillment by the sides of the obligations under the treaty and interim agreement, their observance of the principle of equal security of the sides, and impermissibility of unilateral military advantages will be the decisive factor for successful progress in further strategic arms limitation talks."

In a related development, Jackson accused the Soviet Union Aug. 15 of having "lied" to President Nixon about the number of missile-launching submarines it had deployed. "They said they had 48 submarines. We now know from intelligence sources they didn't have 48. They only had 42." Jackson claimed the Soviet Union had done this in order to give the impression of "more momentum" to its submarine program and thereby obtain a higher ceiling under the interim agreement.

Soviet says U.S. violates arms spirit. The Soviet government newspaper Izvestia charged Sept. 4, 1972 that new efforts by Defense Secretary Melvin R. Laird to secure funds for new U.S. weapons systems were in violation of the spirit of the U.S.-Soviet arms agreements.

Although the article did not mention Laird by name, it said expenditures asked by the Pentagon for development of a B-1 supersonic bomber and a Trident

missile-launching submarine were being justified "to force the U.S.S.R. to take further steps" to limit the arms race.

"It is evident," Izvestia declared, "that without apparently formally violating the letter of the Moscow agreements, one can still fundamentally violate the general spirit of the agreement by unilateral acts, thus jeopardizing the effectiveness of the agreement itself."

SALT talks resume. The U.S.-Soviet strategic arms limitation talks (SALT), in recess since December 1972, resumed March 12, 1973 in Geneva.

The Washington Post March 8 listed the following new members of the U.S. delegation: Army Lt. Gen. Edward Rowny; Boris H. Klosson, formerly with the U.S. embassy in Moscow; Sidney N. Graybeal of the Arms Control and Disarmament Agency; and John C. Ausland, formerly with the U.S. embassy in Oslo. Held over from the previous U.S. negotiating team were Paul H. Nitze, former defense deputy secretary, and Harold Brown, former air force secretary.

Anti-China bid to U.S. reported. According to a book about SALT, the Soviet Union proposed to the U.S. in 1970 that the two nations enter into a joint nuclear defense agreement against China or any other nuclear power. The report was confirmed by "a highly placed Administration official" May 24, according to the May 25 New York Times.

John Newhouse, a former staff member of the U.S. Senate Foreign Relations Committee, reported in "Cold Dawn: The Story of SALT," that Vladimir Semyonov, Soviet SALT negotiator, formally proposed July 10, 1970 at talks in Vienna that the U.S. and U.S.S.R. agree to "joint retaliatory action" in response to "provocative" acts or direct attacks by China. According to Newhouse, the U.S. responded with a "flat negative."

The Soviet embassy denied the report June 1.

Brezhnev Visits U.S.

Soviet Communist Party General Secretary Leonid I. Brezhnev visited the U.S.

June 16–25, 1973 for summit talks with President Nixon.

Brezhnev arrival. Brezhnev landed at Andrews Air Force Base outside Washington June 16, accompanied by Foreign Minister Andrei Gromyko, Foreign Trade Minister Nikolai S. Patolichev, Civil Aviation Minister Boris P. Bugayev, Brezhnev's personal staff chief Georgi E. Tsukanov and his chief foreign policy adviser Andrei M. Aleksandrov. After a brief welcoming ceremony led by Secretary of State William P. Rogers, Brezhnev flew to the presidential retreat at Camp David, Md. for two days of rest and preparation, while Nixon met with advisers in Key Biscayne, Fla. The trip was Brezhnev's first across the Atlantic.

The arrival was shrouded by unprecedented security measures and limitations on news coverage, at the request of Soviet officials.

Henry Kissinger met separately with both Nixon and Brezhnev June 17, reviewing the agenda for the week-long series of talks.

Four accords signed. Nixon and Brezhnev were present June 19 at the signing ceremonies for four executive agreements worked out earlier by representatives of the two countries. The agreements—on oceanography, transportation, agricultural research and cultural exchange—were signed by Gromyko and Rogers, or Agriculture Secretary Earl L. Butz. Although the agreements were considered relatively minor, and in part superfluous, the two leaders had scheduled the ceremony to give concrete evidence of progress in mutual relations.

The five-year oceanography agreement would extend previous cooperative research and set up a joint committee to implement the exchange of data and convene annual conferences and seminars. Fields of research would include ocean currents, biological productivity, deep-sea drilling and ocean-atmosphere interaction. The research could lead to improved weather forecasting and aid in drafting future fishing accords.

The transportation accord, also to last five years, provided for exchange of personnel and information about such matters as efficiency, safety and noise problems in civil aviation; marine cargo handling; construction of bridges, tunnels and railroads under cold climate conditions and automobile safety. A joint committee would meet periodically.

The cultural agreement expanded the current two-year renewable accords, begun in 1958, to a general agreement to last until 1979. New minimums were set on the number of individuals and groups to be exchanged, with a minimum of 40 graduate students, 30 language teachers and 10 professors from each country in each of the next three years, as well as at least 10 major performing groups and 35 individual performers from each country. Both sides agreed to study the possibility of expanding the circulation of America and Soviet Life, distributed on a reciprocal basis, from 62,000 to 82,000.

The agriculture agreement, signed by Butz, provided for a "regular exchange" of information on long-term supply and demand of major crops, to facilitate production for future trade. A working group to study the current harvest was to meet soon. Both sides were asked to ease travel conditions for agriculture specialists of the other country.

Brezhnev asks more trade. Brezhnev met with 25 Congressional leaders for $3\frac{1}{2}$ hours June 19 in a bid for support of most-favored-nation tariff treatment for the Soviet Union.

In response to questions about restrictions on the emigration of Soviet Jews, which had stalled Congressional consideration of the tariff issue, Brezhnev claimed that 97% of all those who had applied for exit visas had been allowed to leave. The Soviet leader said that 68,000 Jews had left the Soviet Union through 1971, another 60,200 were given permission to leave in 1972, and 10,100 of 11,400 applicants had been given visas so far in 1973. The figures were higher than Western estimates.

Brezhnev cited a list of 742 Jews who had allegedly been denied permission to leave. He claimed that over 200 either did not live in the Soviet Union or had not requested exit visas. Another 258 had been given permission to leave just before Brezhnev left Moscow, and cases of 149 who had been denied visas for security reasons were being reviewed.

Sen. J. William Fulbright (D, Ark.) said Brezhnev left the impression that bilateral trade would not be allowed to expand broadly if Congress refused Nixon's request for Soviet most-favored-nation status.

Tax treaty signed. Treasury Secretary George P. Shultz and Soviet Foreign Trade Minister Nikolai Patolichev signed a treaty June 20 to eliminate double taxation of citizens and companies of one country living or working in the other. The U.S. had such treaties with 35 other countries, but none with a Communist country. Senate ratification would be required.

SALT speedup pledged, peaceful atom accord signed. After a day of talks June 20 at Camp David, Md. on control of nuclear weapons, European security talks and the Middle East, Nixon and Brezhnev signed a declaration of principles in Washington June 21 to accelerate the Strategic Arms Limitation Talks (SALT) and complete a new arms limitation treaty by the end of 1974. The two leaders also signed an agreement on cooperation in nuclear energy research.

The declaration, in the form of guidelines to Soviet and U.S. negotiators at the current SALT talks in Geneva, called for a permanent agreement in 1974 to limit and eventually reduce the number and, possibly, the quality of offensive weapons, to replace the interim five-year agreement on offensive arms signed after the first SALT round in 1972.

The declaration said both sides were prepared to sign interim agreements in certain areas, where limiting competition may be urgent. The permanent agreement would allow for modernization and replacement of strategic weapons under negotiated conditions. Each country would verify implementation by the other side through "national technical means," apparently a concession by the U.S., which had in the past demanded on-site inspection.

None of the specifics of a final agreement were mentioned in the accord, but the provision on qualitative limitations could lead to limitations on MIRVs— multiple independently targeted re-entry vehicles—and on strategic bombers, neither of which were included in the 1972 interim accord.

The Soviet Union, whose numerical advantage in missile launchers was accepted in the 1972 accord, had not yet perfected a MIRV system, unlike the U.S., and was expected to use the period until a permanent accord was reached to continue development. The 1972 interim accord had allowed both sides to complete deployment until 1977 of offensive weapons under construction. If deployment were stopped in 1974, the Soviet numerical advantage would be limited.

The agreement on peaceful research cooperation went far beyond previous programs in providing for construction of joint research facilities "at all stages up to industrial-scale operations," and increased exchanges of information and personnel. Work would be concentrated in controlled thermonuclear fusion, fast breeder reactors and the fundamental properties of matter.

U.S. Atomic Energy Commission Chairman Dixie Lee Ray said the agreement could lead to evidence of the feasibility of fusion electricity generation "in the next two to five—at the most 10— years," although industrial use would probably not come until 2000 or 2010.

War curb pact signed. Brezhnev and Nixon signed an agreement in Washington June 22 designed to avert a nuclear war between the two superpowers, or between one of them and any other country.

The U.S. and U.S.S.R. would be obligated under the agreement to begin "urgent consultations" whenever relations between them or between either of them and another country "appear to involve the risk of nuclear conflict." Each nation pledged to avoid worsening relations with any country if a military confrontation or war might result, and to avoid threatening the use of force against any country.

Either side would be permitted to inform its allies, other countries or the United Nations of their consultations. The agreement included a clause disclaiming any effect on the two countries' right to self-defense and obligations to their allies.

The agreement, which was not a treaty

and did not require U.S. Senate ratification, had no enforcement machinery.

Henry Kissinger said at a news conference that the agreement, negotiated in secret for over a year, grew out of a Soviet proposal at the 1972 summit meeting in Moscow for an accord on control of existing nuclear weapons to supplement the Strategic Arms Limitation agreements. The U.S.S.R. had long advocated a mutual pledge not to be the first power to use nuclear weapons, which the U.S. feared would give the Soviets the advantage in Europe, where the Warsaw Pact countries had superior conventional forces.

Kissinger said the accord would not apply to the current U.S. bombing of Cambodia, because it had started while the accord was being negotiated, but he implied the U.S. interpreted the agreement as precluding a repetition of the Soviet invasion of Czechoslovakia. He said the agreement would, in general, ban "the use of force against any country under circumstances that would have wide international repercussions."

Kissinger was reported by a high-ranking U.S. official, according to the New York Times June 26, to have met with Huang Chen, head of Peking's liaison office in Washington, during Brezhnev's visit to allay Chinese fears that the U.S.-Soviet accords, especially the pledge to avoid nuclear war, constituted a superpower alliance against other countries. Peking had charged in the past that the U.S.S.R. was considering an attack on

Text of U.S.-Soviet Agreement on Prevention of Nuclear War

The United States of America and the Union of Soviet Socialist Republics, hereinafter referred to as the parties,

Guided by the objectives of strengthening world peace and international security,

Conscious that nuclear war would have devastating consequences for mankind,

Proceeding from the desire to bring about conditions in which the danger of an outbreak of nuclear war anywhere in the world would be reduced and ultimately eliminated,

Proceeding from their obligations under the Charter of the United Nations regarding the maintenance of peace, refraining from the threat or use of force, and the avoidance of war, and in conformity with the agreements to which either party has subscribed,

Proceeding from the Basic Principles of Relations between the United States of America and the Union of Soviet Socialist Republics signed in Moscow on May 29, 1972,

Reaffirming that the development of relations between the United States of America and the Union of Soviet Socialist Republics is not directed against other countries and their interests,

Have agreed as follows:

Article 1

The United States and the Soviet Union agree that an objective of their policies is to remove the danger of nuclear war and of the use of nuclear weapons.

Accordingly, the parties agree that they will act in such a manner as to prevent the development of situations capable of causing a dangerous exacerbation of their relations, as to avoid military confrontations, and as to exclude the outbreak of nuclear war between them and between either of the parties and other countries.

Article 2

The parties agree, in accordance with Article 1 and to realize the objective stated in that article, to proceed from the premise that each party will refrain from the threat or use of force against the other party, against the allies of the other party and against other countries, in circumstances which may endanger international peace and security. The parties agree that they will be guided by these considerations in the formulation of their foreign policies and in their actions in the field of international relations.

Article 3

The parties undertake to develop their relations with each other and with other countries in a way consistent with the purposes of this agreement.

Article 4

If at any time relations between the parties or between either party and other countries appear to involve the risk of a nuclear conflict, or if relations between countries not parties to this agreement appear to involve the risk of nuclear war between the United States of America and the Union of Soviet Socialist Republics or between either party and other countries, the United States and the Soviet Union, acting in accordance with the provisions of this agreement, shall immediately enter into urgent consultations with each other and make every effort to avert this risk.

Article 5

Each party shall be free to inform the Security Council of the United Nations, the secretary general of the United Nations and the governments of allied or other countries of the progress and outcome of consultations initiated in accordance with Article 4 of this agreement.

Article 6

Nothing in this agreement shall affect or impair:

(a) the inherent right of individual or collective self-defense as envisaged by Article 51 of the Charter of the United Nations,

(b) the provisions of the Charter of the United Nations, including those relating to the maintenance or restoration of international peace and security, and

(c) the obligations undertaken by either party towards its allies or other countries in treaties, agreements, and other appropriate documents.

Article 7

This agreement shall be of unlimited duration.

Article 8

This agreement shall enter into force upon signature.

Chinese nuclear facilities, but the new agreement was interpreted by some observers as restraining such a possibility.

U.S. Secretary of State William P. Rogers made similar disclaimers of a superpower alliance in a June 26 meeting with all ambassadors of North Atlantic Treaty Organization countries.

Brezhnev meets businessmen. Brezhnev delivered a frequently applauded 90-minute address June 22 to 51 American financiers, heavy equipment manufacturers, oil importers and airplane exporters calling for increased trade on a mutually advantageous basis, and proclaiming the end of the cold war period.

At the end of Brezhnev's talk, Soviet Foreign Trade Minister Nikolai S. Patolichev and U.S. Treasury Secretary George P. Shultz signed two trade protocols. One would lead to a "U.S.S.R.-U.S. chamber of commerce" with membership drawn from the American business and financial community. The other announced that both countries had provided space in their capitals for trade centers, and would enlarge their embassies' commercial staffs.

The National Association of Manufacturers, which hosted a luncheon for Patolichev June 22, announced that day it would work to obtain Congressional approval for most-favored-nation tariff treatment for the Soviet Union.

Air service to expand. Soviet Civil Aviation Minister Boris P. Bugayev and U.S. Transportation Secretary Claude S. Brinegar signed a formal protocol June 23 to expand air passenger service.

Pan American World Airways, which already flew to Moscow once a week, would be allowed to fly to Leningrad as well, while Aeroflot, the Soviet airline, would have landing rights in Washington, in addition to its once-a-week current flights to New York. Both lines could schedule three round trip flights a week under the new plan.

The two sides also agreed to facilitate charter flights, under which U.S. airlines might fly to Kiev, Tashkent, Odessa and Khabarovsk, in addition to Moscow and Leningrad.

Talks end. The two leaders flew to San Clemente, Calif. June 22, where Brezhnev

became the first foreign official to be a guest at the Western White House. After a final round of talks June 23 and 24, and a June 24 television speech by the Soviet leader, Brezhnev flew back to Camp David, Md., and left the U.S. June 25.

A joint communique issued June 25 announced that talks on mutual troop cuts in Europe would begin Oct. 30 in Vienna.

In a brief section on the Middle East, the communique said there had been an exchange of opinions, apparently indicating lack of agreement, but said both sides had "expressed their deep concern" and had promised "to continue to exert their efforts to promote the quickest possible settlement." Kissinger said in a news conference explaining the communique, "you have no idea how close we came to war" when Syrian tank forces advised by Soviet military men crossed the Jordan border in 1970 to aid Palestinians fighting the Jordanian army.

The communique called the June 22 agreement to curb nuclear war "a historic landmark," and said the chances were "favorable" that a permanent curb on offensive missiles could be reached in 1974. The document also asked for further talks on limiting chemical weapons, and said a world disarmament conference, long sought by the Soviet Union, could be convened "at an appropriate time."

In economic relations, the communique said both sides "should aim at a total of $2–$3 billion of trade over the next three years," and said Nixon would give "serious and sympathetic consideration" to any natural gas projects contracted by U.S. businesses in the Soviet Union.

The communique hailed the Vietnam cease-fire agreement, and called for "an early end to the military conflict in Cambodia."

Before leaving San Clemente June 24, Brezhnev said he hoped to see Nixon again in "six or eight months," which suggested that he expected early success in either the Strategic Arms Limitation Talks or the European security conference. White House spokesmen later said Brezhnev's remark should not be considered as a definite time schedule. Nixon had announced acceptance June 21 of an invitation to visit the U.S.S.R. sometime in 1974.

Brezhnev's 47-minute taped television

address to the American people June 24 emphasized the "historic significance" of the agreements signed during the talks, which he said were part of "the wider process of radically improving the international atmosphere." He said the U.S. and U.S.S.R., because of "economic and military might" had "special responsibilities for the destinies of universal peace and for preventing war," and said he hoped improved Soviet-American relations would "help draw more and more nations into the process of detente" throughout the world.

Brezhnev stressed the mutual advantage of proposals for U.S. aid in developing Siberian natural gas resources.

Brezhnev was given a 21-gun send-off June 25 presided over by Vice President Spiro T. Agnew, who said the summit talks had brought "all mankind closer to our shared goals of a true and lasting peace."

Brezhnev talks with Pompidou. Before returning to Moscow, Brezhnev spent two days in Paris June 26–27 in talks with French President Georges Pompidou.

In an apparent attempt to allay French fears that the Soviet-American detente might endanger European security, Brezhnev reportedly stressed that his agreement with Nixon did not infringe upon the independence of any third country.

A French spokesman said June 27 that Pompidou was "delighted with the forward step toward detente and peace achieved by the rapprochement between the United States and the Soviet Union," but that this "could not imply the slightest control" over French military forces.

Pompidou also said that agreements to limit nuclear weapons and to prevent their use were only bilateral, and he reiterated the necessity of an independent French deterrent until "general" and "controlled" disarmament was achieved. Brezhnev was reportedly unable to change Pompidou's opposition to European troop cut talks.

Progress & Problems

U.S., Japan in Siberian gas deals. The Soviet government signed two new agreements for exploitation and development of its Siberian gas fields in association with U.S. and Japanese interests.

The larger of the two agreements was signed in Moscow June 29, 1973 with the U.S. firms Tenneco, Inc., Texas Eastern Transmission Corp. and Brown & Root, Inc., all of Houston. Under the pact, preliminary in nature, the U.S. Export-Import Bank and private Western banks would provide loans totaling up to $3 billion for construction of a pipeline and liquefaction plant. The project would ship 2 billion cubic feet of gas daily to U.S. Atlantic coast ports from West Siberia.

The second agreement, signed in memorandum form by Japanese and Soviet officials in Tokyo July 17, provided for development of natural gas facilities in the Yakutsk area by the Soviet Union, Japan and the U.S. American and Japanese banks were to lend $150 million for the project, which would supply the U.S. and Japan with 1.5 million tons of liquefied gas over 20 years.

In other new Soviet-American economic cooperation developments:

■ The International Telephone & Telegraph Corp. (ITT) announced June 14 it had signed a five-year agreement in principle with the Soviet Union to exchange scientific and technical information in the fields of telecommunications, electrical and electromechanical components, consumer products and publishing, in accordance with U.S. government guidelines.

■ Arthur Andersen & Co., one of the leading U.S. accounting companies, signed a cooperative agreement with the Soviet Union, it was reported June 12, to exchange information on accounting and control procedures and on international finance.

■ The Soviet Union signed an agreement July 2 with Bechtel Corp., a leading U.S. engineering and construction firm, to exchange a broad range of information including construction management techniques, pipeline transportation of oil and gas and metal and petrochemical technology.

Nixon, Huang confer at San Clemente. Huang Chen, Chinese representative to the U.S., met with President Nixon July 6 at the Western White House in San Clemente, Calif. They discussed the role China might play in bringing peace to Cambodia.

After his 40-minute meeting with Nixon, Huang talked with Henry A. Kissinger.

Huang was flown to San Clemente from Washington on a presidential aircraft. Observers noted that the treatment accorded Huang was in part intended to counter any possible feeling of concern Peking had over meetings between Nixon and Soviet Communist Party General Secretary Leonid I. Brezhnev.

Although Kissinger declined to discuss the specifics of his meeting with Huang, he noted afterward that "the public expressions of the Chinese leaders have been in the direction of peace throughout Indochina."

Chase in China accord. David Rockefeller, chairman of the Chase Manhattan Bank, said July 4 that he had concluded an accord during a 10-day trip to China to have Chase represent the Bank of China in the U.S.

Rockefeller said his bank expected to "handle a full range of banking services" for the Chinese bank when the two countries had settled outstanding questions of blocked accounts and most-favored-nation trade status. He said Chase would begin immediately to handle foreign remittances and travelers' letters of credit.

Tourist ban continues—Eight visiting U.S. congressmen were told by Peking officials that China would continue to exclude nearly all U.S. tourists, and would grant visas only to Americans with special skills, with few exceptions, it was reported June 9.

Postal service expanded—The U.S. Postal Service July 8 announced parcel post delivery service between the U.S. and the People's Republic.

Chiao scores U.S. & U.S.S.R. Chinese Deputy Foreign Minister Chiao Kuanhua assailed the U.S. and U.S.S.R. before the U.N. General Assembly Oct. 2, 1973.

Chiao criticized the notion of detente, asserting the U.S. and the Soviet Union sought to divide the world into spheres of influence, and were fearful and mistrustful of each other. He was especially critical of Moscow, which he challenged to withdraw its troops from Czechoslovakia and Mon-

golia, and to return the northern Kurile Islands to Japan. He accused the Soviets of reviving "the long-ignored trash known as the Asian collective security system," which he likened to the security pacts of the late U.S. Secretary of State John Foster Dulles.

Chiao charged the U.S.S.R. sought to betray the world's developing countries by posing as a socialist state, while actually practicing "great-power chauvinism, national egoism and territorial expansionism."

Jamming of VOA stopped. The Soviet Union ceased electronic jamming of Voice of America (VOA) and other Western government radio broadcasts in all Soviet languages Sept. 10 for the first time in five years.

However, broadcasts of Radio Liberty, a nonofficial U.S. station, continued to be jammed.

English language VOA and British Broadcasting Corporation (BBC) broadcasts, as well as German language broadcasts from West Germany had not in the past been impeded, but all VOA broadcasts in Russian, Ukrainian, Uzbek, Georgian and Armenian had been jammed since Soviet troops invaded Czechoslovakia Aug. 20, 1968. VOA broadcasts had been unimpeded between 1963–68.

Nixon had opposed such a restriction, arguing that it could jeopardize efforts to establish better relations with the Soviet Union.

Under the bill, Nixon would be required to certify every six months to Congress that nations receiving most-favored-nation status were not denying Jews or anyone else the opportunity to emigrate.

House group vs. emigration bar. The U.S. House Ways & Means Committee Sept. 26, 1973 attached to the Trade Reform Act of 1973 an amendment denying most-favored-nation status to the Soviet Union or any other Communist country unless President Nixon certified to Congress that the nation did not restrict emigration. Nor would anything more than nominal emigration fees be permitted.

"If MFN [most-favored-nation status] is blocked, then the most serious questions have to be raised about the degree to which other countries, in this case the Soviet Union, can rely on a complex negotiation, on the performance of the United States over a period of time, on its commitments," Kissinger said. He recommended that the U.S. utilize private diplomacy to deal with the issue of Soviet emigration.

Kissinger said Sept. 26 that the committee proposal would be "a significant setback" in the U.S. pursuit of detente.

Shultz sees U.S.-Soviet trade gains. U.S. Treasury Secretary George P. Shultz said at the end of a three-day visit in Moscow Oct. 3 that U.S.-Soviet bilateral trade could reach $1.5 billion in 1973. He said it had passed the $900 million mark by July, more than the entire 1971-72 volume.

The same day, the U.S. formally opened a large commercial office in Moscow to facilitate the growing trade. The previous day a group of U.S. businessmen headed by Donald P. Kendall, Pepsico chairman, completed talks on setting up a U.S.-Soviet trade and economic council, to assist American businessmen in the Soviet Union and help U.S.S.R. agencies find U.S. markets. Representatives of the National Association of Manufacturers and the U.S. Chamber of Commerce and 23 major U.S. companies would join with Soviet trading agencies in executive positions on the council.

Shultz noted that the trade increase had come despite the lack of most-favored-nation status for the Soviet Union. He said he had discussed U.S. Congressional opposition to granting most-favored-nation status, and indicated that Soviet Communist Party General Secretary Leonid I. Brezhnev and Premier Alexei N. Kosygin had made no further concession on the issue of emigration. But the Soviet leaders conveyed their confidence in President Nixon's good intentions in the matter, according to the French newspaper Le Monde Oct. 5.

President Nixon asked Congress once again Oct. 4 to give him authority to grant most-favored-nation status to the U.S.S.R.

U.S. firms sign new deals. The Control Data Corp. and the Soviet government announced a 10-year agreement Oct. 24 on cooperative development of computer technology and services. It was the first major U.S.-Soviet deal in the field and the longest Soviet arrangement yet negotiated with a U.S. company.

The agreement, potentially worth $500 million according to a company source, could include joint manufacture of advanced computers and peripheral equipment and joint development of communications systems and software, with possible applications in medicine, education and transportation. The Soviet Union, which lagged behind Western countries in computer technology, had been planning to develop a nationwide computer network to improve process control and planning. Soviet sources said the deal might include investment of U.S. funds, to be repaid in plant output.

The Occidental Petroleum Co. announced an agreement in New York Sept. 19 to construct a $110 million International Trade Center in Moscow. The complex would be designed and construction supervised by Occidental and a subsidiary of the Bechtel Corp., with loans supplied by U.S. banks. The project, to be completed in 1977, would include offices for 400 firms, a 600-room hotel, self-contained living quarters and cultural and business facilities.

The Soviet Union and General Dynamics Corp. announced a "broad, five-year agreement for scientific and technical cooperation" Sept. 26. The agreement provided initially for joint work in shipbuilding, telecommunications, asbestos mining, aircraft, computer-operated microfilm, and navigation and weather equipment.

The Stanford Research Institute signed a five year cooperation accord with the Soviet Union, it was announced Sept. 19. The private institute was the first Western research group to sign an exchange accord with the U.S.S.R. The agreement included joint studies on U.S.-Soviet business opportunities.

Ten major U.S. banks announced Sept. 12 an agreement to provide a $180 million loan for construction of a fertilizer project in the U.S.S.R.

Kissinger becomes Secretary of State. Nixon had announced at his press conference Aug. 22, 1973 that William P. Rogers had resigned as Secretary of State and that Henry A. Kissinger had been appointed to succeed him.

The President said Kissinger, 50, would retain his current post as national security adviser to the President.

Kissinger's appointment was confirmed by 78–7 Senate vote Sept. 21, and he took the oath of office Sept. 22.

U.S. 'Alert' Follows Soviet Mideast Moves

The Arab-Israeli war of October 1973 appeared at more than one point to be threatening a Soviet-U.S. confrontation. The most dangerous event was a worldwide military alert of U.S. armed forces in answer to Soviet military moves.

Soviet action countered. American military forces were placed on a "precautionary alert" Oct. 25 at key bases in the U.S. and abroad. The action was taken in response to a reported alert of Soviet airborne troops and possible Soviet plans to unilaterally send troops into the Middle East war zone under the guise of a peace-keeping force. Although the crisis appeared to have eased by adoption by the U.N. Security Council of a resolution creating a truce observer force of smaller nations, the precautionary alert remained in effect.

Secretary of State Henry A. Kissinger explained the U.S. emergency move in a news conference in Washington.

The alert order was issued from the Defense Department's National Military Command Center and signed by Adm. Thomas H. Moorer, chairman of the Joint Chiefs of Staff, acting under instructions of Defense Secretary James R. Schlesinger. The decision was made by the National Security Council, whose members included President Nixon, Kissinger and Schlesinger.

U.S. suspicions of Moscow's intentions in the Middle East crisis were said to have been aroused by a report, according to American intelligence sources, that 40,-000 Soviet airborne troops had been transferred to staging areas in the southern part of the Soviet Union in the past week for possible airlift to Egypt.

Information also was said to have been received that an unusually large number of Soviet AN-22 transport planes were landing at Egyptian airports. It was not certain whether they were carrying Soviet troops or military supplies. U.S. officials said the Administration also was concerned about the presence of about 6,000 Soviet "naval infantrymen" on ships in the Mediterranean. Some of those vessels were already in Syrian ports, it was believed.

U.S. officials stressed that the precautionary alert did not put the country on a war footing. It provided for cancellation of leaves, the return of men to their units and preparation to move out if necessary. Among the actions taken: 50–60 B-52 heavy bombers were ordered to return from their base at Guam to the U.S. and a third U.S. attack carrier, the John F. Kennedy, was ordered into the Mediterranean from its post in the eastern Atlantic.

Kissinger explains—Kissinger said at an Oct. 25 news conference in Washington that the U.S. had called the military alert as a "precautionary step" in response to evidence that the Soviet Union may have intended to intervene unilaterally in the Middle East.

Kissinger said the "ambiguity" of certain Soviet "actions and communications and certain readiness measures that were observed" led the President to decide to "make clear our attitude toward unilateral steps." He said the evidence that led to the decision would be made available "from the conclusion of the present diplomatic efforts." A questioner cited a report by Sen. Henry Jackson (D, Wash.) that the Soviet Union had delivered a "brutal, tough" note to the U.S. warning of unilateral action. Kissinger said Jackson "does not participate in our deliberations," and he refused to discuss the content of diplomatic communications. But he said the Administration had been "puzzled by the behavior of some Soviet representatives in the discussions that took place."

Kissinger said the U.S. did "not now consider" itself "in a confrontation with the Soviet Union" and was "not aware of any Soviet forces that may have been introduced into Egypt." He reiterated his view that the nuclear superpowers had a special "responsibility" to keep confrontations "within bounds that do not threaten civilized life." He said the latest U.S. move derived from this view and from a resolve to "resist any attempt to exploit a policy of detente to weaken our alliances." He said the introduction of great power forces would either "transplant the great power rivalry into the Middle East" or "impose a military condominium."

Kissinger summarized Soviet-American developments throughout the latest crisis. He said the U.S. had tried "to bring about a moderation in the level of outside supplies that was introduced into the area" in the first week of the fighting, and had "attempted to work with the Soviet Union on a cease-fire resolution." He said the U.S. still aimed to use the present situation to work out a settlement, since "the chances for peace in the Middle East are quite promising."

Kissinger said a question, asking whether the military alert had been designed with domestic political considerations in mind, was "a symptom of what is happening to our country" and denied the charge. He implied that "crises of authority" in the U.S. "for a period of months" may have influenced the Soviet Union to gamble on a unilateral Mideast intervention. He insisted that the alert decision had been made unanimously by the National Security Council.

(Time magazine, in its issue dated Nov. 5, reported that the note sent by Brezhnev to Nixon Oct. 24 had threatened the "destruction of the state of Israel" by Soviet forces if Israel did not stop its advance.

(However, the New York Times cited a U.S. State Department spokesman as denying Oct. 28 that the Brezhnev letter had made any specific reference to Israel or to the trapped Egyptian III Corps.

(Time quoted one official of the Johnson Administration as recalling that Soviet leaders had "made similarly harsh threats toward the end of the 1967 Arab-Israeli war." The source said "Johnson correctly decided that they never intended to act and ignored them.")

Nixon's explanation—Nixon, in a prepared statement at his Oct. 26 news conference, also explained the reasons for the U.S.' actions.

He spoke of the "very significant and potentially explosive crisis" that had developed three days before. The U.S. had obtained information, Nixon said, "which led us to believe that the Soviet Union was planning to send a very substantial" military force to the Mideast. He then had ordered the precautionary world-wide military alert for U.S. forces "to indicate to the Soviet Union that we could not accept any unilateral move on their part to move military forces into the Mideast." He had sent an "urgent message" to Brezhnev, Nixon said, not to take that course but to help support the U.N. resolution to exclude major powers from participating in a peace-keeping force.

Nixon's optimism about a lasting peace was based on the agreement by the Soviet Union and the U.S. to participate "in trying to expedite the talks between the parties involved." This did not mean that the two major powers "will impose a settlement," he said, but "that we will use our influence with the nations in the area to expedite a settlement."

The week's developments, Nixon believed, pointed up that the Soviet Union and the U.S. were in agreement that it was "not in their interest to have a confrontation" in the Middle East despite their "admittedly" different objectives in the area.

The President said there were "enormous incentives" for the major powers to find a solution, "to get the negotiating track moving again" but this time "to a conclusion—not simply a temporary truce but a permanent peace."

During the question period, Nixon described the tenor of the recent exchange of messages with Brezhnev as "very firm" and leaving "very little to the imagination" on both sides. "And it's because he and I know each other," he added, "and it's because we have had this personal contact that notes exchanged in that way result in a settlement rather than a confrontation."

He said the upcoming negotiating would be "very, very tough" but "all parties are going to approach this problem of trying to reach a settlement with a more sober and a more determined attitude than ever before." None of the Mideast countries involved could "afford another war" and both the Soviet Union and the U.S., Nixon said, "now realize that we cannot allow our differences in the Mideast to jeopardize even greater interests that we have, for example, in continuing a detente in Europe. . . ." Nixon suggested "that with all of the criticism of detente," without it, "we might have had a major conflict in the Middle East."

Soviets vs. U.S. action. Soviet Communist party General Secretary Leonid I. Brezhnev accused the U.S. Oct. 26 of the "artificial drumming up" of a crisis to justify its worldwide military alert.

In an address to the World Peace Congress in Moscow, Brezhnev assailed "fantastic rumors" of Soviet plans for unilateral military intervention in the crisis. The Soviet leader, however, did not deny outright that his country had taken precautionary action of its own. He said "events of the last few days forced us to be vigilant. Urgent and decisive measures are necessary to guarantee the fulfillment of the [U.N. Security Council] cease-fire resolution and the withdrawal" of Israeli troops on the Suez front from previously held positions.

Brezhnev disclosed that the U.S.S.R. had sent "representatives" to the Middle East to observe the cease-fire, and expressed hope that the U.S. would do the same.

Brezhnev said Israel had defied the Security Council's resolution to withdraw to the Oct. 22 positions when the Council issued its first truce call. He implied that U.S. arms shipment and support was responsible for the Israeli action.

Despite his criticism of the U.S. role in the latest Middle East crisis, Brezhnev reaffirmed the Soviety policy of maintaining a detente with Washington.

President Nixon's explanation of the U.S. alert at a news conference Oct. 26 was dismissed four hours later by the Soviet government as "absurd." The Soviet regime's statement published by the news agency Tass asserted October 27 that the U.S. alert, "which by no means promoted the relaxation of international tensions, was obviously taken in an attempt to intimidate the Soviet Union." The statement added, "It is appropriate to tell the initiators of this step that they picked the wrong address."

Alert questioned in U.S. Several major American newspapers and news magazines reported public suspicion that the U.S. military alert had been influenced by the political "fire storm" of reaction resulting from the widening Watergate scandal.

This view was rejected by Congressional leaders Oct. 25, immediately after the alert was ordered, although many were reported to have expressed reservations privately. Among those supporting Nixon's action were House Speaker Carl Albert (D, Okla.) and several of Nixon's political opponents, Senators Edward Kennedy (D, Mass.), Edmund Muskie (D, Me.) and Charles Percy (R, Ill.).

Newsweek, in 'its Nov. 5 issue, suggested that the President's "flourish of crisis diplomacy" was a device to divert attention from his domestic political troubles. According to Newsweek, an unnamed Administration aide said that "we had a problem and we decided to make the most of it."

Time's Nov. 5 issue questioned "whether the alert scare [was] necessary." After citing the doubts of "some military experts" that Soviet actions toward the Middle East warranted the military response ordered by the President, Time concluded that "perhaps some less dramatic action might have ended the crisis."

The Wall Street Journal concluded Oct. 26 that the crisis was "real," but it noted that a "few Nixon foes—grown so cynical about presidential actions because of past White House duplicity—may claim that yesterday's exercise was merely a calculated ploy by a man in deep political trouble."

The Washington Post reported Oct. 26 that there was bipartisan support for the President's warning to the Soviets "despite" privately expressed reservations and an "undercurrent of suspicion that the President might have escalated the crisis. . . . to . . . take people's minds off his domestic problems."

U.S. ends military alert. The U.S. ended its worldwide military alert Oct. 31. The Defense Department announced that the nearly 2.2 million troops of the U.S. European command and the sailors of the Atlantic Fleet returned to "normal status." The 30,000 men of the Mediterranean 6th Fleet, however, remained on heightened alert because of the continuing tensions in the Middle East.

Defense Department spokesman Jerry W. Friedheim said it appeared that the 50,-

000 Soviet troops alerted in the Soviet Union and Eastern Europe had returned to normal duties.

The U.S. had moved a naval task force into the Indian Ocean Oct. 30. Its destination was the Persian Gulf. In reporting the decision Oct. 29, the Defense Department at first had said it was in response to a Soviet naval buildup in the Mediterranean and the alert of U.S. troops. Several hours later the department said there was no connection, that the action was taken only "to demonstrate we can operate" in the Indian Ocean. The task force consisted of an aircraft carrier, five destroyers and a tanker.

Nixon asks Soviet trade delay. In response to the tense Middle East situation, the Nixon Administration advised Congress Oct. 29 to delay consideration of most-favored-nation tariff status for the Soviet Union.

Peter M. Flanigan, White House international economic affairs adviser, told a Senate banking subcommittee it would be inappropriate to debate the concessions while "delicate negotiations" were being conducted requiring Soviet cooperation in the Arab-Israeli conflict.

The House Ways and Means Committee had approved the most-favored-nation status, as part of the general trade bill, but with a proviso denying the status to nations restricting emigration, a reference to Soviet curbs on Jewish emigration.

The request for a new delay was explained by Deputy Assistant Secretary of State Robert J. McCloskey Oct. 29 as a need for "the calmest possible atmosphere." The Administration reportedly feared that consideration of the bill before a Middle East settlement was reached would provoke a massive anti-Soviet vote harmful to the spirit of detente.

The Soviet trade union newspaper Trud said Oct. 31 that the Administration's change of plans reflected attempts by anti-Soviet circles to "demolish friendly U.S.-Soviet cooperation."

Further Advances & Difficulties

The U.S.-Soviet difficulties leading to the Mideast alert were followed in late 1973 and early 1974 by indications that *the detente policy, despite continued Soviet-U.S. differences, was meeting with some initial success.*

Medvedev's view. Dissident Soviet historian Roy A. Medvedev circulated a statement, reported Nov. 7, supporting East-West detente as a means to bring about improvements within the Soviet Union. He also criticized Andrei D. Sakharov's call for Western pressure for Soviet democratization.

Medvedev conceded that improved East-West ties had so far been accompanied by a "shift to the right in our politics and our society." He said the gap between the West and the Soviet Union in economic, social and cultural conditions had increased, as had discontent among ordinary citizens and intellectuals. But he said "tactically" it would be a mistake for Western governments to apply direct pressure for improvements, which had to come as a Soviet initiative "from the top."

Science pact OKd. The U.S. and the Soviet Union signed a protocol Nov. 30 in Moscow on the first major exchange of scientists and engineers between the two countries.

Under the accord, as many as 500 U.S. and Soviet scientists in 10 specific fields would spend one or two weeks as guests of each other's country. President Nixon's science adviser, Dr. H. Guyford Stever, said in response to questions that the controversy over physicist Andrei Sakharov "is not an issue in this exchange agreement."

Kissinger in Peking, closer ties set. Henry Kissinger conferred with Chinese leaders in Peking Nov. 10-14, 1973. The two sides then issued a joint communique announcing their agreement to "continue their efforts to promote the normalization of relations" between the U.S. and the People's Republic of China.

Establishment of formal diplomatic relations continued to be blocked by differences over the status of Taiwan. The communique said the U.S. "reaffirmed" its position that "there is but one China and that Taiwan is a part of China." China said full normalization could occur "only on the basis of confirming the principle of one China." China did not specifically call for a U.S. military pull-out from Taiwan.

The communique said "both sides agreed that the scope of the functions of the liaison offices [in Peking and Washington] should continue to be expanded," although no details were specified. Agreement had been reached on expanding people-to-people exchanges, which officials said would include scientists, entertainers and government specialists. The statement took note of a rapid increase in bilateral trade in the past year, and called for "further development of trade on the basis of equality and mutual benefit."

The statement said that "in present circumstances" it was important "to maintain frequent contact at authoritative levels in order to exchange views." U.S. sources said this went beyond previous commitments on negotiation, and said the communique implied the Chinese were willing to discuss a broad range of international questions not limited to mutual problems in the Asia-Pacific area.

China reportedly agreed in principle to allow U.S. news bureaus to set up permanent offices in China, on the basis of reciprocal rights for Chinese newsmen in the U.S., but the presence of Taiwanese newsmen in the U.S. was said to be an obstacle to any practical accord.

Kissinger discussed the full range of bilateral problems in a $2\frac{3}{4}$ hour meeting with Communist party Chairman Mao Tsetung Nov. 13, the longest the Chinese leader had spent with a U.S. official. A communique said the meeting was conducted "in a friendly atmosphere," an unusual compliment for a U.S. official, and an apparent indication that Mao remained committed to improved U.S. ties. The comment was prominently displayed in the Chinese press.

Kissinger also held several long discussions with Premier Chou En-lai.

Kissinger told Chou and others attending a banquet Nov. 13 that "no matter what happens in the United States in the future, the friendship with the People's Republic of China is one of the constant factors of American foreign policy." The Chinese had reportedly been concerned that the weakened domestic political position of President Nixon threatened future bilateral ties.

Kissinger, Teng meet—Kissinger was host to a three-hour working dinner for Chinese Deputy Premier Teng and U.N. representative Huang Hua in New York April 14, 1974.

A U.S. spokesman said the meeting was "very friendly," and the two sides had a "good review" of Chinese-U.S. relations and "a broad review of the world situation." The spokesman said both sides had "confirmed that the Sino-American relationship would continue on the course charted" in the communique issued at the end of President Nixon's trip to China in 1972.

Gromyko confers in U.S. Soviet Foreign Minister Andrei A. Gromyko conferred with President Nixon and Secretary of State Henry A. Kissinger in Washington Feb. 4-5. It was agreed that Kissinger would visit Moscow in March to prepare for a visit by Nixon to the U.S.S.R.

SALT to resume—Kissinger and Gromyko agreed that the strategic arms limitation talks (SALT) would resume in Geneva Feb. 19.

The New York Times reported Feb. 6 that wide differences of opinion remained within the Nixon Administration on the U.S. position in the talks, and that some officials believed a confrontation was developing on the issue between Kissinger and the Joint Chiefs of Staff. Some of the disagreement reportedly centered on the possibility of policing a limitation of multiple warhead missiles (MIRVS), with the military more skeptical than Kissinger.

U.S. grants credits to U.S.S.R. The U.S. Export-Import Bank announced Jan. 18, 1974 it had authorized credits of $37.78 million to the Bank for Foreign Trade of the Soviet Union to help finance purchase of industrial equipment from U.S. companies.

More than $12 million in additional credits would be provided by private U.S. banks.

The loans would allow shipment to various Soviet ministries of iron ore pellet plant equipment, gas reinjection compressors for the oil industry, piston manufacturing machine tools and friction drum equipment for tractor manufacture.

Kaiser in 5-year pact—Kaiser Industries of the U.S. announced Jan. 23 that it had signed a five-year industrial co-operation agreement with the Soviet Union as a basis for further discussion and possible contracts in a broad range of mineral extraction and metallurgical industries.

Veto threat—Kissinger told the Senate Finance Committee March 7 he would seriously consider recommending a veto of the trade reform bill if it did not grant non-discriminatory treatment to the Soviet Union. The House-passed bill contained curbs on Soviet trade tied to Soviet barriers against emigration of Jews.

"If the President asked my opinion today, I'd recommend a veto," Kissinger said. He told the committee: "We cannot accept the principle that our entire foreign policy—or even an essential component of that policy such as normalization of our trade relations—should be made dependent on the transformation of the Soviet domestic structure."

Kissinger cautioned that the trade posture of the U.S. toward the Soviet Union could influence the negotiations between the two countries on other major topics of interest to world peace and that a trade barrier tied to emigration could prove counter-productive and stop such emigration altogether.

Treasury Secretary George Shultz, testifying before the committee March 4, also opposed a trade curb against the Soviet Union.

Senators firm on emigration-trade ties— Sen. Henry M. Jackson (D, Wash.) and Sen. Abraham A. Ribicoff (D, Conn.) met with Kissinger March 15 and reaffirmed their determination to prevent passage of the Administration's trade bill unless the Soviet Union guaranteed the increased emigration of Soviet Jews and others seeking to leave the country.

Soviets press for trade aid—Soviet officials, in the U.S. for meetings, warned that bilateral trade would be jeopardized if Washington refused to grant export credits and most-favored-nation status to the U.S.S.R.

Yuri A. Malov, a Soviet trade official, asserted March 12 that if Congressional curbs were adopted, they "will have an adverse effect on our future trade as well as on political relations in general."

In an interview in the March 18 edition of U.S. News and World Report, Soviet Foreign Trade Minister Nikolai S. Patolichev warned; "The absence of credits might well mean only that your banks and companies would become uncompetitive. And this might lead to a shrinkage in trade . . . We would simply turn for the necessary credits and technology to other markets, such as Western Europe and Japan."

At a Feb. 26 press conference in Washington, Patolichev had called the amended Trade Reform Act linking trade concessions to Soviet Jewish emigration policies "the kind of thinking more typical of the past" (of Cold-War day). He dismissed emigration matters as "purely internal affairs" and, in a remark apparently designed to demonstrate to U.S. businessmen the need for the bill's defeat, noted that "one wanting to sell products would be interested in devising ways to do it."

Treasury Secretary George Shultz Feb. 26 briefed Patolichev, who was in the U.S. leading a 22-member delegation to the first full meeting of the board of the U.S.-U.S.S.R. Trade and Economic Council, and endeavored to reassure him of "the continued interest of President Nixon" in trade and finance with Moscow. Patolichev gave informal assurances that day that the Soviet Union would not use oil or natural gas exports to the U.S. as a political weapon.

Farm groups favor Soviet trade—At Senate hearings on the Administration's trade bill March 25, the American Farm Bureau Federation and other national farm organizations urged that trade concessions be granted the Soviet Union and that the bill be passed without requiring the Kremlin to allow free emigration of Soviet citizens.

Soviet trade with West up 40%. Soviet trade with the Western world rose 40% in 1973, according to statistics published in the Soviet weekly Economic Gazette

April 10. For the first time since World War II, the West accounted for more than 25% of the U.S.S.R.'s global commerce. Trade with the Communist countries represented 58%.

The U.S. doubled its trade with the Soviet Union, realizing a $1 billion surplus. At the Soviet exchange rate, total two-way trade was $1.56 billion.

Kissinger confers in Moscow. After three days of talks with Communist Party General Secretary Leonid Brezhnev, Foreign Minister Andrei Gromyko and other Soviet officials, U.S. Secretary of State Henry Kissinger returned to Washington March 28, 1974 without the "concrete progress" he had predicted upon his arrival in Moscow March 24.

A joint communique, issued March 28, spoke in general terms of "the course taken by the two countries toward a relaxation of tension" and said that both sides were "determined to pursue ... the established policy aimed at making the process of improving Soviet-American relations irreversible." No specific agreements emerged from the meetings, however, and the communique merely acknowledged the "possibilities for reaching mutually acceptable solutions."

Kissinger had established the second round of the strategic arms limitation talks (SALT II) as the topic of highest priority discussed during the Moscow meetings and presented a proposal described as a "conceptual breakthrough" to the Soviet leaders. The presentation March 25 of a Soviet counterproposal, the contents of which were not disclosed, defused the optimism expressed by both sides prior to the meetings.

According to an unidentified U.S. official, Kissinger and the Soviet officials also failed to make progress on the East-West mutual troop reduction talks being held in Vienna.

The U.S. reportedly agreed with the Soviet Union on the value of a 35-nation summit meeting to ratify the final document to be issued from the European security conference being held in Geneva. Previously, the West had demanded Soviet concessions on human rights in exchange for such a meeting.

Kissinger was said to have been given some "clarifications" on Soviet emigra-

tion policy, in the hopes of improving Congress' disposition toward granting better trade terms to the U.S.S.R.

The American official said that the Soviet Union, while pressing for resumption of the Geneva peace conference on the Middle East, gave tacit approval to Kissinger's mediation efforts; he, in turn, offered assurances of closer consultations with Moscow on the negotiations. (Kissinger's "personal diplomacy" had recently been attacked in Soviet periodicals.)

Schlesinger calls U.S. policy firm— U.S. Defense Secretary James R. Schlesinger cautioned the Soviet Union against thinking it could take advantage of President Nixon's troubles over the Watergate scandal to obtain concessions on a strategic arms limitation agreement. "Anyone who knows Mr. Nixon, knows full well he would do nothing to compromise national security ... irrespective of any political disputes that exist within the United States," he said.

The remarks were made at a Pentagon news conference shortly after the issuance of the joint U.S.-Soviet communique in Moscow.

According to Schlesinger, the Kissinger-Brezhnev talks had resulted in a clarification of the basic issues to be resolved but "not a resolution of possible areas of difference." Progress had been made in laying the groundwork for Nixon's June trip to the Soviet Union, he said, adding that the visit did not hinge on an arms agreement alone. "There are a wide range of other things" to be handled, he said.

Schlesinger suggested that the U.S. would show some flexibility when negotiating an arms limitation agreement. It was "inevitable," if only because of their desire to demonstrate the same "high technological capacity" as the U.S., that the Soviets would be allowed to deploy some missiles armed with multiple independently targetable warheads (MIRV), he stated. He expressed hope that the Soviet leaders would understand the "instabilities" that would be introduced into the balance of power by a massive expansion of the Soviet missile program.

Schlesinger reiterated an earlier statement that the U.S. would insist on maintaining "essential equivalence" in nuclear weaponry, a balance that Schlesinger felt currently existed. (Observers construed this as a reference to the U.S. lead in MIRV technology and bombers, which, the U.S. felt, was compensated for by Soviet advantages in other areas.)

Soviets score Western press—The Soviet press criticized as "pessimistic" Western press reports of Kissinger's talks in Moscow.

In an April 4 article, the Communist Party newspaper Pravda accused the New York Times and the Washington Post of "engaging in irresponsible misinformation" by characterizing the talks as "failures." Both U.S. newspapers denied April 5 that their reporting had been so unfavorable. The Soviet press had given more optimistic reports on the meetings.

The U.S. State Department also sought to dispel the impression that the talks had not been successful. In March 29 comments, State Department spokesman George Vest labeled the talks "a definite step forward" and said that the American press reports were "a bit gloomier than the circumstances warrant."

Sen. Jackson visits Peking. A six-day visit to China by Sen. Henry M. Jackson (D, Wash.) July 1–6 was highlighted by a half-hour conference with Premier Chou En-lai in a Peking hospital July 5. The meeting confirmed reports that Chou, 76, had been ill.

Jackson said he had 15 hours of conversation with Chinese officials, including Deputy Foreign Minister Chiao Kuan-hua July 2–3 and Vice Premier Teng Hsiao-ping July 4.

Upon his arrival in Peking July 1, Jackson said he favored "a more expeditious approach" toward U.S. recognition of the People's Republic. Upon returning to the U.S. July 7, Jackson said in Everett, Wash. that the U.S. was developing a "real detente" with the Chinese leaders. "With the Chinese," he said, "the most important consideration is keeping your word" while "the real issue with the Russians is and continues to be whether they will adhere to agreements."

On his return to Washington, D.C. July 8, Jackson urged closer ties with China and was critical of the Nixon Administration's "piecemeal" approach to negotiations with the Soviet Union on

strategic arms limitations. The U.S., he said, should come out forthrightly for disarmament, not arms control, and propose reduction of land- and sea-based and bomber-carried strategic weapons.

He advocated elevation of the U.S. diplomatic status in Peking to an embassy and reduction of the embassy status in Taipei, Taiwan to a diplomatic liaison office.

Jackson suggested that the U.S. and Chinese interests were "parallel" in many areas. He cited Chinese concern over an "expansionist and unreliable" Soviet Union, over the direction of Soviet policy toward "encirclement" of China and over "the weakness of Europe and the need for greater unity among the Western allies."

Arms & Atomic Curbs

Underground A-test curb sought. The State Department announced May 3, 1974 that the U.S. and the Soviet Union had begun negotiating a treaty for a partial ban on underground nuclear tests. The talks were said to have been undertaken in Geneva at the April 28–29 meeting between U.S. Secretary of State Henry A. Kissinger and Soviet Foreign Minister Andrei A. Gromyko.

Officials said the goal was to prepare an accord for signing during the anticipated June meeting in Moscow of President Nixon and Communist Party General Secretary Leonid Brezhnev.

The announcement of the current talks on test limitations, known as a "threshold test ban," rather than a total ban, followed pessimistic reports of the Kissinger-Gromyko meeting stressing the unlikelihood of a comprehensive test ban treaty. The Washington Post reported May 4 that Moscow was believed to have initiated the talks which proposed to limit the size of tests and the number of tests conducted in any given year. (Since 1964, the Soviet Union had conducted 90 underground nuclear tests, the U.S. 255, according to the Washington Post report.)

According to the New York Times May 3, Administration officials had noted that the U.S. position on on-site inspections had recently eased because detection technology had advanced to the point where limitations could be monitored by seismic inspection devices.

In a related development, suggestions that both sides had adopted more flexible positions on the issue of on-site inspections of chemical warfare weaponry were noted by Julian I. Robinson, of the University of Sussex in Britain, in testimony before a subcommittee of the House Foreign Affairs Committee May 2. He reported that at a private scientific meeting held in Helsinki in April, Soviet scientists had intimated that the U.S.S.R. might accept international inspection teams that would go to predetermined locations to monitor compliance; the U.S., he said, had shifted its concentration from the verification issue to the question of benefits and risks of giving up nuclear weapon stockpiles.

Brezhnev asks gradual underground test ban. Soviet Communist Party General Secretary Leonid Brezhnev announced June 14 that the Soviet Union was "ready even now to agree with the United States on the limitation of underground nuclear tests up to their full termination according to a coordinated timetable." He also urged a bilateral agreement "to prevent the creation of ever new systems of strategic arms."

The Soviet leader made the proposals at an election speech in Moscow's Bauman district, in which he was the candidate to the Supreme Soviet. He and many other Soviet officials had stressed the theme of detente in a number of campaign speeches.

Brezhnev's proposals came as U.S. and Soviet negotiators were meeting in Moscow to draft an agreement on a partial limitation of underground nuclear tests. (The U.S. delegation had reportedly been in Moscow since early June.)

NATO & detente. President Nixon and other leaders of the 15 member states of the North Atlantic Treaty Organization (NATO) met in Brussels June 26 and signed a declaration on Atlantic relations that had been approved by their foreign ministers in Ottawa June 18.

In remarks upon his arrival in Brussels June 25, President Nixon stressed the role of NATO in Soviet-U.S. relations: "Without the alliance, it is doubtful that detente would have begun. Without a continuing strong alliance, it is doubtful detente would continue." Nixon attended the NATO meeting en route to his June 27–July 3 summit meeting in the Soviet Union.

During the June 26 meeting of the alliance leaders, Nixon pledged to "consult with our allies" both before and after the Moscow talks "to make sure that our negotiations not only serve the cause of peace, but also the cause of freedom ..."

Nixon also told the allies that the U.S. "would maintain our forces" in Europe "if there is a similar effort by our allies," and pledged not to reduce U.S. forces "unless there is a reciprocal action" by Moscow.

Controversy over '72 pact. Kissinger June 24 denied as "totally false in every detail" allegations lodged June 21 and repeated June 24 by Sen. Henry Jackson (D, Wash.) that Kissinger had engaged in a secret deal in 1972 which allowed the Soviet Union the option of deploying 70 submarine missile launchers beyond the 950 allowed it in the 1972 strategic arms agreement.

In testimony later that day before the Senate Armed Services Subcommittee on Arms Control, Kissinger admitted there had been a "dispute" between the U.S. and the Soviet Union over the interpretation of the number of launchers. He also acknowledged that President Nixon had given a verbal assurance to Soviet Communist Party General Secretary Leonid Brezhnev that the U.S. would not deploy the maximum number of missile launchers permitted it by the pact. Kissinger minimized the significance of either development.

Jackson, who had been among the early critics of the 1972 agreement, claiming that it had given the Soviet Union a numerical advantage in missile strength over the U.S., said June 24: "The issue here is not 70 missiles more or less. The issue is the withholding from the Congress and the American people of a secret agreement that had the clear effect of altering the terms of the SALT interim agreement."

Jackson said the "loophole" in the secret agreement that would have allowed the Soviet Union the extra missile launchers was closed with a "clarification" signed June 18. Administration officials acknowledged this June 25.

The charge that a secret deal had been made arose from testimony given June 20 before the Senate subcommittee on arms control by Paul H. Nitze who had resigned as top Pentagon negotiator at the Strategic Arms Limitation Talks (SALT) a week earlier, strongly denouncing the form and content of the Administration's nuclear policy.

In his own subcommittee testimony June 24, Kissinger explained that the language of the 1972 protocol as submitted to Congress had contained an ambiguity with regard to the number of Soviet submarine missile launchers. He acknowledged that the Soviet Union had "disputed our interpretation."

According to Nixon Administration officials, Kissinger met with Soviet Ambassador Anatoly Dobrynin June 17, 1972 to discuss the issue and signed an "agreed clarification" July 24, 1972. This secret agreement contained language which, by virtue of a key definition of modern ballistic missiles on submarines, would have allowed the Soviet Union an additional 70 launchers of a type not deployed since 1965. In a press conference June 24, Kissinger dismissed the clause as "a sort of legalism that would be totally rejected by the U.S." and added that it was "an absurdity to assume that the Soviet Union would develop a special missile for a submarine that is in itself obsolescent."

With respect to the President's verbal assurance that the U.S. would deploy fewer than the 710 submarine launch missiles allowed it by the terms of the 1972 agreement, Kissinger said the pledge referred to the Trident submarine which would not, in any event, have been operational until after 1977 when the interim agreement was scheduled to expire. Kissinger further characterized the President's guarantee as "a relatively minor gesture designed to retain general confidence." However, the secretary acknowledged that the "gesture" was "not necessarily" binding.

U.S., U.S.S.R. speed arms development. Both the U.S. and the Soviet Union were reportedly accelerating the testing of strategic weapons in order to perfect their development before April 1976 when the treaty banning the testing of underground nuclear weapons whose yield exceeded 150 kilotons would go into effect.

U.S. Administration officials said July 11 that the Atomic Energy Commission had submitted a request for an additional $100 million to conduct in 20 months tests that would normally be carried out over a period of three years. The tests related to the development of three new missile warheads: MIRV (multiple independently targetable re-entry vehicle) warheads for the Minuteman III intercontinental ballistic missile (ICBM) and for the Trident submarine-launched missile; and either a bomb or missile warhead for the B-1 supersonic bomber.

The Soviet Union, the U.S. Defense Department said July 25, was also accelerating its development of strategic missiles. The department said the U.S.S.R. was testing four missiles with multiple warheads—the SS-16, -17, -18 and -19—and had launched four test flights in June, compared with three test flights for the entire year beginning April 1973. Moscow was also accelerating the development of from 10 to 12 new long-range land-based and submarine missiles, the Pentagon said.

The 1974–75 edition of the authoritative Jane's Fighting Ships, released Aug. 28, evaluated the Soviet Navy as "a very powerful fighting force" which "leads the world in seaborne missile armaments, both strategic and tactical, both ship and submarine launched." The U.S. Navy, it said, because of a "direct policy" of slashing its strength from 1,000 ships in 1968 to 514 in 1974, "bears a desperately heavy burden" and was in the vanguard of navies "subjected to misinformed, illogical and irrational attacks by some of those who depend upon it most."

A comparison of the fleets, with the Soviet figure preceding the U.S.:

Total number of ships: 1,062/514; nuclear submarines: 131/102; conventional submarines: 236/15; cruisers: 34/6; and frigates, destroyers and escorts: 102/196.

The Chinese navy, Jane's said, was "the forerunner of one of the world's greatest navies of the near future." Peking had 51 submarines—seven more than a year ago and at least one of them nuclear.

A survey published June 18 by the Stockholm International Peace Research Institute recorded that the U.S. had nearly 6,000 independent warheads on strategic missiles, outnumbering the U.S.S.R. in deployment of both land-based and submarine missiles with MIRV warheads. The Soviet Union had about 2,200 independent strategic missile warheads, including four new intercontinental ballistic missiles (ICBMs) tested in 1973; three of them had MIRV warheads for releasing 4–7 re-entry vehicles.

The U.S. also had a greater number of strategic bombers: 448, compared with the Soviet Union's 130, according to figures reported in the New York Times March 2.

CIA: Soviet arms spending exceeds U.S. —A U.S. Central Intelligence Agency (CIA) analysis showed that the Soviet Union's military budget had increased in recent years to the point where Moscow had spent more on military expenditures in dollar terms in 1973 than had the U.S. Details of the comparative analysis were released July 19 by Sen. William Proxmire (D, Wisc.) in a declassified version of secret testimony April 24 by CIA Director William E. Colby before the Joint Congressional Economic Committee, of which Proxmire was chairman.

The CIA report estimated that the Soviet defense expenditure had grown at a rate of 3% annually since 1960. The report said U.S. defense spending had been increasing by 5%–6% annually—largely to offset inflation, it said—but had shown a relative decline, measured in constant dollars. The U.S.S.R.'s defense effort was estimated to be the equivalent of $80 billion in 1973; U.S. defense spending for that year totaled about $76 billion.

The Soviet defense program, the report estimated, absorbed 6%–10% of the Soviet gross national product, which was figured to be the equivalent of $660 billion annually. As a share of the U.S. GNP, American defense spending had declined from 9.4% in 1968 to about 6% in the last two years. The U.S. GNP equalled $1.1 trillion in 1973.

Colby also said there was an "across the board" technological lag in the Soviet Union, notably in computers and in the complexity and accuracy of missiles. In terms of readiness, he said, the U.S.S.R. exercised its forces "at less intensity" than the U.S.

China "lags five to 10 years or more" behind the other large industrial nations in various branches of technology, Colby said. He noted a generally upward trend in Chinese military procurement over the last decade.

(According to the Stockholm International Peace Research Institute, in its survey published June 18, international military expenditures had remained roughly stable at $200 billion over the past five years. The share of world military spending accounted for by the U.S., U.S.S.R., France and Great Britain had fallen from 82% in 1955 to 70% in 1973, because of a mounting military buildup elsewhere in the world.)

U.N. panel warning on Diego Garcia. A report issued by a three-member United Nations panel of experts May 10 warned that plans to expand Diego Garcia into a fully-developed U.S. naval and air base would almost certainly provoke the Soviet Union into establishing a similar installation in the Indian Ocean and lead to a new arms race in the region.

The report, requested by the U.N. General Assembly in December 1973, said "the instabilities inherent in the Indian Ocean area will not easily permit a mutual balance to be maintained successfully by the two great powers over a period of time" and could result in U.S.-Soviet competition "interacting with local conflicts, and then escalating."

The report noted that the U.S. and the Soviet Union had increased their naval forces in the Indian Ocean since the 1973 Middle East war.

The Soviet Union May 8 had reaffirmed the right to send its warships into the Indian Ocean. It accused China of deliberately misrepresenting the Soviet naval presence there in an attempt to foment anti-Soviet feelings in the region and of "playing into the hands of the imperialist West." The statement, published by the news agency Tass, complained that China had been falsely charging that the passage of Soviet ships through the Indian Ocean constituted a threat to Asian and African peoples. Tass said the countries bordering the Indian Ocean were opposed only to foreign "military bases," a reference to U.S. plans for Diego Garcia.

3rd Nixon-Brezhnev Meeting

Richard M. Nixon flew to Moscow June 27, 1974 for his third summit meeting with Soviet Communist Party General Secretary Leonid I. Brezhnev.

Minor accords. In a gesture that broke protocol, Brezhnev met Nixon at Moscow's Vnukovo Airport on the latter's arrival June 27 for a series of meetings that, according to observers, produced no major agreements. Three nuclear accords were considered minor.

With Brezhnev at the airport to meet President and Mrs. Nixon were Soviet President Nikolai V. Podgorny and Premier Alexei N. Kosygin. Also in the welcoming delegation was Culture Minister Yekaterina Furtseva, participating in her first public ceremony since being dropped from the Supreme Soviet June 19.

Brezhnev and Nixon issued a joint statement June 27 in which they pledged to make their negotiations serve "the strengthening of universal peace." In dinner speeches that night, they lauded the improvement in Soviet-U.S. relations in recent years. Brezhnev noted resistence to progress in improving relations, however, from "those who oppose international detente, who favor whipping up the arms race and returning to the methods of the cold war."

Nixon and Brezhnev began their formal talks in Moscow June 28, after the President paid a morning visit to the Tomb of the Unknown Soldier. Three agreements emerged from the day's negotiations: a five-year housing accord calling for exchange of information and experts and for future joint projects in the housing and construction fields, with emphasis on residential building in earthquake-prone zones; a five-year energy accord calling for a range of joint scientific and technological research and development programs in non-nuclear forms of energy and related subjects such as environment and conservation; and a three-year medical research accord calling for cooperation in improvement in the design of synthetic cardiac valves and for development of artificial hearts. None of the three agreements were of major significance; they merely complemented already-existing accords signed in 1972.

A 10-year economic agreement was signed June 29, calling on Moscow and Washington to facilitate trade and improve working conditions for trade representatives. Like the accords signed June 28, it augmented 1972 agreements.

Nixon, Brezhnev and their entourages, including Secretary of State Kissinger and Soviet Foreign Minister Andrei A. Gromyko, flew to Yalta, the Crimean Black Sea resort, where talks continued June 29-30. The White House had originally opposed the trip because of the connotations and associations such a visit would have with the 1945 "Big Three" Yalta conference which had been denounced by many, including Nixon.

Because Moscow had already carried out extensive preparations for the visit, the President's party acceded to the trip, insisting, however, on referring to the site as Oreanda, the precise location, although Oreanda was itself part of greater Yalta. Soviet reports were deferentially datelined either "Oreanda" or "from the Crimean press center"; Western reports were consistently datelined "Yalta."

The President July 1 flew to Minsk, the capital of Byelorussia, where he visited two World War II memorials. Brezhnev, Gromyko, Kissinger and other officials returned to Moscow from Yalta for further talks.

Nixon and Brezhnev continued their talks in Moscow July 2. In a television address delivered to the Soviet people that day, Nixon noted the "dramatic change in the nature of the relationship between our two countries" in the past two years, but observed that "we have many difficulties yet to be overcome."

In a farewell dinner speech that evening, Brezhnev revealed that the three partial nuclear accords had been reached. A communique issued in Moscow July 3 before the President's departure took note of other areas in which agreements had been made: environmental protection, space ventures, transportation innovations, cultural exchanges and the establishment of new consulates.

Nixon stresses personal relations—In his dinner addresses June 27 and July 2, President Nixon underscored the "personal" basis on which Soviet-U.S. negotiations were conducted and the vital role of "personal relationships" in the evolution of detente. In his June 27 speech, Nixon said previous Soviet-U.S. agreements had been possible "because of a personal relationship that was established between the general secretary [Brezhnev] and the President of the United States." He stated July 2 that "our differences . . . could never be solved unless we met as friends."

Brezhnev, for his part, was less inclined to balance detente on the shoulders of individuals. While he too, in his addresses at the Moscow welcome and farewell dinners, noted the good personal relations between himself and the President, Brezhnev did not repeat the theme as forcefully as Nixon. Observers viewed this as an acknowledgement of the collective structure of the Soviet leadership, which would discourage founding detente on individual personal relations. Moscow and Washington sources also saw it as an indication that Moscow was not anxious to link detente to a President whose viability was undermined by the threat of impeachment.

A brief controversy arose June 28 over the official Soviet translation of Nixon's June 27 speech. As published in the Soviet newspapers, the Tass translation omitted the word "personal" from a phrase in which it had been used by the President: "Because of our personal relationship," Nixon had said, "there is no question about our will to keep these agreements [that had been made in the past] and to make more where they are in our mutual interest."

Leonid Zamyatin, director general of Tass, the Soviet news agency, denied June 28 that there was any significance to the alteration of the text.

Nuclear & other accords—The minor agreements on nuclear arms were signed by Nixon and Brezhnev July 3. In first revealing them July 2, Brezhnev had said that the accords "could have been broader."

Kissinger had conceded June 28 that the impact of Watergate and impeachment efforts would hamper attempts by Nixon to exert leadership in the negotiations. In a Moscow press conference July 3, Kissinger laid blame for failure to achieve more substantial agreements on factionalism within both governments: "Both [Washington and Moscow] have to convince their military establishments of the benefits of restraint, and that does not come easily to either

side." Kissinger and U.S. Secretary of Defense James Schlesinger had expressed contrasting views on the issue of limiting nuclear arms.

Nixon and Brezhnev signed a communique committing their countries to negotiate a new interim accord dealing with both quantitative and qualitative limitations of strategic nuclear arms to cover the period until 1985. The present interim agreement, signed in 1972, was due to expire in 1977.

In a separate treaty and protocol, the U.S. and the Soviet Union agreed not to conduct any underground nuclear weapons test with a yield exceeding 150 kilotons (more than seven times the power of the bomb used over Hiroshima, Japan in 1945). U.S. officials said the level was far above what either side considered necessary for most tests. The treaty, which did not cover underground nuclear explosions for peaceful purposes, was to become effective March 31, 1976.

A second protocol limited each side to a single area for deployment of antiballistic missile (ABM) systems. The 1972 ABM treaty had allowed both countries two such areas, but officials confirmed that neither side intended to avail itself of the option to maintain the second.

Other instruments included:

A joint statement in which the two sides agreed to begin discussions on controlling the use of environment-modification techniques, including climate modification, for military purposes;

Two secret protocols, to be submitted to U.S. Congressional leaders, on the dismantling and replacement of missiles under provisions of the 1972 defensive missile treaty and interim accord on offensive arms. Kissinger said they were made secret at the request of the Soviet Union, but that "they break no new ground, they change no provisions";

An unwritten agreement in principle by Brezhnev to permit on-site inspection of explosions carried out for peaceful purposes. The signed treaty limiting underground tests called only for the use of "national means of verification" and the exchange of various data on the conduct of the tests.

Soviets arrest dissident Jews. More than 50 Jews were arrested in Moscow,

Leningrad, Odessa and Kishinev June 21–24 in an apparent effort to forestall demonstrations during President Nixon's visit to the Soviet Union. Among those arrested June 21 were Drs. Viktor Brailovsky, Mark Azbel and Alexander Voronel, prominent scientists who were organizers of a scientific meeting planned for July to support Jewish scientists excluded from work in the Soviet Union.

Nixon bars emigration role—Before his trip, Nixon had stressed in a commencement speech at the Naval Academy June 5 that "we cannot gear our foreign policy to the transformation of other societies." In an apparent allusion to the effort in the Senate to withhold trade favors from the Soviet Union unless its curbs on Jewish emigration were removed, Nixon said, "Eloquent appeals are now being made for the United States, through its foreign policy, to transform the internal as well as the international behavior of other countries, especially the Soviet Union." And while foreign policy "must respect our ideals and ... reflect our purposes," he said, there were limits to what could be achieved.

"Not by our choice but by our capability," he said, "our primary concern in foreign policy must be to help influence the international conduct of nations in the world arena. We would not welcome the intervention of other countries in our domestic affairs, and we cannot expect them to be cooperative when we work to intervene in theirs .... In the nuclear age, our first responsibility must be the prevention of a war that could destroy all society."

We must recognize, the President told the graduates at Annapolis, that "we are more faithful to our ideals by being concerned with results, and we achieve more results through diplomatic action than through hundreds of eloquent speeches."

Kissinger got pledge—Kissinger was reported to have received assurances from Soviet Foreign Minister Andrei A. Gromyko that the restrictions on Jewish emigration would be eased. The report emerged from a meeting Kissinger held June 5 with Sens. Henry M. Jackson (D, Wash.), Jacob K. Javits (R, N.Y.) and Abraham Ribicoff (D, Conn.) to discuss Jackson's amendment tieing the trade curbs to the Jewish emigration issue.

Telecasts on dissidents blacked out—Moscow cut off the TV broadcasts of three major U.S. networks July 2 as American correspondents tried to send filmed reports on Soviet dissident activities. Two of the broadcasts included interviews with physicist Andrei Sakharov who had begun a hunger strike on behalf of political prisoners June 29.

Despite several attempts to broadcast explanations of the interruptions as well as the reports themselves, the networks were each time blacked out within seconds.

A White House spokesman said: "It is the White House position that the networks should be able to send anything they wish." He said the White House would protest the action "if the networks wish it."

A CBS correspondent asserted that the Soviet action appeared to be in violation of an agreement that Moscow would allow transmission of any and all news relating to the summit meeting.

Valentina Zheleznova, a Soviet television official, took the position that the telecasts had no relation to the President's visit. Before the evening's broadcasting began, she had warned an ABC producer that the technicians did not like "the anti-Soviet material" being prepared and said they would refuse to transmit it.

Detente & the Ford Administration: 1974-75

Ford Continues Detente Policy

Richard M. Nixon resigned as President Aug. 9, 1974 under pressure of the Watergate scandals. He was succeeded as President by Gerald R. Ford, who promised that Henry A. Kissinger would remain Secretary of State and that the policy of detente would not be dropped.

Ford picks up reins. Before the Nixon resignation, but after the announcement of it, Ford assured reporters at his home near Alexandria, Va. Aug. 8 that he would retain Henry Kissinger as secretary of state and continue the foreign policy of the Nixon Administration. On Aug. 9, Ford and Kissinger met at the White House with nearly 60 ambassadors or chiefs of mission, in groups and individually, to assure continued friendly relations. A personal message from Ford was sent to Soviet Communist Party leader Leonid I. Brezhnev. The diplomatic sessions were continued at the State Department Aug. 10.

Policy outlined. Ford appeared before a joint session of Congress Aug. 12 to deliver a televised address in which he asked for Congress' cooperation in confronting the nation's problems. He cited inflation as the major issue.

On foreign policy, Ford pledged "continuity" in all areas of "the outstanding foreign policy" of his predecessor. "Let there be no doubt or misunderstanding anywhere. There are no opportunities to exploit, should anyone so desire. There will be no change of course, no relaxation of vigilance, no abandonment of the helm of our ship of state as the watch changes. We stand by our commitments and will live up to our responsibilities, in our formal alliances, in our friendships and in our improving relations with any potential adversaries."

Ford also affirmed a goal stated by the late President Kennedy in his 1961 inaugural address, "Let us never negotiate out of fear, but let us never fear to negotiate."

Ford said:

Successful foreign policy is an extension of the hopes of the whole American people for a world of peace and orderly freedom. So I would say a few words to our distinguished guests from the governments of other nations where, as at home, it is my determination to deal openly with allies and adversaries.

Over the past five and a half years, in Congress and as vice president, I have fully supported the outstanding foreign policy of President Nixon. This I intend to continue.

Throughout my public service, starting with wartime naval duty under the command of President Franklin D. Roosevelt, I have upheld all our Presidents when they spoke for my country to the world. I believe the Constitution commands this. I know that in this crucial area of international policy I can count on your firm support.

Let there be no doubt or misunderstanding

171

anywhere. There are no opportunities to exploit, should anyone so desire. There will be no change of course, no relaxation of vigilance, no abandonment of the helm of our ship of state as the watch changes. We stand by our commitments and will live up to our responsibilities, in our formal alliances, in our friendships and in our improving relations with any potential adversaries. On this, Americans are united and strong. Under my term of leadership I hope we will become more united. I am certain we will remain strong. A strong defense is the surest way to peace. Strength makes detente attainable. Weakness invites war, as my generation knows from four bitter experiences.

Just as America's will for peace is second to none, so will America's strength be second to none.

We cannot rely on the forebearance of others to protect this nation. The power and diversity of the armed forces, the resolve of our fellow citizens, the flexibility in our command to navigate international waters that remain troubled—all are essential to our security. . . .

■ To the Soviet Union, I pledge continuity in our commitment to the course of the past three years. To our two peoples, and to all mankind, we owe a continued effort to live and where possible, to work together in peace; for, in a thermo-nuclear age, there can be no alternative to a positive and peaceful relationship between our nations.

■ To the People's Republic of China, whose legendary hospitality I enjoyed, I pledge continuity in our commitment to the principles of the Shanghai communiqué. The new relationship built on those principles has demonstrated that it serves serious and objective mutual interests and has become an enduring feature of the world scene.

Soviet reaction. Soviet commentators emphasized that the change in U.S. presidents would not affect relations between Moscow and Washington.

An article in the government newspaper Izvestia Aug. 9 by its political commentator, Vikenti Matveyev, declared: "In the development and improvement of relations between the United States and the Soviet Union and the question of detente in general, there is a basis of national support in the U.S.A., that does not depend on membership in the Democratic or Republican Party, or some other vacillation in the country's political atmosphere."

"The forces which originated [the improvement] will continue to act further, independently of inter-party struggle or other events . . ." the article stated. The optimism of the commentary was supported by publication alongside it of a new poem by Yevgeny Yevtushenko praising detente.

Gromyko, Ford hold talks. President Gerald Ford held discussions with Soviet Foreign Minister Andrei A. Gromyko Sept. 20 and 21 on the Middle East, strategic arms limitations and issues of bilateral relations. Although the talks in Washington yielded "no breakthroughs, no agreements," according to a White House spokesman, the discussions were seen as contributing to the improvement in Soviet-U.S. relations.

Ford had met with Sen. Henry M. Jackson (D, Wash.) Sept. 20 before seeing Gromyko. Jackson later told reporters that "the Russians have come 180 degrees" with respect to concessions on the emigration issue. He noted that the disagreement over the Administration's trade bill was no longer between Moscow and the U.S. Congress, but, rather, between the U.S. Administration and Congress, with the difficulty concerning the legislative form and language in which to acknowledge the emigration/trade concession agreement and provide for U.S. review.

(According to a key official in the Ford Administration, Moscow and Washington had reached agreement on the emigration issue; it was reported Sept. 7 that the U.S.S.R. had agreed to permit at least 60,000 Jews and other Soviet citizens to emigrate each year, a 70% increase over 1973's record emigration figures.)

Arms & Arms Control

SALT negotiations resume. The second round of the Strategic Arms Limitation Talks, known as SALT II, resumed in Geneva Sept. 18, 1974.

Under the terms of the July summit agreement signed by President Nixon and Communist Party General Secretary Leonid Brezhnev, the SALT delegations were to negotiate a new interim accord to cover the period 1975-1985. A five-year interim agreement was signed in 1972 and did not include limits on long-range bombers or multiple nuclear warheads (MIRVs).

Western sources were doubtful that the mandated pact could be achieved before the projected date of 1975. Fundamental incompatibilities in the U.S. and Soviet positions remained unreconciled: the U.S.S.R., which in its arms programs stressed large land-based missiles, sought parity with U.S. forces, whereas the U.S., whose defense programs balanced land, sea and air forces, sought essential equivalency with the Soviet Union.

The issue of U.S. nuclear forces in Europe was also unresolved, Moscow held that since these forces could be directed against the U.S.S.R., they should be taken into account in determining weapons levels, while the U.S. maintained that its European forces were part of the North Atlantic Treaty Organization (NATO) defense and fell outside the realm of the SALT talks.

Kissinger on SALT role. Kissinger told the Senate Foreign Relations Committee Sept. 19 that efforts to limit strategic weapons competition constituted "perhaps the single most important component of our policy toward the Soviet Union." He delivered his 10,000-word, largely philosophical statement on Soviet-U.S. relations during the committee's detente hearings which had begun Aug. 8 in the charged atmosphere surrounding the policies of then-President Nixon.

Kissinger described the renewed Strategic Arms Limitation Talks (SALT-II) as "a means to achieve strategic stability by methods other than the arms race" and enumerated Washington's specific objectives at the talks: "to break the momentum of ever-increasing levels of armaments; to control certain qualitative aspects, particularly MIRVs [multiple independently targetable re-entry vehicles]; to moderate the pace of new developments; and, ultimately, to achieve reductions in force levels." He stressed the need to concentrate on establishing weapons ceilings, as in the 1972 interim agreement which quantitatively limited antiballistic missile defenses and froze the level of ballistic missile forces, rather than, as others had proposed, insisting on immediate arms reduction talks.

The secretary of state acknowledged the "subjective judgment" involved in determining comparability between Soviet and U.S. forces, but expressed confidence that the difficulties could be resolved. He warned, however, that "if we are driven to it, the U.S. will sustain an arms race."

With respect to the U.S. negotiating position, Kissinger said the Ford Administration had chosen not to work out a concrete proposal to submit at the SALT talks, but to concentrate on broad principles. He said concrete proposals would emerge by the time of his scheduled trip to Moscow in October.

Challenged by Sen. Clifford Case (R, N.J.) that the Soviet Union had gained more from detente than had the U.S., Kissinger countered that the gains had been in Washington's favor. He said Moscow had helped the U.S. "extricate" itself from Vietnam and had shown restraint in many areas, including Central Europe. The secretary also pointed out that the Soviet Union had weakened its position in the Arab world because it had not taken a stronger pro-Arab position in the October war, with the result that the Arab countries had since sought closer relations with the U.S.

Kissinger predicted "disastrous" results if the senators sought to exact too many concessions from the Soviet Union, a reference to the proposed trade bill amendment which would link U.S. trade concessions to Moscow's emigration policy.

U.S. seeks ban on peaceful explosions. The U.S. and the Soviet Union undertook negotiations in Moscow Oct. 7 on broadening the scope of the underground nuclear weapons test agreement to include peaceful explosions. The talks recessed Nov. 6, apparently stalled on the issue as Moscow maintained its opposition to restricting such explosions.

Nuclear tests for peaceful purposes had been excluded from the U.S.-Soviet treaty and protocol signed in Moscow in July by Nixon and Leonid Brezhnev. However, according to the New York Times Oct. 7, the Ford Administration, faced with what it considered almost certain Senate rejection of the agreement in that form, sought to expand the domain of the treaty to be negotiated to include peaceful tests. Noting that U.S. draft treaties had never before distinguished between peaceful and military nuclear explosions, one Washington official said: "President Nixon and Secretary of State [Henry] Kissinger caved in to Soviet pressures."

A State Department spokesman denied Nov. 21 that the Moscow talks had recessed in a deadlock and said there had been satisfactory progress. The U.S. delegation was headed by Ambassador Walter J. Stoessel. Igor Morokhov, first deputy chairman of the committee on peaceful uses of atomic energy, headed the Soviet delegation.

SALT pact violations charges exchanged. Two U.S. senators charged that the Soviet Union was violating the strategic arms limitation treaty of 1972 by constructing new missile silos beyond the limit set, developing a new mobile radar system, confusing agreed-upon verification systems, and modifying certain missiles to a degree exceeding that permitted by the treaty.

Sen. James L. Buckley (R-Con., N.Y.) made such allegations in New York Oct. 31 and in London Nov. 19. Sen. James A. McClure (R, Idaho) reiterated them in the Senate Nov. 20. Buckley was in the Soviet Union Nov. 9–15.

The Pentagon disclaimed the charges Oct. 31, a spokesman repeating the Oct. 10 statement of Gen. George S. Brown, chairman of the Joint Chiefs of Staff: "I can state that we have no information that the Soviet Union is failing to abide by [the SALT] agreements." The spokesman said it was "a fair inference" that construction work detected was not related to new missile silos, but was instead for underground command and control facilities.

Gen. Vladimir F. Tolubko, commander of the Soviet missile forces and deputy defense minister, labeled the violations charges "fabrications" and asserted Nov. 15 that "not a single silo for a ground-based launching pad has been set up since May 1972. No tests of new intercontinental mobile systems are being made."

Soviet Premier Alexei Kosygin said Nov. 14 that Soviet officials had complained to Washington that some U.S. strategic missiles had been covered with tents and possibly camouflaged. The Pentagon Nov. 15 denied camouflaging Minuteman missile silos and said the Air Force had erected large aluminum shields to protect newly poured concrete.

1917 Revolution anniversary rites. The Soviet Union's traditional military parade through Moscow's Red Square in commemoration of the Bolshevik Revolution of 1917 was held Nov. 7.

In a departure from past practice, no major new weaponry was unveiled, but a small shoulder-held, heat-seeking anti-aircraft missile used in Vietnam and by Arab forces in the Middle East was shown for the first time.

In his Red Square speech, Soviet Defense Minister Andrei Grechko declared that the Soviet Union would continue to build up and modernize its armed forces, but he noted that "the danger of nuclear war has been lessened."

U.S.-Soviet Developments

U.S.-Soviet trade compromise. A formal compromise to extend U.S. trade and credit benefits to the U.S.S.R. in return for the assured relaxation of Soviet emigration policies was detailed in an exchange of letters between Kissinger and Sen. Henry Jackson.

In his letter to Jackson, Kissinger wrote that "on the basis of discussions that have been conducted with Soviet representatives . . . we have been assured" that harassment of would-be emigrants would end.

No statement or acknowledgement was issued by Moscow which, according to Administration sources, was anxious to mute the impact of the reported agreement.

In his response, Jackson indicated that 60,000 emigrants annually would be considered a "minimum standard of initial compliance . . . and we understand that the President proposes to use the same benchmark."

(The White House issued a clarifying statement Oct. 21 emphasizing that Washington had received no guarantee of a "specific number" of emigrants, saying that "all of the assurances we have received from the Soviet Union" were enumerated in Kissinger's letter which cited no figure except to note: "It will be our assumption that . . . the rate of emigration from the U.S.S.R. would begin to rise promptly from the 1973 level.")

On the basis of the Congressional-Administration compromise, the trade bill to be presented to Congress when it returned from recess in November would authorize President Ford to extend most-favored-nation trade status and the credit facilities of the Export-Import Bank to the Soviet Union for 18 months. The power to discontinue the benefits after this period if Soviet compliance were not deemed adequate would be vested in Congress.

U.S. allows limited Soviet grain purchases. Treasury Secretary William E. Simon announced Oct. 19 that the Soviet Union would be allowed to purchase up to 1.2 million metric tons of U.S. wheat and 1 million tons of corn, valued at an estimated $380 million, through June 30, 1975. The Soviets had agreed not to make any "further purchases in the U.S. market this crop year," Simon added.

Recent Soviet efforts to buy 3.4 million tons of grain had been blocked by President Ford, who feared that massive sales would cause further disruptions in the U.S. grain market, already buffeted by poor crop reports, smaller than usual domestic reserves, and rising export demands from other nations.

Kissinger in U.S.S.R. Kissinger conferred with Soviet leaders in Moscow Oct. 23-27, 1974 during a three-week world tour. He said on leaving that on the basis of these discussions, there was a "reasonable chance" a strategic arms limitations agreement could be reached in 1975.

His talks at the Kremlin were described by U.S. officials accompanying Kissinger as "very tough," but more constructive than had been expected, according to Oct. 27 reports. The discussions had concerned not only procedural issues on the negotiation of a comprehensive agreement on offensive weapons, but also on the numerical limits that would be placed on them.

During a break in talks begun Oct. 24, each side issued a statement expressing strong support for increased cooperation and detente. The release of statements so early in the talks was uncharacteristic and was considered indicative of the mutual desire to clarify relations between Moscow and the Ford Administration.

It was announced Oct. 26 that President Ford would meet with Soviet Communist Party leader Leonid Brezhnev Nov. 23 and 24 in the vicinity of Vladivostok. It was reported that Soviet

Foreign Minister Andrei Gromyko had suggested such a meeting during a discussion with President Ford in Washington in September.

Although a joint communique issued Oct. 27 stressed that "relations between the U.S. and the U.S.S.R. continue to improve steadily," policy differences persisted at the meetings between Kissinger, Brezhnev and other Soviet and U.S. officials:

■ Brezhnev was said to have reacted "violently" to the publicity given in the U.S. to Moscow's assurances on ending the harassment of would-be emigrants in return for Congressional approval of trade benefits.

■ Strong Soviet resentment was expressed on the cancellation and only partial restoration by Washington of a U.S.S.R. grain purchase.

■ Policy differences reportedly persisted on Middle East diplomatic efforts, with Moscow opposing the personal shuttle style of Secretary of State Kissinger, and the step-by-step approach pursued by the U.S. in Middle East negotiations.

Oil offered for technology. Soviet Oil Minister Valentin Shashin told visiting U.S. Sen. Walter Mondale (D, Minn.) Nov. 12 that the Soviet Union was "ready to repay technical cooperation" in increasing Soviet oil production with "a certain part of the oil extracted."

Shashin noted that two U.S. firms, Union Oil Co. of California and Standard Oil of Indiana, "had shown an interest in this Soviet proposal," but he added that cooperation was also being encouraged with other countries, particularly France, Great Britain and Japan.

In conceding the need for U.S. technology, Shashin said new American methods could raise the extraction rate of some Soviet oil fields from the 10%-15% possible with traditional methods to "50% or even higher."

Ford Meets Brezhnev in Vladivostok

Arms pact includes MIRVs. U.S. President Gerald Ford and Soviet Communist Party General Secretary Leonid Brezhnev held talks in a suburb of the eastern

U.S.S.R. port city of Vladivostok Nov. 23-24 and reached a tentative agreement to limit the numbers of all strategic offensive nuclear weapons and delivery vehicles, including multiple independently targetable re-entry vehicles (MIRVs), through 1985.

The arms agreement was described Nov. 24 by Secretary of State Henry Kissinger, who attended all the meetings and who had set the foundation for the accord in talks in Moscow in October, as a "breakthrough" which would "mean that a cap has been put on the arms race for a period of 10 years."

Kissinger noted that the Soviet Union had made a basic concession in ceasing to insist that the U.S. forward-based fighter bomber system deployed in Europe be included in the total of U.S. strategic delivery vehicles. He also said precise numerical limits on MIRVs and delivery vehicles had been agreed on at the talks, but these figures were not released.

The agreement released Nov. 24 established the principle of equivalency in strategic forces, in contrast to the 1972 agreement which set unequal force-balancing quotas.

However, both sides would be permitted to employ whatever mix of delivery vehicles they chose—land-based or submarine-launched strategic missiles or strategic bombers; the 1972 pact had not included bomber forces.

The agreement also set broad limits on the deployment of MIRV warheads, previously excluded from bilateral accord. The pact envisioned restriction only on the number of MIRV-equipped vehicles, however, and would not limit the number of individual MIRV warheads.

In reviewing the negotiations leading to the Vladivostok accord Nov. 24, Kissinger noted that President Ford had "decided on a proposal which did not reflect any of the [five] options [considered before the October talks] precisely, but represented an amalgamation of several of the approaches."

The preliminary arms agreement had not been anticipated by the press or hinted at by the Administration prior to the Vladivostok meeting, scheduled to acquaint Ford and Brezhnev with each other and to re-establish a sense of policy and commitment to detente in the new Ford Administration. A final communique issued Nov. 24 reaffirmed Soviet and U.S. determination "to continue, without a loss in momentum, to expand the scale and intensity of their cooperation efforts in all spheres."

The communique also broached other topics discussed in the meetings: Both sides "expressed their concern with regard to the dangerous situation" in the Middle

---

Text of U.S.-Soviet Nuclear Arms Agreement

During their working meeting in the area of Vladivostok on Nov. 23-24, 1974, the President of the U.S.A., Gerald R. Ford, and General Secretary of the Central Committee of the C.P.S.U., L. I. Brezhnev, discussed in detail the question of further limitations of strategic offensive arms.

They reaffirmed the great significance that both the United States and the U.S.S.R. attach to the limitation of strategic offensive arms. They are convinced that a long-term agreement on this question would be a significant contribution to improving relations between the U.S. and the U.S.S.R., to reducing the danger of war and to enhancing world peace. Having noted the value of previous agreements on this question, including the interim agreement of May 26, 1972, they reaffirm the intention to conclude a new agreement on the limitation of strategic offensive arms, to last through 1985.

As a result of the exchange of views on the substance of such a new agreement, the President of the United States of America and the General Secretary of the Central Committee of the C.P.S.U. concluded that favorable prospects exist for completing the work on this agreement in 1975.

Agreement was reached that further negotiations will be based on the following provisions:

1. The new agreement will incorporate the relevant provisions of the interim agreement of May 26, 1972, which will remain in force until October 1977.

2. The new agreement will cover the period from October 1977, through Dec. 31, 1985.

3. Based on the principle of equality and equal security, the new agreement will include the following limitations:

A. Both sides will be entitled to have a certain agreed aggregate number of strategic delivery vehicles.

B. Both sides will be entitled to have a certain agreed aggregate number of ICBMs and SLBMs equipped with multiple independently targetable warheads (MIRV's).

4. The new agreement will include a provision for further negotiations beginning no later than 1980-1981 on the question of further limitations and possible reductions of strategic arms in the period after 1985.

5. Negotiations between the delegations of the U.S. and U.S.S.R. to work out the new agreement incorporating the foregoing points will resume in Geneva in January 1975.

East and urged that the Geneva Conference "should resume its work as soon as possible." The two parties also saw a "possibility" that the Geneva Conference on Security and Cooperation in Europe could conclude successfully with a summit meeting of participating nations' leaders.

(The port city of Vladivostok, closed to Soviet tourists as well as Westerners for almost three decades "because it is a military base," according to a Soviet shipping official, was opened to Western newsmen traveling in President Ford's entourage Nov. 24. Soviet leader Brezhnev had extended the invitation to the press corps and himself took the President on a tour of the city that day. It was reported that U.S. visitors had not been in Vladivostok, less than 50 miles from the Chinese border, since 1922.)

Congressional leaders briefed—President Ford returned to Washington from the Soviet Union Nov. 24 and held a briefing Nov. 26 for 26 Congressional leaders to inform them of the exact figures and other details of the arms limitation accord which, as issued Nov. 24, had not cited missile and warhead numbers. Ford told the congressmen he did not want to make the numbers public pending further correspondence with Soviet leader Brezhnev and asked them to maintain secrecy until that time.

Sen. Mike Mansfield (D, Mont.) was among a number of congressmen attending the Nov. 26 briefing to react favorably to the agreement. Strong reservations were expressed, however, by Sen. Henry Jackson (D, Wash.) who was not invited to attend the White House meeting, but who was briefed separately by an assistant to Secretary of State Kissinger. Jackson said Nov. 26 that setting so high a MIRV-vehicle limit "will make possible the addition of thousands of nuclear warheads," a reference to the fact that the agreement did not directly affect the number of warheads, but only the vehicles on which they could be deployed.

Jackson also charged that the Administration had "failed to bring the potential Soviet missile build-up under control" and expressed his disappointment that the agreement "did not provide for mutual force reductions."

President Ford asserted at he White House briefing: "This is not an arms reduction system, but it has got to start

somewhere." He also said the ceilings provided in the agreement were considerably below the Soviet plan for offensive nuclear weapons, but slightly above the U.S. plan.

Peking briefed on pact—Kissinger arrived in Peking Nov. 25, his seventh visit to the People's Republic of China, to brief Chinese leaders on the summit meeting between President Ford and Secretary Brezhnev. The Peking talks also focused on Sino-U.S. relations, specifically the Taiwan issue, Chinese assets frozen in the U.S. and U.S. property claims against China.

Kissinger visited with Chou En-lai Nov. 25 in a Peking hospital where the Chinese premier had been convalescing for the past five months. The secretary of state left China Nov. 29 without having been accorded a visit with Chairman Mao Tse-tung, a gesture that was seen as an indication of Chinese displeasure at the lack of momentum in Sino-U.S. relations.

Kissinger held formal talks Nov. 26–28 with Chinese Deputy Premier Teng Hsiao-ping and the new foreign minister, Chiao Kuan-hua.

Ford details Soviet agreement. President Ford, at a news conference Dec. 2, disclosed details of the tentative arms agreement he had reached with Brezhnev in Vladivostok. Ford stressed that the accord had put "a firm ceiling on the arms race." Ford said that he and Brezhnev had agreed it was "realistic to aim at completing this agreement next year."

This was possible, he said, "because we made major breakthroughs on two critical issues:

"(1) We agreed to put a ceiling of 2,400 each on the total number of intercontinental ballistic missiles, submarine-launched missiles and heavy bombers.

"(2) We agreed to limit the number of missiles that can be armed with multiple warheads (MIRV's). Of each side's total of 2,400, 1,320 can be so armed."

Ford said these ceilings were "well below the force levels which would otherwise have been expected over the next 10 years and very substantially below the forces which would result from an all-out arms race over that same period."

"What we have done," Ford said, "is to set firm and equal limits on the strategic forces of each side, thus preventing an arms race with all its terror, instability, war-breeding tension and economic waste. We have in addition created the solid basis from which future arms reductions can be—and hopefully will be—negotiated."

"We have made a long step forward toward peace," Ford said.

The President disagreed with a questioner's interpretation that "this pact permits the nuclear buildup to go ahead." "This does not permit an agreed buildup," he said. "It puts a cap on future buildups and it actually reduces a part of the buildup at the present time." "If we had not had this agreement," Ford said, the U.S. would have had "to substantially increase its military expenditures in the strategic areas . . . It's a good agreement. And I think that the American people will buy it because it provides for equality, and it provides for a negotiated reduction in several years ahead."

The President said "we do have an obligation within the limits of 2,400 on delivery systems and 1,320 on MIRVs to keep our forces up to that level."

Ford was questioned about the acknowledged lead of the Soviet Union in rocket power and warhead-power on MIRVs. What would the U.S. position be if each side went to the maximum number of 1,320 on the MIRV limit, he was asked. Ford replied that "on delivery systems we are equal" and "on the MIRVing we are equal." It was recognized, he said, that the Soviet Union had "a heavier throw weight" but the agreement did not preclude the U.S. from increasing its throw weight capability. Years ago, he said, "our military decided that we wanted smaller missiles that were more accurate," but the U.S. had "the capability" to increase its throw weight and could do so under the agreement if the military recommended it and Congress provided the funds. He said the Soviets had the same option to increase throw weight "but for, I think good reason, they have no justification for doing so." The President viewed the "flexibility" on the throw weight factor as "one of the benefits of this agreement."

Was Ford "satisfied that the Soviets are carrying out the spirit and the letter of the 1972 arms limitation agreements?" Ford said he knew of no violation by either side. There were "some ambiguities," he said, but there was provision for a standing consultative commission to meet and analyze "any allegations as to viola-tions." Ford said the U.S. intended to call for a meeting of the commission early in 1975 for that purpose.

Ford said he did not anticipate an increase or decrease in the defense budget as a result of the agreement. Strategic arms costs "will hold relatively the same," he said, except for increases resulting from inflation, which would also be reflected in other military programs.

Ford said there was no commitment made with Brezhnev at Vladivostok concerning mutual balanced force reductions in Western Europe. "We did agree to continue negotiations," he said, and "it is hopeful that we can make some reductions both in numbers of military personnel between ourselves and the allies on the one side and the Warsaw Pact nations and the Soviet Union on the other as well as any arms reduction."

As for conventional weapons, the President considered it "of mandatory importance" for the U.S. to maintain its capability because, "through a responsible military program," the U.S. could maintain the peace.

Ford said he and Brezhnev had discussed the Middle East "at some length" and while there were "some differences" they were "not as major as it would appear."

Kissinger cites arms pact change. In a Dec. 22 interview published in the Dec. 30 issue of Newsweek magazine, Secretary of State Henry Kissinger said the Soviet Union had agreed to a change sought by the U.S. in the wording of the Vladivostok nuclear arms agreement in order to insure that reductions in strategic forces could be negotiated before the accord expired in 1985.

Kissinger said the change had been made in the formal aide-memoire containing the November pact. The still secret aide-memoire was initialed by Kissinger and Soviet Ambassador Anatoly Dobrynin Dec. 10— 18 days after the Vladivostok meetings; the delay was attributed to negotiations in rewording the pact.

Sen. Charles Mathias, Jr. (R, Md.) Dec. 28 saw the modification as a move intended to strengthen Kissinger's hand in the face of anticipated Congressional opposition to the accord. Sen. Henry Jackson (D, Wash.) Dec. 6 had called on the Administration to renegotiate the pact in order to lower the arms levels agreed on at Vladivostok. Kissinger Dec. 7 warned that Congressional insistence on changes in the arms limits could pose "serious consequences" to relations with the Soviet Union.

Trade & Emigration

Late in December 1974 the U.S. Congress passed the controversial trade reform bill with the disputed rider authorizing trade benefits to the U.S.S.R. on the understanding that the Soviets had agreed to end restrictions on the emigration of its Jewish citizens. The Soviet Union denied having made such a commitment, and it decided early in January 1975 to cancel the 1972 U.S.-Soviet trade agreement because of Congress' requirement that it stop harassing would-be emigrants in order to qualify for the U.S. trade aids.

U.S. trade bill OKd despite Soviet disavowal. A comprehensive foreign trade bill was passed by the U.S. Congress Dec. 20, despite strong Soviet denials that the Kremlin had pledged freer emigration of Jews as a condition for trade benefits.

The Senate passed the bill by a 72–4 vote; the House passed it by a 323–36 vote.

In its final version, the bill gave the President the authority to eliminate tariffs of 5% or lower and to reduce by three-fifths tariffs above 5%. The President could negotiate elimination of non-tariff barriers, on an industry-by-industry basis, subject to Congressional approval.

Tariffs could be eliminated on goods from developing nations, with exceptions for Communist countries (but not Rumania and Yugoslavia), any country restricting supplies to the U.S. in a cartel-like operation and countries discriminating against the U.S. on trade or refusing compensation for confiscations.

A major provision of the bill would grant trade concessions to the Soviet Union if Soviet emigration curbs were eased, especially against Jews. Other Communist countries also would be permitted the "most favored nation" tariff status. In the case of Czechoslovakia, the status was tied to settlement of World War II claims to U.S. citizens.

Moscow denies 'understanding'—The U.S.S.R. Dec. 18 had disavowed any compromise agreement on the extension of U.S. trade benefits in exchange for freer Soviet emigration.

The denial, revealed prior to agreement on the bill by a House-Senate conference committee that night, was brushed aside by congressmen as a "face-saving" gesture.

The statement distributed by the official Soviet press agency Tass asserted that "leading circles" in the U.S.S.R. "flatly reject as unacceptable" any attempts to attach conditions to the extension of trade benefits or to otherwise "interfere in the internal affairs" of the Soviet Union.

Accompanying the statement, Tass also circulated a letter, dated Oct. 26, from Soviet Foreign Minister Andrei Gromyko to U.S. Secretary of State Henry Kissinger, in which Gromyko rejected the content of the letter exchange documented by Jackson as presenting "a distorted picture of our position." (The letter was said to have been handed to Kissinger during his visit to Moscow Oct. 23–27.)

In the letter, Gromyko stated that "we resolutely decline" any interpretation or assumption that there would be an increase in emigration from the Soviet Union in the future. The foreign minister alleged that in his talks with Kissinger, "the point was quite the contrary, namely about the present tendency toward a decrease in the number of persons willing to leave the U.S.S.R."

Although the Tass report repudiating the understanding and disclosing the Oct. 26 letter to that effect cast a shadow over Kissinger's relations with Congress, since he had not informed the body of the letter, Congressional reaction was calm. Sens. Jackson, Abraham Ribicoff (D, Conn.) and Jacob Javits (R, N.Y.), prime supporters of the amendment linking the trade concessions to freer emigration, were unanimous in their belief Dec. 18 that the Soviet action was chiefly "face-saving" and in maintaining confidence that the arrangement was not in jeopardy.

(In testimony before the Senate Finance Committee Dec. 5, Kissinger had said: "I must state flatly that if I were to assert that a formal agreement on emigration exists between our governments, that statement would immediately be repudiated by the Soviet government." He said he could give no "assurance concerning the precise emigration rate that may result," assuming the extension of most-favored-nation status to the Soviet Union. Kissinger did not mention the Gromyko letter. According to a New York Times report Dec. 19, with the Tass release of Dec. 18, the secretary of state had authorized an aide to say Kissinger had intended to inform the senators of the letter, but "forgot.")

Moscow circulated additional repudiations of the alleged understanding Dec. 21–25 in the Communist Party newspaper Pravda and other publications. A Dec. 25 article in the journal Literaturnaya Gazeta charged that reports of Soviet concessions on emigration in return for U.S. trade benefits had been "invented" to give members of Congress a face-saving explanation for not voting against the trade reform bill because such a negative vote might cost them support of U.S. businesses which, on a whole, favored the liberalization of trade with the Soviet Union.

Congress curbs Eximbank credits. A bill putting restrictions on U.S. government credit to the U.S.S.R. was passed by Congress Dec. 18–19.

It set a $300 million ceiling on credit to the Soviet Union, which the President could raise if he found it in the national interest, subject to Congressional approval. The bill also barred any Eximbank credit for production, transport or distribution of energy from the Soviet Union. A $40 million ceiling was set on loans or guarantees for exploration of energy in the Soviet Union.

The Senate approved the bill Dec. 19 by 71–24 vote. The House had passed it by a 280–96 vote Dec. 18, the same day it emerged from a second Senate-House conference.

Both the Soviet Union and the U.S. State Department expressed displeasure at the adoption of the restrictions.

State Department officials said Soviet Ambassador Anatoly Dobrynin had told Secretary of State Henry Kissinger Dec. 18 that Moscow regarded the credit limitation as a failure of the U.S. to live up to its side of detente. Dobrynin had also reiterated the Kremlin's disavowal of the informal understanding on freer Soviet emigration in exchange for U.S. trade benefits.

A State Department spokesman Dec. 19 characterized the unprecedented credit ceiling as "grossly discriminatory." It was the first time Congress had set a limit on loans involving a single country.

Soviets cancel '72 trade pact. The Soviet Union informed the U.S. Jan. 10, 1975 that because of the curbs imposed by Congress, Moscow would not put into force the 1972 Trade Agreement "which had called for an unconditional elimination of discriminatory trade restrictions." Secretary of State Henry Kissinger announced the action Jan. 14.

Although both countries reaffirmed their commitments to the policy of detente, Kissinger said in a Jan. 15 interview that "I think detente has had a setback."

The Soviet Union considered both the limitation placed on the amount of Export-Import Bank credit available to it and the trade act rider linking most-favored-nation status to freer emigration as "contravening both the 1972 Trade Agreement . . . and the principle of noninterference in domestic affairs."

In making the announcement, which followed several days of negotiations with Soviet officials, Kissinger reaffirmed Washington's commitment to detente and said the Administration would "pursue all available avenues" to improve overall Soviet-U.S. relations, "including efforts to obtain legislation that will permit normal trading relationships."

He added, however: "Should the [Soviet] decision herald a period of intensified pressure, the United States would resist with great determination and as a united people."

The nullification of the Trade Agreement, Kissinger explained, meant that the U.S.S.R. would not make any further payment on its Lend-Lease debts beyond 1975; a pledge to repay the World War II loans had been included in the 1972 Trade Agreement. It also meant, more significantly, that the Soviet Union would not receive most-favored-nation trade status and would not be entitled to any further Eximbank loans.

(According to a New York Times report Jan. 15, Kissinger had remarked of the four-year $300 million credit offered the Soviet Union: "That's peanuts." The Eximbank had, in fact, extended $469 billion in credits to the U.S.S.R. in the less than two years since Soviet loan facilities were first activated.)

Ford on detente—At his press conference Jan. 21, Ford was asked to evaluate the state of detente with the U.S.S.R. "in the light of what happened with the trade agreement."

The President said detente "will be continued, broadened, expanded." He said he was "disappointed" that the trade agreement was canceled but believed that "we can continue to work with the Soviet Union to expand trade regardless" and hoped to work with Congress "to eliminate any of the problems in the trade bill that might have precipitated" the Soviet action.

Ford was asked to comment on his plea to Congress not to legislate curbs on his conduct of foreign policy, specifically

whether he had in mind Sen. Henry Jackson's (D, Wash.) amendment on emigration of Soviet Jews involved in the trade pact. "I don't wish to get in any dispute with members of Congress," Ford said, and he declined to speculate on what actually precipitated the Soviet cancellation of the pact. He said several current restrictive amendments, such as imposed on the Soviet Union and on Turkey, were "harmful to a President in the execution and implementation of foreign policy."

Sen. Jackson and other congressmen most closely involved in the legislative actions to secure the amendment in question issued a statement Jan. 15 charging Moscow with blame for the collapse of the agreement: "The compromise of Oct. 18, which was freely entered into by all concerned, appears to have lost its appeal to the Soviets only when it became apparent that the Congress would not approve government credits for multibillion dollar development programs in the Soviet Union."

Text of Kissinger's Jan. 14 Statement

Since the President signed the trade act on Jan. 3, we have been in touch with the Soviet government concerning the steps necessary to bring the 1972 U.S.-Soviet Trade Agreement into force.

Article 9 of that agreement provides for an exchange of written notices of acceptance, following which the agreement, including reciprocal extension of nondiscriminatory tariff treatment, would enter into force. In accordance with the recently enacted trade act, prior to this exchange of written notices, the President would transmit to the Congress a number of documents, including the 1972 agreement, the proposed written notices, a formal proclamation extending MFN [most-favored-nation trade status] to the U.S.S.R. and a statement of reasons for the 1972 agreement. Either house of Congress would then have had 90 legislative days to veto the agreement.

In addition to these procedures, the President would also take certain steps, pursuant to the trade act, to waive the applicability of the Jackson-Vanik amendment [authored by Senator Henry M. Jackson, (D, Wash.) and Representative Charles A. Vanik, (D, Ohio)]. These steps would include a report to the Congress stating that the waiver would substantially promote the objectives of the amendment and that the President has received assurances that the emigration practices of the U.S.S.R. will henceforth lead substantially to the achievement of the objectives of the amendment.

It was our intention to include in the required exchange of written notices with the Soviet government language, required by the provisions of the trade act, that would have made clear that the duration of three years referred to in the 1972 Trade Agreement with the U.S.S.R., was subject to continued legal authority to carry out our obligations. This caveat was necessi-

tated by the fact that the waiver of the Jackson-Vanik amendment would be applicable only for an initial period of 18 months, with provision for renewal thereafter.

The Soviet government has now informed us that it cannot accept a trading relationship based on the legislation recently enacted in this country. It considers this legislation as contravening both the 1972 Trade Agreement, which had called for an unconditional elimination of discriminatory trade restrictions, and the principle of noninterference in domestic affairs.

The Soviet government states that it does not intend to accept a trade status that is discriminatory and subject to political conditions, and accordingly, that it will not put into force the 1972 Trade Agreement.

Finally, the Soviet government informed us that if statements were made by the United States, in the terms required by the trade act, concerning assurances by the Soviet government regarding matters it considers within its domestic jurisdiction, such statements would be repudiated by the Soviet government.

In view of these developments, we have concluded that the 1972 Trade Agreement cannot be brought into force at this time and that the President will therefore not take the steps required for this purpose by the trade act.

The Administration regrets this turn of events. It has regarded and continues to regard an orderly and mutually beneficial trade relationship with the Soviet Union as an important element in the overall improvement of relations. It will, of course, continue to pursue all available avenues for such an improvement, including efforts to obtain legislation that will permit normal trading relationships.

Kremlin denies blame, detente shift— The Soviet Union said in a Jan. 16 statement released by the official news agency Tass that "no changes have or could have taken place in the Soviet policy of detente" as a result of the decision to annul the 1972 Trade Agreement.

The Tass commentary, Moscow's first official response since the Jan. 14 disclosure in Washington, added: "As for trade, it is not a unilateral process. We want and are prepared to trade with the West, but, needless to repeat, only on the basis of full equality and mutual benefits."

"The Soviet people . . . would never make their right to decide their own internal affairs an object of bargaining. It would never occur to them to predicate their normal state-to-state relations with the U.S., say, on abolition of private ownership of the means of production. Why, then, do some American senators . . . think that someone would allow them to instruct the U.S.S.R. in the 'correct way of life'?"

Weapons & Arms Control

SALT negotiations resume. The second round of the Strategic Arms Limitation Talks (SALT II) resumed in Geneva Jan. 31 after a three-month recess.

In the U.S., fresh impetus for concluding an arms pact under the Vladivostok guidelines came Jan. 17 when Sens. Edward Kennedy (D, Mass.), Charles Mathias (R, Md.) and Walter Mondale (D, Minn.) issued a statement calling for Congressional support for the accord. The statement emerged, according to a New York Times report Jan. 29, from an agreement between the senators and Secretary of State Henry Kissinger for their support for a strategic arms pact if negotiations were undertaken to set lower arms ceilings and to curb the development of new weapons; the Vladivostok accord had come under strong criticism for not fixing a lower ceiling on arms levels.

Schlesinger defends Pentagon budget. Secretary of Defense James R. Schlesinger warned Congress that U.S. military might remained essential to preserving the peace in a "turbulent world." He ex-

pressed concern that the military power of the Soviet Union was continuing to grow and warned that the U.S. would arm itself up to the levels permitted in the 1974 Vladivostok agreement unless the Soviets exercised restraint in their armaments program.

Schlesinger's statement, contained in the secretary of defense's annual report to Congress Feb. 11, paralleled Congressional testimony he gave in support of the Pentagon's proposed fiscal 1976 budget.

In a era of U.S.-Soviet nuclear parity, he said in the annual message, general-purpose forces assumed greater importance. Noting that his report in 1974 had emphasized modernization of the U.S. nuclear arsenal, Schlesinger said, "This year it is equally essential to think in fresh terms about the role of our non-nuclear forces."

Schlesinger defended current U.S. war plans for dealing with a major and a minor contingency simultaneously. His most pressing concern was Central Europe, where "a powerful assault force, nearly half of it Soviet in origin," stood poised. This threat had to be countered with increased combat strength in Europe.

Schlesinger reported that he was "cautiously optimistic" on the U.S.-Soviet naval balance. While U.S. naval power had seriously declined and needed to be resuscitated, he said, it was "clear" that the naval forces of the U.S.S.R. and its allies were "not generally superior" to those of the U.S. and its allies. Overall, U.S. ships were "larger, more sophisticated and have a greater capacity for sustained action" than Soviet ships. These advantages tended to offset Soviet numerical superiority, he added.

He said that U.S. movement toward new strategic weapons systems would "depend on future developments of the Soviet strategic missile forces." Taking note of the section of the Vladivostok agreement limiting each side to 2,400 strategic missiles, Schlesinger said, "Assuming that the Soviet leaders exhibit restraint in their application of the agreement's principles, we are prepared to exercise restraint as well. However, until we obtain solid evidence of Soviet restraint, we shall plan for deployment of approximately 2,400 strategic delivery vehicles and 1,320 MIRV missiles. How we proceed . . . will depend essentially on the actions of the Soviet Union."

Unlike Soviet programs, which were proceeding as expected, Schlesinger said, the Chinese nuclear effort had slowed. He ascribed the loss of momentum in the Chinese missile program to "technical difficulties."

U.S., Soviet warships exchange visits. The U.S. and the Soviet Union exchanged visits of warships May 12 in ceremonies commemorating the 30th anniversary of the end of World War II. It was the first time since 1945 that ships of either country had visited the other.

The Soviet guided-missile destroyers Boikiy and Zhguchiy docked in Boston harbor for a five-day visit, while the U.S. guided-missile destroyer Tatnall and the guided-missile frigate Leahy moored at Leningrad's Vasilyevsky Island port.

U.S. submarine spying reported. The U.S. Navy had for almost 15 years been using specially equipped nuclear submarines to spy on Soviet missile submarines, the New York Times reported May 25.

Sources in Washington who confirmed the existence of the mission, code-named Holystone, also affirmed that the U.S. vessels had repeatedly violated the territorial waters of the Soviet Union and other nations.

According to the Times report, by correspondent Seymour Hersh, supporters of the program maintained that the highly classified missions had supplied vital information on the configuration, capabilities, noise patterns and missile-firing abilities of the Soviet submarine fleet. However, critics within the government charged that the program was inconsistent with detente policy; that much of the information gathered by the submarines could be obtained through other means, such as satellites; and that a number of accidents involving the U.S. fleet had occurred.

Washington sources said the Soviet Union was aware of the Holystone program.

Cruise missile developments emerge. The long-range cruise missile (LRCM), a new type of weapon with the "potential to make war more casual and less politically responsible," was being developed by the U.S. Air Force and Navy, according to an article by Kosta Tsipis, a nuclear physicist at the Massachusetts Institute of Technology's Center for International Studies, in the April issue of the Bulletin of the Atomic Scientists. The LRCM developments were also detailed in the New York Times June 16.

Able to fly at low altitudes for up to 1,500 miles, the LRCM could deliver a thermonuclear warhead, similar to the Minuteman III warhead, with very high accuracy, within 30 yards of target. Recent advances in the development of small highly efficient turbo-fan jet engines had made the long-range flights possible; new developments in the microminiaturization of electronic components had made possible the high-precision guidance system, based on terrain matching and recognition.

The LRCM's high accuracy made it a potential first strike weapon that could be used in a pre-emptive attack to eliminate an enemy's missile force, Tsipis stated. "Since high accuracy and large payload make the lethality of the cruise missile quite high. . . , the kill probability of this weapon against any target will be virtually 100 percent."

Citing an analysis by Tsipis in the Stockholm International Peace Research Institute Center's Yearbook, the Times quoted him as saying the technological advances represented in the cruise missile "could drastically alter the conduct of both tactical and strategic warfare." The installation of cruise missiles on nuclear attack submarines would "aggravate what perhaps is the only chronic problem of the sea-based deterrent, its command and control. The proliferation of nuclear weapons on [nuclear attack submarines] will complicate further the operation and control of these weapons and could increase the probability of accidental launch or misperceived attacks," Tsipis said in the Bulletin article.

The cruise missile had thus far aroused little debate in Congress. The Times reported that a recent attempt by Sen. William D. Hathaway (D, Maine) to cut funds for the cruise missile program had been defeated in the Senate, 72-16. Secretary of Defense James R. Schlesinger had argued in favor of LRCM development when he made his annual speech to Congress in February. He said that the air-launched cruise missile would "enhance the capability" of manned bombers to penetrate heavy defense and that the submarine-launched cruise missile would provide a "unique potential for unambiguous controlled, single-weapon response from relatively invulnerable submarines." He also pointed out that, while cruise missiles were "relatively low" in cost, they "would impose on the Soviet Union large additional expenditures for air defense to counter them." (The U.S. reportedly had 486 cruise missiles with a 450-mile range, the U.S.S.R. none.)

The cruise missile, not limited by any strategic arms agreement, [See above] also raised the specter of critical verification problems, for the long-range strategic version was virtually indistinguishable, without dismantling, from the short-range tactical version, the Times noted.

China's arms spending reduced. A report made public by the U.S. Congress July 15 said China's military spending had reached a record in 1970–71, but had been reduced by 25% since then. No specific figures were given in the report, published by the Joint Economic Committee and based on a survey of the Central Intelligence Agency.

One paper, by Sydney H. Jammes of the CIA, said: "Much of the decline reflects a sharp curtailment of acquisition of aircraft, but other weapons production programs have also slowed down." The sharp drop, Jammes said, "suggests that it is not simply the consequence of a coincidental cutback in several weapons programs; rather, it is the result of some general cause or causes."

Ford warns Soviets on arms race. President Ford warned Aug. 19 that unless a nuclear-arms agreement were reached with the Soviet Union he would "have no choice" but to ask Congress for an additional $2 to $3 billion for strategic weapons in the current and coming fiscal years.

He gave the warning in a warmly ap-plauded speech before the 57th national convention of the American Legion in Minneapolis.

"Peace is crucial but freedom comes first," he told the Legionnaires, declaring that detente meant "a fervent desire for peace but not peace at any price."

The President said he hoped to hold down spending on nuclear forces, a judgment he said that was "tentative" and "conditioned on real progress" in the SALT II talks with the Russians.

Ford also talked of detente in the context of the political turmoil in Portugal. He said Soviet policy in Portugal would be a test of the U.S.S.R.'s attitude toward detente and cooperation in European security.

U.S., U.S.S.R. ask environmental war ban. The U.S. and the Soviet Union Aug. 21 submitted to the United Nations Conference of the Committee on Disarmament (the Geneva Committee) a draft treaty that proposed the banning of attempts to manipulate the weather or otherwise modify the environment for military or other hostile purposes.

Presentation of the jointly-drafted text, which emerged from bilateral talks initiated following the July 1974 U.S.-Soviet summit meeting in Moscow, marked the first major advance at the 31-nation Geneva Disarmament Conference since the adoption in 1971 of an accord prohibiting germ warfare and other forms of biological warfare.

The proposed nine-article convention would, in part, bind signators "not to engage in military or any other hostile use of environmental modification techniques having widespread, long-lasting or severe effects as the means of destruction, damage or injury to another state" that was party to the accord.

Underground test, SALT talks resume. The U.S. and the U.S.S.R. resumed talks in Moscow Sept. 5 on restricting the underground explosion of nuclear devices for peaceful purposes. The previous round of negotiations had recessed March 22.

Strategic Arms Limitation Talks (SALT II) being conducted in Geneva resumed July 2 after a two-month recess.

U.S.-Soviet Space Mission

U.S. & Soviet spaceships link up in orbit. American and Soviet spacecraft linked together in space July 17, 1975 and, in what was seen as a symbolic gesture of goodwill, astronauts/cosmonauts from the two countries shook hands.

The event was the highlight of the Apollo-Soyuz Test Project (ASTP), a joint effort in space between the two countries once considered fierce rivals in the field. Although several important joint and individual experiments were scheduled by the two ships, the two-day linkup, with and its symbolic evocation of detente, was considered ASTP's main mission.

The Apollo first made physical contact with the Soviet Soyuz at 12:09 p.m., Eastern daylight time (7:09 p.m. in Moscow), several minutes earlier than expected. The ships were 140 miles over the earth and 620 miles west of Portugal over the Atlantic Ocean.

The Apollo carried a 10-foot-long docking module that it attached to the Soyuz. Three and a half minutes after contact, a firm linkup was acknowledged by Apollo commander, Gen. Thomas P. Stafford of the Air Force, with the words "We have capture," which he radioed in Russian to the Soyuz commander, Col. Aleksei A. Leonov. The two crews, who had spent a good deal of time in training learning their counterpart's language, spoke to each other in the listener's tongue.

The linkup was made by the Apollo crew after pulling up from below and behind the Soyuz craft. Apollo then went beyond the Soyuz, half-looped back, and made what Stafford referred to as a "soft docking." The Soyuz remained the passive partner throughout the linkup.

The docking module then served as an airlock for the transfer of the crewmen between the different atmospheres of the Apollo and Soyuz. The Americans remained in the airlock until the atmospheres were made compatible enough for a meeting of the crewmen to take place.

Peering through the opened hatch into the docking module, three hours and two orbits after docking, Leonov welcomed Stafford with "Glad to see you" in English. Stafford replied in Russian with "Ah, hello, very glad to see you." The spacecraft were passing over Amsterdam at the time, traveling at 17,300 miles an hour. Both the docking and the historic handshake were broadcast live in color around the world.

Stafford and Donald K. (Deke) Slaton of the Apollo crew, then crawled into the Soyuz where they presented a gift of U.S. flags to the Soviet cosmonauts, Leonov and Valery N. Kubasov.

The mission was hailed by U.S. and Soviet leaders as a significant step in improving U.S.-Soviet relations.

After the historic meeting between the two spacecraft, both heads of government radioed their congratulations to the crews. Soviet Communist Party General Secretary Leonid I. Brezhnev said, in a message read by mission control in Moscow, "The successful docking proved the correctness of the positions which were carried out in joint cooperation and friendship between Soviet and American designers, scientists and cosmonauts." He then put forth the hope that ASTP would be the "prototype of future orbital stations."

President Ford, in a telephone link-up with the ships, extended his congratulations to the five men on the docking. Using the symbolism of the hatch being opened between the two spacecraft he said, "It's taken us many years to open this door to useful cooperation in space between our two countries." Leonov, the Soyuz commander, said in reply, "I want to thank you for those warm words."

The day the two spaceships were launched, Ford referred to the two crews as "opening a new era in exploration" and said they were blazing a "brand-new trail of international space cooperation." He made his remarks in the State Department auditorium in Washington before viewing the televised blastoff of the Soviet cosmonauts July 15.

The same day, Brezhnev sent his greetings to the Soviet cosmonauts and their American counterparts. He wished them a happy journey and a successful mission.

ASTP came about only after high-level discussions were able to resolve difficulties inherent in such a joint mission. The first draft of such a project was drawn up in the spring of 1972. It was formally signed in May 1972 by President Nixon and Soviet Premier Alexei N. Kosygin on Nixon's visit to Moscow.

Although it had been argued that the Soviet Union, whose space program was considered not as advanced as the U.S. program, would gain valuable information from ASTP, it was pointed out that only basic knowledge vital to ASTP was being transferred. Furthermore, while the U.S. had always given out information on its program, Russia's space program had generally operated in secrecy, and ASTP had reportedly unlocked several secrets about the Soviet's space organization.

Finally, it was noted that Apollo was the last spaceship of its kind in the U.S. space program, and would be followed by the more technically advanced Space Shuttle. Although the U.S. had built and defrayed the full cost of the 10-foot docking module which was used to connect the two spacecraft, it was generally conceded that the Soviets had spent a sum on ASTP roughly equal to the $245 million spent by the U.S. (Soviet space costs were kept secret, according to policy.)

U.S. astronauts visit Soviet base— American astronauts, following a tour of the Soviet launching facilities before the Apollo-Soyuz mission, said May 14 they were impressed by what they had seen. The crew of Thomas P. Stafford, Donald K. (Deke) Slayton and Vance Brand said that the facilities were three to four times bigger than Florida's Kennedy Space Center.

Although each nation's crew had made several trips to the other's country, this was the first time the Americans had been to the Soviet launching site.

The Baikonur facilities, as they were called, and the adjacent space city of Leninsk, where the Soviet space personnel lived, was so secret that they had been omitted from unclassified Soviet maps and census reports (they were listed as Tyuratam).

The terrain of the launching facilities, located 1,400 miles southeast of Moscow, was described by the Americans as made up of "rolling hills" similar to the topography of Southern California. They said the living facilities for Soviet astronauts at Leninsk were better than those for Americans at Cape Canaveral, Fla. The as-

tronauts were flown into the Leninsk airport at night and were flown out the next night presumably to keep them from getting an overall view of the city.

China assails ASTP. The Chinese Communist Party newspaper, People's Daily, criticized the Apollo-Soyuz Test Project (ASTP) July 26. The newspaper said the flight, ostensibly made as a show of friendship between the U.S. and the Soviet Union, was really a "duel in space."

Referring to the linkup in space, the daily said, "The peoples of the world understood very well that the astronauts had knives concealed in the hands that they stretched out." It said each side sought to "uncover the technical secrets of the other side in order to obtain superiority in space."

China added to its own space program July 26 with the launching of its third satellite. Peking radio said it went successfully into orbit and its instruments were working "properly." No indication was given as to the purpose of the satellite. However, its trajectory took it over a major Soviet military base in the central part of the U.S.S.R.

Kissinger & Gromyko

U.S. State Secretary Kissinger and Soviet Foreign Minister Gromyko took advantage of several opportunities during 1975 to meet and discuss problems.

Meeting in Geneva. U.S.-Soviet differences over the Middle East were discussed by Kissinger and Foreign Minister Gromyko in Geneva Feb. 16–17. A communique issued after the talks did not reflect a reported rift in which Gromyko accused the U.S. of excluding Moscow from diplomatic efforts to help resolve the Arab-Israeli dispute. The joint statement merely said that both sides "believe that the Geneva conference should play an important part" in establishing peace and "should resume its work at an early date."

Other topics discussed included the Cyprus crisis, U.S.-Soviet trade, strategic arms and the European security conference.

At a joint news conference Feb. 17, Gromyko was asked whether critical remarks on Middle East peace moves made Feb. 14 by Soviet Communist Party Secretary General Leonid Brezhnev were an allusion to Kissinger's diplomatic efforts. Gromyko said Brezhnev had no one in particular in mind. (The Soviet leader had said that "certain persons apparently would like to offer the Arab peoples something like a soporific, hoping that they will be lulled and will forget their demands for restoration of justice and full liquidation of the consequences of aggression.")

Meeting in Vienna. Kissinger and Gromyko then conferred in Vienna May 19–20.

Both men described the talks as "useful" and agreed to meet again for further discussions in July. Kissinger noted in remarks to newsmen May 20 that "progress was made on issues that were discussed." Gromyko, who was present, seconded Kissinger's comment.

On the Middle East, agreement was reached to cooperate on a framework for reconvening the Geneva Conference in late summer or the autumn. No details on the two powers' Middle East positions emerged from the Vienna talks.

Some progress was reported on issues related to the Strategic Arms Limitation Talks (SALT II).

Also discussed was the Conference on Security and Cooperation in Europe and the possibility of holding a high-level summit meeting at the Conference's conclusion.

(In a speech May 12 before the World Affairs Council of St. Louis, Mo., Kissinger, commenting on the Communist victories in Asia, had warned the Soviet Union that its "willingness . . . to exploit strategic opportunities—even though some of these opportunities presented themselves more or less spontaneously and not as a result of Soviet action—constitutes a heavy mortgage on detente." Gromyko, speaking at a Warsaw Pact anniversary meeting in Moscow May 14, publicly rebuked Kissinger by name—a highly unusual gesture—for certain of his May 12 remarks. He said that Kissinger's espousal of detente and his opposition to military budget cuts "do not quite jibe, to put it mildly.")

2nd Geneva meeting. Kissinger and Gromyko met again in Geneva July 10–11.

Kissinger observed: "We reviewed the outstanding issues in a number of categories and progress was made in narrowing the differences and understanding each other's position." He said the two nations would work "with optimism for concluding an agreement on the basis of the Vladivostok principles," giving impetus on the stalled Strategic Arms Limitation Talks (SALT II).

Gromyko confirmed at a July 11 press conference that an "understanding" had been reached with the U.S. for on-site inspection of peaceful nuclear explosions. However, Gromyko added that, generally, "we believe national means of verification are adequate," indicating that the verification issue remained a thorny one in the context of strategic arms.

European Security

Helsinki summit meeting. The largest summit meeting in European history took place in Helsinki, Finland July 30–Aug. 1, 1975. The leaders of 35 Eastern and Western European states, the U.S. and Canada attended this third and final stage of the Conference on Security & Cooperation in Europe (CSCE) and signed its final document Aug. 1.

With declared goals of "peace, security, justice and cooperation," the non-binding document, in its six official languages—English, French, German, Russian, Italian and Spanish—comprised four sections dealing broadly with aspects of European security (including confidence-building measures); economic and other forms of cooperation; humanitarian issues and increased human contacts between the East and West; and, finally, provisions for a follow-up conference.

The 35 leaders completed their individual speeches to the assembly Aug. 1. In his address that day, U.S. President Gerald R. Ford declared: "Peace is not a piece of paper . . . History will judge this conference not by what we do today, but by what we do tomorrow—not by the promises we make, but by the promises we keep." He assured his fellow participants of the U.S.' "vital interest in Europe's future" and, citing "our common heritage, our common destiny," Ford said the U.S. "therefore intends to participate fully in the affairs of Europe and in turning the results of this conference into a living reality."

In his July 31 address to the assembly, Soviet Communist Party General Secretary Leonid I. Brezhnev said "the outcome of the prolonged negotiations ... has been a victory for reason." He lauded the CSCE's accomplishments and praised the spirit of compromise which had permitted them.

Although his appearance successfully culminated the long Soviet effort to convene a European security conference that would recognize the permanence of borders created in Europe after World War II, Brezhnev said the conference's "major [conclusion] that is reflected in the final document is this: No one should try to dictate to other peoples, on the basis of foreign policy considerations of one kind or another, the manner in which they ought to manage their internal affairs." This was seen as a reference to continued Soviet opposition to Western attempts to promote greater tolerance of domestic dissent within or emigration from the U.S.S.R. It also seemed to suggest, however, that Moscow might be mollifying its position with regard to the so-called "Brezhnev doctrine," which asserted the U.S.S.R.'s prerogative to intervene militarily when Communist governments were threatened in Eastern Europe, as happened in Hungary in 1956 and Czechoslovakia in 1968.

U.S. Secretary of State Henry Kissinger, who accompanied President Ford to the Helsinki summit, said Brezhnev's statement could be read "both ways" and described the speech as "on the whole, moderate and conciliatory." The Soviet leader also said that progress on the reduction of troops in Central Europe, the subject of East-West talks being held in Vienna, must become a "priority goal."

In a gesture of apparent acknowledgment of criticism being leveled against President Ford in the U.S. for participating in the conference and accusing him of having capitulated to the Communist bloc of nations, Brezhnev asserted that "the outcome [of the CSCE] ... is such that there are neither victors nor vanquished, winners nor losers."

Ford-Brezhnev meetings—Ford and Brezhnev met twice in private in Helsinki during the conference. The first talk, on strategic arms, took place July 30, and Ford said it had been "constructive." They met again to discuss the issue Aug. 2 and reported "encouraging progress."

Ford defends summit participation—In his departure statement before leaving Washington July 26 for Europe, President Ford sought to reassure his domestic critics and defend his participation in and support for the summit finale to the Conference on Security and Cooperation in Europe (CSCE) and its final document which he would sign in Helsinki. He stated that although "the outcome of this Helsinki conference remains to be tested ... it is at least a forward step for freedom."

According to a June 30 N.Y. Times report, Sen. Henry Jackson (D, Wash.), echoing the opposition of emigre groups in the U.S., said the CSCE declaration would represent "a sign of the West's retreat" from "a crucial point of principle," the right of self-determination of the Baltic and Eastern European states. (The U.S. had never formally acknowledged the incorporation of Estonia, Latvia and Lithuania into the U.S.S.R. during World War II; emigres and other presidential critics maintained that, in accepting a document which affirmed the permanence of borders in Europe, Ford was giving de facto recognition to the Baltic states' absorption by the U.S.S.R.)

In his July 26 statement, Ford said: "Our official policy of non-recognition is not affected by this conference. We are not committing ourselves to anything beyond what we are already committed to by our own legal and moral standards." He stressed that the Helsinki declaration did not comprise any legal commitments.

Ford also sought to appease critics by noting that the Soviet Union and the other Eastern bloc nations had made a concession to the West by accepting the possibility of peaceful adjustments of frontiers, as provided for in the final document.

Other criticism was leveled by exiled Soviet writer Alexander Solzhenitsyn who declared July 21 that the U.S. participation in the conference was "a betrayal of Eastern Europe." He also rejected an "open invitation" from the White House to meet with President Ford, saying that only a formal invitation would be acceptable. The informal welcome was issued July 15 after a furor arose among the President's critics when Ford refused, at the urging of his advisers, to hold a meeting with Solzhenitsyn.

Grain Deals

China cancels U.S. wheat orders. China canceled contracts to purchase 601,000 tons of U.S. wheat, Cook Industries, Inc. announced Jan. 27, 1975. The firm, a trading company based in Memphis, Tenn., was to have delivered the grain between February and September. The shipment accounted for about 60% of the 991,000 tons of U.S. wheat that was to have been sent to China between then and June 30, 1976, according to U.S. Agriculture Department records.

Peking's cancellation of the wheat order was attributed by diplomatic sources in Washington Jan. 28 to concern over its foreign exchange drain and debts abroad.

China canceled an order for another 382,000 metric tons of U.S. wheat, the U.S. Agriculture Department announced Feb. 27. This order and the previously canceled one covered all the wheat that China had contracted to receive from U.S. exporters during 1975.

Moscow cancels wheat purchase. The Soviet Union had cancelled orders for 3.7 million bushels (100,000 tons) of U.S. wheat and was negotiating for the cancellation of a further 7.5 million bushels ordered in 1974, it was disclosed Jan. 29.

The cancellations would represent about a third of the remaining Soviet wheat orders from the 1974 crop. The original purchase had been reduced by the U.S. government in October 1974.

It was reported that the Soviet cancellation had been arranged weeks earlier by executives of Cook Industries, Inc., one of two major U.S. sellers involved in the controversial 1974 grain sale.

The Agriculture Department Feb. 4 approved the sale of 100,000 tons of corn to the Soviet Union, Cook Industries, Inc.

said. Moscow had asked to make the corn purchase in place of the canceled wheat shipment, Agriculture officials confirmed.

According to Feb. 4 reports, the trade developments came as revised data was released on 1974 Soviet grain crops, showing that wheat production had fallen sharply from the 1973 level and was well below December 1974 forecasts.

The reported crop failure suggested, according to the New York Times Feb. 4, that the Soviet wheat purchase cancellation had stemmed partly from temporary congestion at some ports. It was also noted that wheat prices had dropped since the Soviet Union had made its purchases in 1974 and that the cancellation indicated Moscow's unwillingness to take a loss if forced to resell the wheat.

U.S. grain export curbs eased. U.S. Agriculture Secretary Earl Butz announced Jan. 29, 1975 that export curbs on wheat and soybeans would be eased. The restrictions had been set in October 1974 because of soaring food prices and fears of domestic shortages, prompted in part by a controversial Soviet grain purchase.

Butz said the action "returns the export trade in wheat and soybeans virtually to a free basis, following a period in which tight supplies forced us into a program where the possibility of export controls was to a degree implicit." The new regulations doubled to 100,000 tons the quantity of wheat or soybeans that an exporter could sell to any one destination in a single day without government approval and to 200,000 tons the quantity permitted sold to a single destination in a week. Butz noted that U.S. supplies of wheat and soybeans had increased and that it therefore was unnecessary to keep so close a watch on export sales.

However, the 50,000-ton-a-day and 100,000-ton-a-week regulations would be maintained on corn and feed grains until the supply situation became clearer.

Soviet buys wheat from U.S., Canada. A major purchase of wheat by the Soviet Union from U.S. exporters and from Canada was announced July 16-17.

The agreements with American companies, disclosed July 16, involved 3.2 million metric tons of wheat, or about 117 million bushels. Cook Industries of Memphis was to supply 2 million metric tons, Cargill, Inc. of Minneapolis 1.2 million tons.

A 2-million-ton sale was first announced by the Agriculture Department without disclosing the name of the company. The department said the sale was a direct commercial deal without government subsidies or credit involved.

Confirmation came from Edward W. Cook, chairman of Cook Industries, who landed July 16 in Memphis on return from Moscow and the negotiations. He said the transaction was conducted "with the full knowledge" of the Agriculture Department and the Ford Administration and "it was personally reported" to the department and the Senate Permanent Investigations subcommittee upon his return that day to the U.S.

Cook revealed that the agreement permitted "shipment from origins other than" the U.S. "While most will probably be shipped from the United States," he said, "it is also highly probable that some will be shipped from other grain-producing countries."

Announcement of the Cargill sale was made by the company that night in Minneapolis. Some of the U.S. winter wheat was to be delivered in the summer of 1976.

The Canadian sale—of two million metric tons of high grade wheat for delivery in the fall—was announced by the Canadian Wheat Board July 17.

Reports of the Soviet interest in grain purchases had been circulating. Sources at the U.S. Agriculture Department said July 10 the size of the U.S. sales could total 10 million metric tons. The U.S. wheat crop estimate for 1975, released at the same time, was 59.5 million metric tons, 22% higher than in 1974. The corn crop was expected to be 30% higher than 1974's, at 118.1 million metric tons.

Agriculture Secretary Earl L. Butz, in testimony to the Senate Agriculture Committee July 11, said that 38 million tons of the bumper wheat crop was expected to be available for export. Confirming that U.S. businessmen were in Moscow negotiating a new grain sale, Butz said the U.S. could sell the Soviet Union up to 10 million tons of grain "with a minimal impact on the price of bread here." "I said a minimal impact," he added, "not a zero impact."

Soviet gold sales seen as purchase hint— Early indications that the Soviet Union

might be preparing for North American grain purchases had been seen in growing Soviet activity in Western currency, Eurodollar and gold markets in order to acquire substantial dollar balances, according to a July 8 report from the British news agency Reuters.

Bankers in Zurich, Reuters said, calculated that Soviet sales of gold in recent weeks could have created a dollar income of up to $100 million weekly.

The U.S.S.R. was also believed to have sold as much as 50 tons of gold directly to Middle Eastern buyers, the Journal of Commerce reported July 10, thus circumventing European bullion markets which, under present trading conditions, would have registered sharp price declines with the appearance of such a large amount of gold.

In another development, the Soviet Bank of Foreign Trade had completed a record $250 million medium-term loan in Western Eurocurrency markets, it was reported July 8.

More wheat bought. Further large Soviet purchases of grain in the world market were disclosed July 21–22.

The second round of sales involved 4.5 million metric tons, or 177 million bushels of corn and 1.1 million metric tons, or 50.5 million bushels of barley from the Continental Grain Co. of New York, which said July 21 there was an option in the arrangement to substitute corn for the barley.

The next day, Cook Industries, Inc., which had announced a wheat sale to the Soviet Union the week before, said it had sold an additional 36.7 million bushels (1 million metric tons) of wheat to Russia. Delivery was to be completed in 1976.

The Australian Wheat Board also announced July 22 a sale of 27.5 million bushels (.75 million metric tons) of wheat to the Soviet Union, with shipment between September and May 1976.

The Soviet grain purchases announced in the two-week period totaled 12.55 million metric tons, or 482.2 million bushels. The total value of the shipments was estimated at more than $1.3 billion. This included 381.7 million bushels of wheat, corn and barley from U.S. export firms.

Unions boycott Soviet grain loadings. The sale of U.S. grain to the Soviet Union ran into opposition from organized labor over the sale's alleged impact on consumer prices in mid-August.

Maritime unions of the AFL-CIO called a boycott Aug. 18 against loading grain shipments to the Soviet Union. "We are not going to load any grain to the Soviet Union," AFL-CIO President George Meany explained, "unless and until a policy is set forth and agreed to that will protect the American consumer and also the American shipping interests."

Meany protested that Soviet purchases from the U.S., amounting to 9.8 million tons of grain since July 1, would "cost the American consumers billions of dollars." He said Americans were "still paying" for the massive grain sales to the Soviet Union negotiated in 1972.

Part of the union discontent with the 1972 grain shipments stemmed from the alleged failure to implement arrangements that one-third of the loads would be carried in American ships. The agreement had not been honored, according to an AFL-CIO executive council statement July 31, which said only 11% of the shipments were made aboard U.S. ships manned by American seamen.

President Ford sought to cool the dispute. During a visit to the Iowa State Fair in Des Moines Aug. 18, he endorsed the Soviet sales, saying they were "in the interest of all Americans—farmers and consumers alike." Farm exports, he said, were "a vital part" of the country's diplomacy. Ford said that he expected "further purchases of grain" by Russia but that American exporters had been asked to hold off on further grain sales until more crop estimates were in and a firmer estimate could be made of the impact of the sales on U.S. prices. The order to exporters had been announced Aug. 11 after the corn crop estimate had been reduced because of a persistent dry spell.

An accord was reached Sept. 9. The union leaders agreed to suspend the boycott for a month, and the Administration pledged to try to negotiate new long-term purchasing and shipping arrangements with the Russians and to extend the current moratorium on new grain sales to the Soviets until mid-October.

A negotiating team headed by Undersecretary of State Charles Robinson arrived in Moscow Sept. 11 and

Robinson reported Sept. 16 that a long-term agreement on grain purchases was acceptable to the Soviet team, which included Nikolai Patolichev, minister of trade. Robinson said "we are very optimistic" and an agreement was "very likely" to be set "in the next few weeks."

Another U.S. team, led by Assistant Secretary of Commerce Robert J. Blackwell, was in Moscow negotiating the shipping rate, and it was reported from Washington sources Sept. 17 that the Soviet Union had agreed to pay $16 a ton to American ships carrying the grain. This was well above the previous rate of $9.50 a ton negotiated in 1972. The break-even point for the American ships reportedly was $12 to $13 a ton.

President Ford met Sept. 15 with William J. Kuhfuss, president of the American Farm Bureau Federation, which had objected to the moratorium the Administration had settled upon further grain sales to the Soviet Union. Kuhfuss was given assurance by Ford that more sales could be made to the Soviet Union of this year's grain crop but the President said the moratorium would not be lifted until a long-term agreement designed to protect domestic food prices was consummated.

The union's boycott, actually, was of little effect realistically since shippers had obtained court orders, obeyed by the locals involved, requiring the loading, generally on a ship-by-ship basis.

Other Developments

Kissinger defends detente. Secretary of State Henry A. Kissinger defended detente and U.S. support of authoritarian regimes in a speech in Minneapolis July 15 focusing on "the moral foundations" of American foreign policy.

Addressing the Upper Midwest Council, Kissinger said "in an era of strategic nuclear balance—when both sides have the capacity to destroy civilized life—there is no alternative to coexistence." "The world's fears of holocaust and its hopes for a better future have both hinged on the relationship between the two superpowers," he said, and "in such conditions the necessity of peace is a moral imperative."

The choice, he said, was "not between

morality and pragmatism. We cannot escape either, nor are they incompatible. This nation must be true to its own beliefs or it will lose its bearings in the world. But at the same time it must survive in a world of sovereign nations and competing wills."

The "immediate focus" of U.S. policy toward the Soviet Union was on "international actions" because that was "the sphere of action that we can most directly and confidently affect," Kissinger said. "As a consequence of improved foreign policy relationship, we have successfully used our influence to promote human rights. But we have done so quietly, keeping in mind the delicacy of the problem and stressing results rather than public confrontation."

Kissinger questioned whether detente encouraged repression. "Or is it detente," he posed, "that has generated the ferment and the demands for openness that we are now witnessing?"

As for the morality of relations with countries whose domestic policies were repugnant to America, Kissinger asked "to what extent are we able to affect the internal policies of other governments and to what extent is it desirable?" "We have used, and we will use, our influence against repressive practices," Kissinger declared, but "truth compels also a recognition of our limits. The question is whether we promote human rights more effectively by counsel and friendly relations . . . or by confrontation propaganda and discriminatory legislation."

Alliances and political relationships served "mutual ends" and were "not favors to other governments," he argued, and should be withdrawn "only when our interests change and not as punishment for some act with which we do not agree."

Opposes Solzhenitsyn visit—In a news conference in Milwaukee July 16, Kissinger had high praise for exiled Russian novelist Alexander Solzhenitsyn, who was visiting the U.S., but said it would be "disadvantageous" to U.S. foreign policy for President Ford to meet with Solzhenitsyn because of the writer's outspoken opposition to the Soviet leadership and to detente. The White House previously had said Ford was too busy to schedule a meeting with Solzhenitsyn but the denial of a visit later was said to have been based on the advice of aides, including Kissinger.

At the news conference, Kissinger acknowledged giving the advice, saying it was "no reflection on the literary greatness of Solzhenitsyn or on the importance of some of his message."

Soviet taps of U.S. phones reported. The Chicago Tribune reported June 22 that the Soviet Union had put into effect a massive operation to monitor, record and identify private phone calls within the U.S. The Soviets had long possessed the technology necessary to intercept microwaves, which were used in the U.S. to transmit 70% of all long distance telephone calls, but had only recently developed the computer technology required to separate the conversations and identify the callers, the Tribune said.

The disclosure, the Tribune said, had prompted investigations by the White House and congressional committees to determine how much information was being gathered, how it was used and what, if anything, was being done by U.S. intelligence agencies to stop the monitoring by the KGB, the Soviet security police.

The newspaper indicated that the information had been disclosed in testimony to the Rockefeller commission during its probe of domestic U.S. intelligence but that the testimony had been heavily censored from the commission's final report for reasons of national security.

Congress members & Brezhnev. A group of 14 U.S. senators visited the Soviet Union June 29–July 2 and met with Communist Party General Secretary Leonid I. Brezhnev, as well as with several dissident Jews who had been seeking, unsuccessfully, to emigrate. The senators' trip was made at the invitation of the Supreme Soviet, reciprocal to a visit last year to Washington by a cognate Soviet delegation.

The U.S. delegation, headed by Sens. Hubert H. Humphrey (D, Minn.) and Hugh Scott (R, Penn.), was told in a June 29 meeting with 16 leading Jewish dissidents that Soviet emigration policies had of late become much more harsh. The group of senators raised the issue in their July 2 meeting with Brezhnev, but detected no softening of the Soviet refusal to offer assurances on emigration in exchange for most-favored-nation trading status and credits.

Sen. Humphrey indicated that he had detected a modification of past Soviet views with respect to the problem of verification in the context of arms control, describing the Soviet attitude as "flexible." Brezhnev impressed the senators as having been genuinely concerned about the arms race. The Soviet leader also reportedly emphasized that he had had no specific weapon in mind when, in a June speech, he called on the U.S. to join in banning all "new" weapons of mass destruction.

Brezhnev later met with a group of 18 U.S. congressmen Aug. 14 at Yalta on the Crimean coast. The delegation, headed by House Speaker Carl Albert (D, Okla.), visited the Soviet Union in return for a visit by a group of Supreme Soviet deputies to Washington in the spring of 1974.

Brezhnev reportedly sought to reassure the legislators that the Soviet Union would fulfill the freedom of information clause included in the Final Act of the Conference on Security and Cooperation in Europe, but indicated that Moscow would insist upon further discussions with individual countries before implementing the document's humanitarian provisions.

During the meeting, details of which were provided by Rep. John Brademas (D, Ind.), one of the 18 congressmen present, Brezhnev said Moscow favored "strict noninterference in Portugal," where the U.S.S.R. had recently been accused of manipulating events.

Mini-calculator pact with U.S. The General Instrument Corp. announced June 19 the signing of a multi-million dollar contract that would enable the Soviet Union to begin mass production of hand-held calculators. It was reportedly the first contract between the Soviet Union and a U.S. electronic-component maker and had been approved by Washington.

Index